Hospices de Beaune

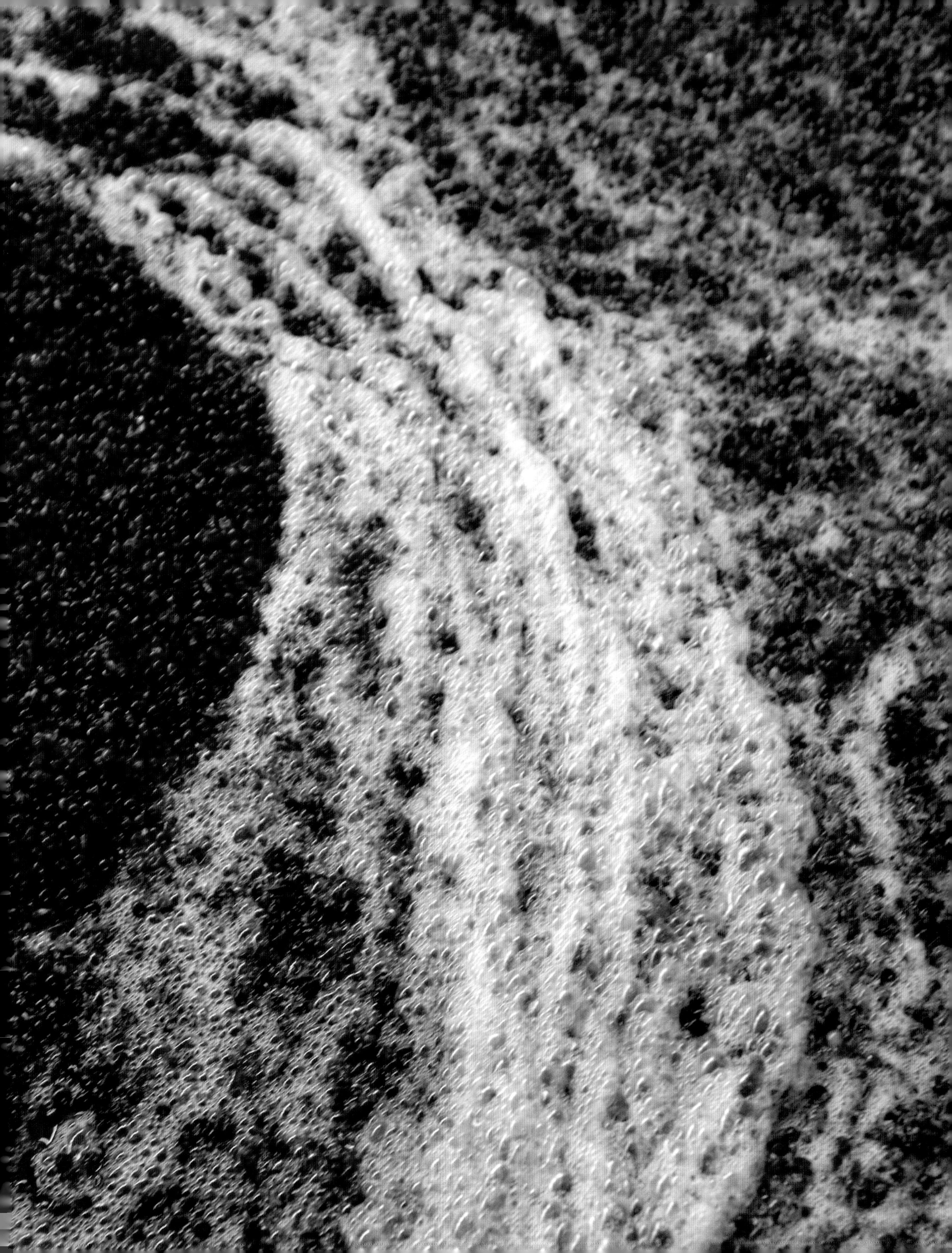

Laurent Gotti

Hospices de Beaune

The Saga of a Winemaking Hospital

Translated by Delia Dent

FÉRET

A bird's-eye view of Beaune.
Previous page: *Wine fermenting in vat at the estate of the Hospices de Beaune.*

To Amandine and our three children, Valentin, Céleste, and Faustine, who were born at the Hospices Civils de Beaune.

"Where peril grows,
so does that which saves."
Friedrich Hölderlin

A Unique Testimony to the Civilization of Wine

The third Sunday of November. As every year, Beaune, the wine capital of Burgundy, is ebullient. The famous Hospices of the town is putting its wines up for sale. The crus that come from these sixty hectares are among the most in demand by connoisseurs of great wine. These cuvees, sold to the highest bidders throughout the afternoon, capture the attention of an entire profession and the passion of those who taste them. The buyers are from Japan, Germany, the United States, the Middle East, etc. The world's oldest charity auction began working its magic in 1859. But the Hospices de Beaune is much more than a historical act of altruism. A new page in the chronicle of this unusual "winemaking hospital" is written each year, with each new vintage. The supervisor of the wine estate and his team of twenty-two *vignerons* have the privilege and also the heavy responsibility of promoting a jewel of the Burgundian cultural patrimony, an estate that dates back to 1457 but which is still in the news every year. It has even been enhanced over the last few decades by the addition of certain exceptional *terroirs*: Pommard, Clos de la Roche, Bâtard-Montrachet, Meursault, etc. Made up mainly of premier cru and grand cru vineyards, the estate owes its existence exclusively to donations from local winemaking families.
The institution prides itself on using all available means to bring the best out of these coveted *terroirs*.

Why the fascination? The famous polychrome roofs of the Hôtel-Dieu of Beaune are the "emblem" of Burgundy, a very popular tourist destination that captivates almost 400,000 visitors each year. Jean-Philippe Lecat, former French Minister of Culture, drew attention several years ago to the symbolism of this masterpiece of Flemish architecture: "The stones assembled for pleasure, power, and glory have been overturned. The house of the poor is intact." Part of the credit goes to the beneficial effects of wine, a symbol of generosity, comfort, and conviviality. It seems a lot like a Biblical parable.... Built in 1443 by Nicolas Rolin, chancellor to Duke Philip the Good, the Hôtel-Dieu continued to receive the sick until 1971! Today the profits from the estate's wine auction still contribute considerably to the modern hospital and the restoration of the Hôtel-Dieu.

This passion is also fueled by the media frenzy surrounding the auction. Many big names from show business, literature, and science have presided over the event: Catherine Deneuve, Lino Ventura, Barbara Hendricks, etc. In the spotlight, the wines are sold well above market prices. The rises and drops that mark the history of the auction are widely publicized, sparking a reaction that goes far beyond the confines of the institution: journalists descend en masse to attend and report on the event. For them, it is often the first glimpse of the new vintage, the incontrovertible opportunity to gauge Burgundy. In the heart of the vineyards, the impact of the auction on the local economy is hotly debated: originator or merely an indicator of trends? In the end this is unimportant; the wines of the Hospices de Beaune are a gift from history to today's wine connoisseurs. And more broadly speaking, they are a striking testament to the vivacity of the civilization of wine!

Left page:
The multicolored roof of the Hôtel-Dieu de Beaune.

The Origins

OVER FIVE CENTURIES AGO, NICOLAS ROLIN, CHANCELLOR TO THE DUKE OF BURGUNDY, AND HIS WIFE, GUIGONE DE SALINS, FOUNDED THE HÔTEL-DIEU OF BEAUNE. ROLIN ACHIEVED AN IMPRESSIVE SOCIAL ASCENSION: HE WAS NOT OF NOBLE BIRTH, BUT HE KEPT COMPANY WITH GREAT MEN AND FREQUENTED THE MOST PROMINENT ARTISTS. IT WAS AN ERA OF SUMPTUOUS BANQUETS AND JOUSTING TOURNEYS AMONG THE RULING CLASSES. AND YET SPIRITS WERE LOW; FAMINE AND PLAGUE POCKED A CENTURY OF WAR. SO THE CHANCELLOR BECAME A PHILANTHROPIST AND CHOSE BEAUNE TO ESTABLISH HIS CHARITY. BUT HE NEVER SUSPECTED THAT WINE WOULD INVADE THE HISTORY OF HIS INSTITUTION, RIGHT FROM THE START.

A Saga in the Golden Age of Burgundy

A tower and three keys: these are the omnipresent symbols of the wine of the Hospices de Beaune. On the label of each bottle, on the oak barrels that sit in the cellar, above the entrance to the winery, on the signs that announce the vineyard parcels worked by the prestigious estate, etc. It is a veritable treasure hunt! This coat of arms deserves to be deciphered. It harks back to the founding of the Hospices de Beaune, more than five centuries ago, and refers to the creators of the institution, Nicolas Rolin and Guigone de Salins.

The three keys are those of Nicolas Rolin, ducal chancellor of Burgundy for forty years (1422-1462). He was, in a manner of speaking, the Burgundian prime minister. The keys represent certain ancestors of his who held public office. State affairs were certainly not unknown to the Rolin family. Nothing could have better prepared Nicolas for such prestigious duties. This contemporary of Joan of Arc and vassal of Philip the Good left his mark on a particularly crucial and turbulent page of his region's history: murder, treason, conspiracy, kidnapping, chivalry, and great fortune…. All against the background of the Hundred Years' War pitting the French against the English. The elements that make up our imagery of the Middle Ages are all gathered in the story of the chancellor, a saga tracing the paths of power that nevertheless would not

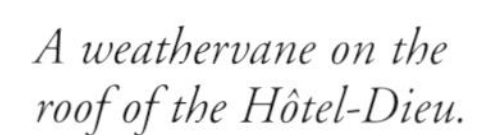

A weathervane on the roof of the Hôtel-Dieu.

Left page: *The entry gate to a courtyard of the Hôtel-Dieu.*

prevent Nicolas Rolin from dying peacefully in his hometown of Autun. Prosperous and assured of a prestigious descent, he passed away at 85 years old, a venerable age for that era. The chancellor would go down through history as one of the most feared and esteemed men of state of his time, a key player in Burgundy as it reached the peak of its influence throughout Europe. A highly unlikely destiny for the son of a family with no noble blood. Throughout his life Rolin frequented the most powerful men of his time and the most brilliant artists. Yet as history has a knack for irony, it was his institution serving the poor and the sick, founded toward the end of his life, that secured his name for posterity: the Hôtel-Dieu of Beaune.

An Ambitious Attorney

Nicolas Rolin's origins lie in Autun, an ancient town (popular today for its Roman theatre) in the northern part of the Saône-et-Loire department in southern Burgundy. The youngest son of a clerk, Nicolas came from a prosperous bourgeois family. As important landowners, the Rolins already had a foothold in the vineyards of the Couchois (also in the Saône-et-Loire) and the Côte de Beaune. Nicolas' mother also had family ties to wine-growing; she came from Pommard, a few miles away from Beaune.

When his basic schooling was done, Nicolas Rolin chose to study law like his brother Jean. He attended the University of Avignon – which enjoyed the reflected prestige of the papacy and therefore international renown – where he acquired juridical knowledge of the highest degree. His studies completed, Rolin set his sights on becoming a lawyer and returned to Burgundy, where in 1401 he participated in the parliamentary assemblies of Beaune, the highest court of the duchy. It was here that the dukes of Burgundy held court during the Capetian dynasty. Meanwhile, the deaths of his parents placed the young man at the head of a significant estate. Among other things, he inherited vineyard parcels in the Côte de Beaune in Saint-Aubin, Meursault, Auxey-Duresses, Volnay, Pommard, and Beaune.

At the time, Philip the Bold had established a prosperous realm as the head of the duchy. Son of King John II aka John the Good, Philip founded in 1364 a Burgundian dynasty that was particularly successful and ambitious (see inset). John the Fearless, his son, succeeded him in 1404 and recognized the great juridical aptitude of Nicolas Rolin, who within a few years had become part of the new duke's entourage. Off to Paris, Rolin was named attorney to the duke of Burgundy by the parliament and consequently assembled a team of a dozen jurists who were among the most qualified in the kingdom. It was also in the capital that he would meet his second wife, Marie de Landes, a young lady from a rising family in finance and administration. Rolin's social ascension was obvious.

A view of Pommard from the premier cru vineyard Les Arvelets. The Hospices owns a parcel here (cuvee Billardet).

John "the Fearless," duke of Burgundy, in 1404 (1371-1419) *by Alexandre Laemlein (1813-1871).*

BURGUNDY AT THE FOUNDING OF THE HOSPICES

In the 14th century, the borders of the duchy of Burgundy were very different from those of the region we know today. Burgundy had become French less than a century earlier, after Philip of Rouvres died without an heir, struck down in his youth by the plague in 1361. The Capetian dynasty of the dukes of Burgundy died with him. The king of France, John II "the Good" snatched up the duchy to put it under the rule of one of his sons: Philip, who would go down in history under the name Philip the Bold. Philip significantly expanded his realm by marrying Margaret of Flanders. Burgundy would thus extend its flag over a large part of modern-day Belgium, up to the Dutch coast of Friesland and encompassing Picardy, Hainaut, Artois, etc. Fourteenth-century Burgundy included not only Dijon, but also Brussels, Antwerp, Bruges, Ghent, Mechelen, Lille, Cambrai, etc. – numerous cities with flourishing economies. The duchy also extended east into what was then called the Comté of Burgundy (now the Franche-Comté), where the most important cities were Dole and Salins. The Mâconnais and the Charolais were the southernmost reaches of the "Burgundian state." The territory remained rather fragmented but enjoyed a dominant position in Europe during that period.

The Swords are Unsheathed

The period was marked by an abhorrent atmosphere in the French court, with a backdrop of bloody battles against the English: the Hundred Years' War was in full swing. John the Fearless had at best stormy relations with part of the court of King Charles VI of France. Rivalries were exacerbated by the ill health of the sovereign who, seized by dementia, was unable to exert his power. Various clans struggled for power in the council of regents, over which Queen Isabeau of Bavaria presided. In this destructive context John the Fearless had his cousin and rival, the Duke of Orleans, killed in 1407. Grudges among the nobility of the period were grave matters, and John the Fearless died violently in his turn: in 1419, the duke of Burgundy was killed in an ambush by partisans of the heir to the French crown. Relations between France and Burgundy were at their worst. The rift led to the Treaty of Troyes between Burgundy and England, signed on May 21st, 1420 and confirming the English king's claim to the French crown. Burgundy had now firmly sided with the English. The murder of John the Fearless had grave long-term consequences. It also had significant short-term effects: this bloody episode opened political doors for Nicolas Rolin.

A Brilliant Argument

The widow and the son of the assassinated duke chose the young jurist from Autun to demand justice and restitution. The future chancellor was given the task of establishing "The Complaint to the King Regarding the Death of John the Fearless." The argument was presented in Paris in 1420 to the kings of France and England, Charles VI and Henry V. "*As was the custom in important affairs, Rolin was assisted by other lawyers, there to encourage him by their presence and possibly to make suggestions; he had no less than 12 associates, most of whom practiced law in Paris. He recounted the drama, enhancing it with details that would provoke indignation. His eloquence conquered the audience,*" report Marie-Thérèse Berthier and John-Thomas Sweeney in their book on the chancellor. The theatrics used by lawyers today are nothing new. Rolin touched his listeners. The qualities he demonstrated while in service to the ducal family, in this historic moment for the house of Burgundy, were certainly crucial to his later appointment to more prestigious positions. His ascension to the chancellery would be effected two and a half years later. In the interim, Rolin strengthened his ties to the duchy by practicing in the parliament in Dole. In 1422 Philip the Good took over for his late father, John the Fearless. The designation of an attorney was already a historic event. A jurist became a chancellor, and not an ecclesiastical dignitary, as was the rule. In 1521, while François I was visiting the Burgundian capital, a monk with a sharp sense of humor presented the skull of John the Fearless to the king. As he pointed out the marks of the blow that killed the duke of Burgundy, he said, "Sire, this is the hole through which the English entered France." It is also the hole through which Rolin reached the chancellery…

The Very Picture of Nobility

The team of Philip the Good and Nicolas Rolin would rule Burgundy for four decades: forty years that would leave their mark on local history. The duchy would reach the height of its power, driven by the ambition and the political ingenuity of Philip the Good. "I want it to be known that I could have been king had I wished it," the duke liked to say. In his biography of Philip the Good, Emmanuel Bourassin paints a grandiose portrait of the Burgundian sovereign: "*A generous, even extravagant patron, likeable and welcoming, but above all a shrewd politician. He amassed property – not necessarily honestly – by a succession of inheritances – and what inheritances! – that he managed to gather or capture. The prince of knights, the very picture of nobility, he hardly had to draw his sword to become 'The Great Duke of the West,' richer than ten kings. That was his ultimate tactic: act only when you are sure of hitting your mark.*"

His dream was to build a bridge between the Latin and Germanic worlds. He established himself as a successor to Charlemagne, no more and no less, but also as a precursor to Charles V, his great-grandson… Philip the Good found in Rolin someone truly reliable to aid him in his work: "*His pro-Burgundian sentiments made quite an impression on Duke Philip, who appreciated his great abilities, his arduous*

Philip "the Good," duke of Burgundy (1396-1467).

Left page:
Valentina of Milan implores King Charles VI for justice after the murder of the Duke of Orleans in 1407 *by Alexandre-Marie Colin (1798-1873).*

enthusiasm, and his sense of the State. Already an attorney in the parliament of Dole, Nicolas Rolin was promoted to chancellor of Burgundy in December 1422 and until his death forty years later filled this role so efficiently and with such authority that his master never made an important decision without consulting him first. His functions did not stop at doling out justice in the Burgundian states though: not content to counsel the duke, he made important decisions for his chief," explains Emmanuel Bourassin.

For the Ailing Poor

Many long years would pass before Rolin's most lasting and famous work was completed. The creation of the Hôtel-Dieu of Beaune came about during the second half of his long tenure as chancellor. The project began in January 1442, when the chancellor was 66 years old, with the first acquisitions of land destined to hold the hospital. The official launch of the charitable work was solemnly held in the open narthex of the collegiate church of Beaune in late August, 1443. Rolin dictated to notaries the founding act before the prominent men of the town and a crowd of onlookers. "*Beginning now, and in perpetuity, I hereby establish and build by endowment a hospital in the city of Beaune of the diocese of Autun, for the reception, use, and housing of the ailing poor.*" His hospital would be placed directly under the authority of the Pope.

What were the chancellor's motives? Nicolas Rolin had already outlined them: "*Relinquishing all affection and concern for worldly matters, and turning my thoughts to my own salvation: desiring, by a blessed enterprise, to exchange my temporal gifts that have increased by God's grace with those of Heaven, and to leave that which is ephemeral to enjoy eternal gifts (...) I hereby establish...,*" etc.

The famous Salle des Pôvres or Poor Men's Hall at the Hôtel-Dieu. The nuns welcomed their first patients here in 1452.

In the cabinets of the apothecary: the materia medica of the era holds a few surprises....

A Blessed Enterprise

Nicolas Rolin's charitable work, this "blessed enterprise," obviously was not as selfless as it might seem. In his twilight years, the chancellor seemed seized by a fear of the Last Judgment. Rolin wanted to earn a place in Heaven. But when he examined his conscience, the salvation of his soul and his eternal rest did not seem certain. Did this man of power, admired and feared, have sins to pardon? His political career shows no great blemish nor infamy. On the contrary, an unwavering fidelity to the Duke of Burgundy seems to have been his guiding principle. But perhaps that is where the fault lies? This undying allegiance, including in base deeds of wartime, persistently troubled him. For a good part of his career, Nicolas Rolin spent his energy making his prince's desire for revenge or for power a reality. His treasons too. This man must have ridden throughout the entire duchy collecting taxes destined to finance the war effort or mobilize the men at arms who would go off to battle. The chancellor even assumed some of the direction of military affairs just as a Chief Commander would do.

This "Armagnac-Burgundian" Civil War was the major event of Rolin's political career. The French fought amongst themselves over the future of the royal throne. The English claims further fanned the fire. It is this conflict that would permit a simple bourgeois from Autun to ascend to the highest function he could possibly have imagined. It was also the interminable saga that spanned the first half of his term in office. For if Rolin played a primary military role, the conflict also established his talents as a diplomat and negotiator throughout an era rife with maneuvers and realignment of alliances.

Right page:
Six scenes from the life
of Joan of Arc.

Calming the Ire

It would be careless to depict Rolin as a pacifist. At the beginning of his career, under John the Fearless, he also sided with the English as that position struck him as more beneficial to the interests of Burgundy. He deserves credit, however, as an author of the reconciliation with France in the early 1430s. Might this have been the effect of a certain pragmatism instilled in him by regularly dealing with the conflict? At the time the duchy was harassed by the Armagnacs, who ravaged many districts of Burgundy; the townspeople appealed to their lord for help. But the fact remains that Rolin had a crucial influence in calming the ire of the duke of Burgundy against his family in the French court. Philip the Good was still scarred by the "criminal homicide" of his father. This murder was a lasting blow to his spirits. The duke was also bound by an oath to the English to fight for their cause. These sentiments and this obligation were coupled with a clear economic interest: England provided wool to Flanders, where a cloth-making industry flourished. It seemed difficult for Burgundy's Flemish states to jeopardize such an important economic partnership.

One famous episode of the Anglo-Burgundian alliance would prove fatal to the most famous historic figure of the period: Joan of Arc. She who had a divine mission to restore the authority of the king of France and reunite his kingdom fell into Burgundian hands in 1430 when she was captured by one of Philip the Good's captains. Joan's downfall came during the siege of Compiègne that was led by the duke.

A Medieval Pontius Pilate

It was this great capture that brought about a lucrative trade between Philip the Good and his allies across the Channel: the English paid a great sum for her. Nothing would come between Joan of Arc and her martyrdom any more. By a singular destiny, mixing mysticism and patriotism, Joan's messianic aura appeared quickly to her contemporaries. Doctors of theology pored over her case weeks before she assembled the French troops. In this medieval gospel, Philip the Good, and his loyal chancellor with him, played a very somber role: that of Pontius Pilate washing his hands of the fate of the prisoner. It was undoubtedly a sad scene when the duke met with his captive. A chronicler was present to witness the event, but his account is enigmatic. "Yes, they spoke, but I don't remember what they said," he essentially reported. "It's a state secret!" we would say today….

Historians have made no mention of even the slightest remorse on the part of the duke regarding this episode; but there is no doubt that the court could not ignore the gravity of the situation, nor the immense popularity of Joan of Arc. Hardly fifteen years after she was burned at the stake, the young woman's reputation (she was just 19 years old) was restored. Her so-called judges, devoted to the English cause, had died in the interim; Philip the Good and his chancellor, however, were still much alive. Even worse for the duke, Joan had always shown Philip great respect. She wrote him two letters trying to convince him to recognize Charles VII as the legitimate king of France, reminding him that royal blood ran through his own veins. But her letters went unanswered….

Rolin followed the affair very closely. After convening the war council in Châlon-sur-Saône, a few days after Joan's capture, he returned directly to the council and rejoined his duke. Who knows if the chancellor was thinking of repentance and redemption for turning Saint Joan over to her enemies when he created the Hospices de Beaune?

46 10
71 25
73 34
80 48
61
78
87
JEANNE EST FAITE PRISONNIÈRE DEVANT COMPIÈGNE
(24 Mai 1430)
MME
1429)
50
60
53 11
64 18
79 30
85 35
JEANNE-d'ARC DEVANT ses JUGES (Février-Mars 1431)
ON (Mars 1429)
57 12
69 27
83 38
88 50
SUPPLICE DE JEANNE-d'ARC (30 Mai 1431)

The Treaty of Arras, December 23rd, 1482.

Pardon Granted

In September of 1435 the Treaty of Arras would bring the Armagnac-Burgundian War officially to an end. In a public ceremony, a representative of the king of France knelt before Duke Philip and, in the name of the sovereign, begged him to pardon his "step cousin" for the assassination of John the Fearless. He claimed that the murderous dauphin was still young at the time and ignorant of public affairs. Philip, in turn, swore never to bear a grudge against the king and to purge his heart of any wish for revenge. The Hundred Years' War was far from over, but the peace between the Burgundians and the French could begin. Yet it would be foolish to imagine any great friendship between the French crown and the ducal house of Burgundy: this would never come to be. There was no love lost between the next generation of sovereigns, Charles the Bold in Burgundy and Louis XI of France. The people, meanwhile, weary of the ravages of war, rejoiced at the news of the reconciliation. Burgundy emerged from this episode with reinforced autonomy and borders. The many reparations contained in the forty three articles of the treaty were flattering: compensation for the death of John the Fearless, exemption from the duties of vassalage, and a substantial allocation of territories. Once again, Rolin's talents as a jurist awed his audience.

Exaction and Plundering

Rolin could nevertheless see that this vicious family quarrel had, and would have, lasting effects on the lives of the commoners. The consequences of the conflict were sorely felt; Burgundy suffered through miserable times, including during breaks in the fighting and even when peace returned. The victories of diplomacy did not put an end to the violence and plundering. Men of arms had been paid to fight on behalf of the warring factions and found themselves without any revenue when calm returned. Mercenaries on both sides were disinclined to put away their swords and sowed terror throughout the countryside. The sobriquet they earned speaks for itself: the Flayers.

In their work on Nicolas Rolin, Marie-Thérèse Berthier and John-Thomas Sweeney cite an almost apocalyptic description of the state of Burgundy in the mid-15th century: "*In the towns, the poor would gather around heaps of refuse and there die of hunger. There were those who sought to rid themselves of this spectacle by chasing off the destitute; others would eliminate any possible source of nourishment. It was forbidden to remove grain, to feed dogs, to use wheat to make beer or other liquor; but these measures were not sufficient to bring back prosperity. The shortage was a result of the laborers, forced to remain inside cities or fortresses, neglecting to work the land, so that produce sold for ten times more than it had in previous years. The famine was followed by plague, which devastated the towns of Burgundy. Wolves became accustomed to feasting on human cadavers and came right up to cities to attack the*

A statue of Nicolas Rolin in the courtyard of the retirement home at the Hôtel-Dieu.

Pillage of a Village *by Sebastiaen Vrancx (1573-1647).*

living. And the Flayers, even worse than these carnivorous animals, kept a stranglehold on the towns with their constant attacks: theft, murder, arson, and rape on all sides were the terrible tracks left by these bandits."

Distributing Bread

This profile is undoubtedly somewhat of a caricature or at least depicts a particularly critical moment for the duchy; under Philip the Good, most Burgundians ate their fill, and the economy performed well. In 1438 however, five years after the creation of the Hospices, Burgundy suffered one of its worst famines of the Middle Ages. Moreover, Beaune and its surroundings were forced to face the menace of the Flayers. It is worth noting that the day after the official establishment of the Hôtel-Dieu, and before the hospital was even built, Rolin began distributing bread at the basilica of Beaune. Every day at 8 o'clock in the morning rations were given out to "Jesus Christ's poor." The portions of bread doubled during Lent.

A comparison between the living conditions of commoners and the luxurious habits of the nobility shows the social reality of the period to be particularly unjust. The Congress of Arras provides a striking example: the event drew a great number of dukes, counts, and important clergymen from France, England, and Burgundy. Horse shows and other festivities were staged, and the champions faced off in a tournament. Members of rival factions participated in various diversions. This was surprising behavior in light of the grave business at hand: princes and lords had come to debate a war that would determine the fate of millions of men. But the time to celebrate an end to the horrors of battle had not yet come. On the contrary, the discussions would end in a partial failure. Though the French and the Burgundians signed the "Treaty of Arras," it was only to improve the war. Starting the following spring, the Burgundian troops would fight alongside their former enemies and together they would liberate Paris from the English occupation.

A Matter of Chivalric Honor

In 1436 Philip the Good demonstrated remarkable zeal in planning the Siege of Calais. The Picards, the Flemish, the local militia, and his own officers were united under the duke for an expedition that would end in a terrible defeat. English reinforcements would chase their counter-offensive all the way to Flanders, an industrious and prosperous country that had not seen the ravages of war in a long time. Blood was shed in vain. His northern subjects resented the duke: their economy, already largely deflated by the demands of the ducal causes, slumped. Philip was also much maligned by the English; he was called a traitor, a coward, and all the other insults deserved by a man who had stained the name of chivalric honor.

Rolin was therefore well placed to witness the growing mistrust of a people towards their sovereign. Shortly after this defeat, there was a revolt in Bruges. The mutiny was brutally suppressed and the main players condemned to death, but this wind of rebellion was just a taste of the tempest that would soon devastate Flanders. Ghent shortly followed suit, the financial burden of the duke's political exploits being their primary grievance: the people of the city refused to accept a new tax.

A Bloody Retaliation

Entry of Philip the Good, duke of Burgundy, into Ghent in 1448.

Philip the Good, determined to re-establish his authority, took retaliatory measures against the people of Ghent. The situation turned ugly, and numerous acts of violence were committed against the servants and officers of the duke. The show of force ended in a pitched battle in July 1453. The inexperienced militiamen of the town had only their determination in their favor when they faced the army of Philip the Good. The duke led his troops himself, surrounded by his best horsemen. The evening after the battle, twenty thousand bodies were scattered over the fields and in the Escaut River, according to contemporary reports. The duke, in a moment of lucidity and compassion, found it to be a bitter victory: "Alas, who has won? I'm the one who has lost; you can see that these are my subjects." Emmanuel Bourassin believes that Philip had shortly recovered: "On July 30th the duke, quickly consoled after the massacre there, entered the subdued city; a delegation of two thousand townsmen, barefoot and wearing nothing but their undershirts, threw themselves at his feet yelling, 'Thanks to the duke!' in French, which for the Flemish was the ultimate humiliation."

Rolin was closely involved in these events, as witnessed by the death threats that were sent to him from Flanders. The culprits of this "lese-chancellor" were condemned to death.

A Wave of Fury

In the meantime, a wave of discontent swept through the very heart of the duchy (though it never reached the same extremity as in the Nordic countries). In 1451 the parliaments of both Dijon and Dole addressed their grievances to the chancellor: they were tired of the increasingly restrictive taxation. At the height of these troubles, the Hospices de Beaune had already been established for several years and Rolin was in his seventies. Perhaps this shrewd politician had foreseen the accumulation of anger and the depth of the rift. In the context of these events, the initiative to found such an institution could only insure a rise in popularity and guarantee him a place in history. Regardless, this act highlights the contradiction of an era when, in the name of chivalry, great men could just as easily massacre their subjects as build them havens for the day when they would fall ill. "It is more a prince's palace than a poor man's hospital," people said of the Hôtel-Dieu.

Worldly Matters

As for the worldly matters that Rolin mentioned in the founding deed of the Hospices de Beaune, he did not abandon them so quickly. Life at the ducal court was extravagant. In fact, Philip the Good is known to have hosted one of the most sumptuous banquets of the Middle Ages, the "Feast of the Pheasant" held in Lille in 1454. The finest wines of the ducal cellars flowed freely, and the profusion of foods, garnished with the most precious spices, was presented at great expense, with flair and imagination. If the word "Burgundian" is a synonym for bon vivant, it certainly took on this meaning in the Middle Ages. Throughout the banquet there were theater performances, acrobatics, songs, and music. One of the plays, in three acts, represented current affairs of the day: Constantinople had fallen to the Turks. A grief-stricken woman – an allegory of Christianity – called princes and knights to aid her: in short, she was calling for another crusade. At the end of the play the duke vowed to take up arms; but such an expedition would also mean raising more funds. Rolin, at 78, was too old to make the holy voyage, but he wanted to send one of his children, accompanied by twenty-four armed and mounted noblemen. The chancellor would finance their equipment. At least, this is what he agreed to during the banquet.

The court of Burgundy was known for its splendid banquets. The Book of Conquests and Feats of Alexandre.

Unrivaled Splendor

Neither Philip the Good nor his chancellor would have to finance a crusade. Although the topic was raised again several times, Philip would not go to war in the name of the cross. In fact, under his rule, Burgundy would not launch any military offensives to expand its territory even though, as demonstrated previously, there were numerous opportunities to do so. The duke needed money to support his men at arms, but another matter was also straining the budget: the most extravagant expenses were not even questioned, even though they would have to be paid with funds raised through blood and anger.

Left page:
The garden of love in the court of Philip III the Good, duke of Burgundy, in the gardens of the castle of Hesdin in 1432 (celebrations held on the occasion of the marriage of chamberlain André de Toulongeon).

Philip the Good would be known to history for the incomparable luxuriousness of his court. Some historians even see in it "a foreshadowing of Versailles under Louis XIV." Emmanuel Bourassin is quite convinced of this: "Unrivaled splendor: you would have to trace back to the sumptuous period of Byzantium to find a court conducted with such ceremony, with so many dignitaries and officials, and displaying, even in daily life, such solemn pomp. (...) Everything was a pretext for a party: receiving great men or ambassadors, baptisms, marriages. Countless occasions to empty the coffers of the duke's treasury."

Luckily, Nicolas Rolin's administrative skill and his close relations with important bankers, the Arnolfini family (refer to Jan Van Eyck's famous painting "The Arnolfini Portrait") and the Portinari family, northern Italians who had settled in the duchy, averted bankruptcy.

The Arnolfini Wedding
by Jan Van Eyck (circa 1390-1441).

A Friend of the Arts

Today we can glimpse the splendor of Philip's court in the ducal palace in Dijon, a place Philip the Good actually visited rather infrequently. Much less often, at least, than Rolin, who owned a vast town house in the same city. And yet the duke had large kitchens built there around 1435. Six immense fireplaces to prepare feasts, each with its own particular use: one for roasting cuts of meat, entire cows or quarters of venison, roe deer, or wild boar; in another the sauce chefs prepared their sauces; while meat boiled in gigantic cauldrons in yet another. The kitchens were staffed by a large team led by the head chef, whose appointment was a very solemn moment. In a strange show of democracy in the life of the palace, the head chef was essentially chosen by his peers.

It would nevertheless be unfair to depict Philip the Good as a crude, unscrupulous hedonist. The influence of the duke of Burgundy on the art of his era was considerable; his court had no equal in Europe as an artistic center. The list of artists who received commissions from the duke was impressive and knew no boundaries. Among the sculptors were Juan de la Huerta of Aragon and Antoine le Moiturier of Avignon; the two of them executed the tomb of John the Fearless and Marguerite of Bavaria (now in the Museum of Beaux-Arts in Dijon). In music, the English composer John Dunstable stands out for his international renown and his profound influence on certain composers of the early Renaissance. Guillaume Dufay was another important musical figure of the period; he composed the musical element of the famous Feast of the Pheasant discussed above. His best-known work is the "Homme Armé" mass, which is a

The polyptych of the Last Judgment *by Rogier Van der Weyden. In the museum of the Hôtel-Dieu, a magnifying glass allows visitors to admire the remarkable precision of the details. This masterpiece of Flemish painting is over six yards wide.*

A PATRON

Rolin's charity was an object of admiration for generations. This great official of the Burgundian state invested one fifth of his fortune, a quantity deemed "considerable" by historians, in charitable works. Aside from building the Hôtel-Dieu of Beaune, he had the parish church of his childhood, in Autun, rebuilt into a collegiate church. Avignon has him to thank for a chapel built in the Celestine church there. This charitable and religious work also had artistic implications: the famous painting by Jan Van Eyck, Madonna with the Chancellor Rolin, *would be placed in the collegiate church of Autun, while the triptych of the* Last Judgment *by Rogier Van der Weyden was destined for his foundation in Beaune. His actions sometimes had unexpected effects. Louis XI had a cruel comment when he learned of the construction of the Hôtel-Dieu: "He has made enough people poor in his lifetime to shelter them today!" Historians are not much more kind, seeing above all the preoccupation of a man full of his newly won nobility and fixated on the image he would leave for posterity.*

musical depiction of chivalric values. The court painter, Henri Bellechose, came from the northern states of the duchy; archives have shown that he was richly paid.

This was also the advent of Burgundo-Flemish art, to which the architecture of the Hôtel-Dieu of Beaune bears witness, as does the altarpiece of the Last Judgment attributed to Rogier Van der Weyden (still displayed in Beaune). Van der Weyden had been a student of Jan Van Eyck, a leading figure of pictorial art of the period who had close ties with Philip the Good: the duke was his son's godfather. Van Eyck remained in the duke's service until he died. Philip also encouraged the production of tapestries and illuminated manuscripts.

Charity Begins at Home

Such abundance and splendor, while the peasants struggled to survive: was Rolin partly responsible? Nothing could be more certain. After all, the social pyramid of the period was rarely challenged; the inevitability of being high- or low-born had long been the rule. Rolin, who was not of noble birth, could undoubtedly demonstrate great sensitivity toward the lot of his less affluent contemporaries; so we cannot exclude the possibility that creating the Hospices de Beaune was the manifestation of a profound feeling of atonement and compassion. Be that as it may, it is certain that Rolin adhered to the famous proverb, "Charity begins at home." He knew perfectly well how to take advantage of his power. The chronicler Georges Chastellin jocularly described Nicolas Rolin at work: "the Chancellor had the habit of governing everything alone, managing everything himself, and being responsible for everything, whether in matters of war, peace, or finances. In all things, the duke left everything up to him… and there was not a single task or profit, in the cities or in the country, in any of these provinces, no donation or loan that he hadn't arranged… So in addition to honor and confidence, and beyond everyone revering him, he made more and greater profits than words can express…." In short, his worldly assets were not "amplified" exclusively by divine grace.

A reconstruction of a scene in the everyday life of the Hôtel-Dieu. This room, Saint Hugh, welcomed patients as recently as the 1980s.

Nicolas Rolin as depicted by Jan Van Eyck (15th century).

“Rolin, Noble Man”

In 1423, after his accession to the chancellery, Rolin the bourgeois became a noble lord. It was at this time that he acquired the seigneury of Authumes on the plain of Bresse (east of Chalon sur Saône), which included land, hamlets, the town, and an impressive castle. “Noble man master Nicolas Rolin,” said the deed of sale, consecrating the new social rank of the chancellor. Other seigneuries fell under his control soon after: a survey of Rolin’s holdings in Burgundy and the Franche-Comté spans both regions from north to south and east to west. Castles, fortresses, towers, and hotels, not to mention the income raised from salt mining, etc. The inventory is dizzying.

Emmanuel Bourassin drives the point home : “*It must be admitted that Nicolas Rolin did not always show great delicacy in handling public funds but, after all, great servants of the state like Sully, Richelieu, and Mazarin were no different. He was generous with the riches he had amassed and enriched his natal town of Autun with artistic treasures that are mostly gone today since the collegiate church of Notre Dame did not survive the turmoil of the revolution.*” The creation of the Hospices was another proof of his generosity, a virtue that was closely linked to a movement that took on great importance under Philip the Good: the glorification of chivalry.

The Golden Fleece

It was Philip the Good who founded “The Most Noble Order of the Golden Fleece” in order to bring together the most valiant knights of the duchy. The golden fleece was a reference to Greek mythology: the wool of a winged ram allows Phrixus and Helle to flee their stepmother, who is plotting against them. A fugitive, Phrixus offers the ram’s pelt to his new protector, the king of Colchis (modern-day Georgia). Later, Jason organizes his famous adventure of the Argonauts to seize the golden fleece. But the order also claims Biblical references, again in a symbol of protection: in the Old Testament (Book of Judges), a certain Gideon is chosen by God to save his people and draw them away from idolatry. Fearful, Gideon asks for signs from God to confirm His will: he asks that a sheepskin be damp when the weather is dry and dry when it is humid. His request is granted.

But the creation of this new order drew its most direct inspiration from the stories of King Arthur and the Knights of the Round Table. Such a great initiative had precedents: the Most Noble Order of the Garter, founded by the king of England in 1344 and placed under the patronage of Saint George. Its motto, “Evil unto him who evil thinks,” has passed into posterity. Even earlier (11th century), the Order of Malta had been created to serve the crusades. It claims the distinction of having survived through the centuries, although only with the least militaristic of its original purposes: to help the poor and the sick, just like the Hospices de Beaune. This is not the only similarity to the Burgundian duke’s creation: “The spirit of the order was structured around the unrealized dream of a crusade that would haunt Philip the Good for the rest of his life,” comments Emmanuel Bourassin.

Honoring the Code

Only sixty-four knights were admitted to the Order of the Golden Fleece under Philip the Good. Logically, Rolin was not inducted. It was hardly within his jurisdiction to take up arms, even though Philip the Good had knighted him in 1424. The chancellor knew the rites involved in the knighting of a noble combatant: the vigil over his arms, the accolade, receiving his sword, etc. But his chivalric motto attested that he did not consider it his office to carry a sword: "*It is useless to plead without obtaining repentance and humility or, even better, the atonement for wrongs.*" Here Rolin reaffirms that he was foremost a jurist and that he prized efficiency above all; this latter point was unquestionably part of his personality. But he still participated in the life of the group: for the festival of the Fleece, celebrated in The Hague in 1456, he served as chancellor of the order. This was a very solemn task because each year on the feast of Saint Andrew, patron saint of Burgundy, there was an inspection into the conduct of the members. They must not have yielded to heresy, nor to treason or cowardice. Even the duke himself was subject to this test! In this particular year, the knights were found to have honored their code, and Rolin complimented them. The ceremony was followed by festivities that lasted a whole week.

This chivalric spirit is not entirely dead. The famous Chevaliers du Tastevin, created in 1934, based its rituals heavily on the imagery that surrounds these medieval orders, and particularly that of the Golden Fleece. Of course, the goal is no longer to go into battle and protect widows and orphans, but rather to belong to an elite club of connoisseurs of the great wine of Burgundy. It is a vine rather than a sword that is now placed on the shoulder of the applicant! The way this brotherhood thrives today shows just how profoundly and enduringly the reign of Philip the Good marked the people of the region.

The first chapter of the Order of the Golden Fleece, held by Philip III the Good, duke of Burgundy, in the church of Saint Peter in Lille, November 22nd, 1431, by Joseph Albrier (1791-1863).

Right page:
The beams of the Salle des Pôvres. Note the omnipresence of the letter S from Rolin's motto, Seule étoile *or "only star." Patients also had a view of the altarpiece of the Last Judgment.*

"Only Star"

Visitors to the Hôtel-Dieu today can still see the spirit of chivalry that motivated Rolin. The motto of his marriage to Guigone de Salins appears on the tiling and the polychrome beams of the "salle des pôvres" or room of the poor. It can also be seen on a tapestry in the chapel:

"Only Star"

For once it is not courage in combat that is exalted, but rather the purity and fidelity of a knight's sentiments for his lady. Each tile carries the motto "Only" with a six-pointed star (like a spur, perhaps?) repeated in a circle; in the middle of the circle the initials of Nicolas and Guigone are intertwined with oak branches. The oak was a favorite motif of the chancellor; first used in his townhouse in Dijon, it reappears in several of his castles (Authumes, Présilly, etc.) and again in Beaune.

There is also an echo of the motto that Philip the Good adopted upon his marriage to Isabelle of Portugal in 1430:

"No other shall have
Lady Isabel as long as she lives"

Philip III the Good in the robes of the Grand Master of the Order of the Golden Fleece, by Eugène Devéria (1805-1865).

A floor tile from the Hôtel-Dieu. Note in the center the initials of Nicolas and Guigone, the founders.

"How generous, loving, and romantic it is!" visitors sometimes say as they leave the Hôtel-Dieu, but unfortunately this is a false impression. Neither Rolin nor Philip the Good was a model of fidelity; both of them had bastard children.

Until his death, Rolin remained dedicated to chivalry. He asked to be displayed after his passing dressed in his gown and with all his insignia of knighthood. On his bronze funerary plaque, Rolin is depicted in armor.

Like the Duke

The most thorough historical studies of Nicolas Rolin's patronage find an effort to imitate Duke Philip the Good. They do not neglect the great particularity of the chancellor's destiny: his spectacular social ascension. "The foundation of the Hôtel-Dieu of Beaune by the man who was particularly attached to his title of Lord of Authume fit the dual goal of a charitable work that was also associated with the memory of himself and his wife, in the aristocratic tradition," notes the historian Hannelore Pepke-Durix. In short, Rolin wanted to be seen as more noble than the nobility and to be remembered that way. It also seems that Philip the Good liked his court to follow in his footsteps. An anecdote bears witness: in 1461, the duke had his head shaved due to an illness. His pride hurt, he ordered all the lords, knights, and squires to have their heads shaved just like the duke. Those who refused to cooperate were hounded relentlessly by the duke's servants.

While this context is clearly vital to understanding the creation of the Hospices de Beaune, and consequently its wine estate, the private world of the chancellor reveals certain elements that may also have had an impact. Illness had not spared those close to him: his mother, Amée, his first wife, and his sister-in-law were certainly all victims of the Plague, and moreover in Beaune. The epidemic that swept through Burgundy at the beginning of the 15th century undoubtedly killed these three relatives. At least, that is the theory presented by Marie-Thérèse Berthier and John-Thomas Sweeney in their book on the chancellor. "*Amée and her two daughters-in-law were probably struck by this epidemic, because in February 1401 they had left this world.*" It is not unreasonable to think that the chancellor was showing his compassion in creating a hospital.

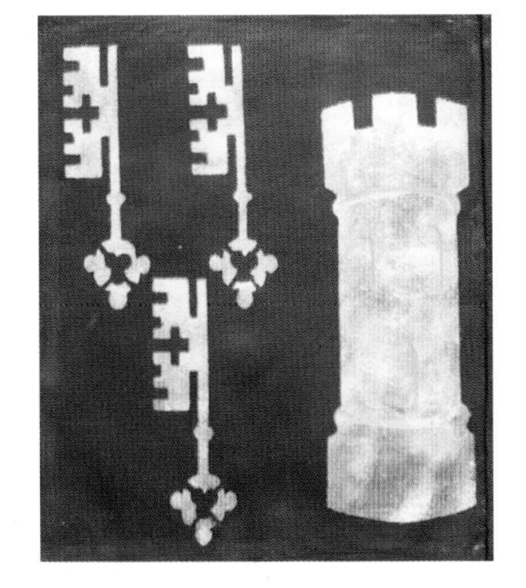

A Tower with Three Crenellations

All of this almost makes us forget that the three keys of Rolin are not alone on the coat of arms of the Hospices de Beaune: the tower with three crenellations, the symbol of Guigone de Salins, Rolin's wife, was also essential to the creation of the Hôtel-Dieu. "*She was the private advisor of the chancellor. Very pious, she was concerned for the soul of her husband and actively encouraged him to do charitable acts,*" assert Marie-Thérèse Berthier and John-Thomas Sweeney. This was the duty of all noblewomen of the Middle Ages.

Guigone de Salins was descended from the Asinari, a noble family from Piedmont, in northern Italy. Their coat of arms had a golden tower on a blue background. They were in finance, running lending banks. Their business led them to establish commercial ties in various regions and to develop trade abroad, thus bringing a branch of the family to the Franche-Comté, which was at the time under Burgundian control. Less exotic, Guigone was also descended from members of the nobility of the Franche-Comté who had lands in Salins, in the Jura. Finally, to add a chivalric touch, her mother was from a family that had given the region some of its most valorous fighters.

When they were married in 1423, Guigone was not yet 20 years old; Nicolas was 48. This young noblewoman was his third wife. At the time, Rolin had already begun negotiations for a reconciliation between Burgundy and France, a long process that would take another twelve years. Moreover, he had already been noble for several months, a change in social status that facilitated the union.

Her Father's Footsteps

One important element shows Guigone's crucial role in the creation of the hospital. Her father, Etienne de Salins (a knight who was killed in combat) had himself founded a hospital in Ivrey for the pilgrims and the poor, and Guigone followed in her father's footsteps. The family of the young lady may also have had an influence on the location chosen for the project. Beaune was not an obvious choice; historians have wondered why it was selected. More important cities of the duchy (Bruges, Bruxelles, Malines, Valenciennes, Lille, etc.) undoubtedly occurred to the chancellor, not to mention Autun, his natal town, where he would have had several advantages in completing his project. His oldest son, Jean, had become bishop of this powerful diocese that covered the entire western part of modern Burgundy and beyond. There were many arguments for the bishop's see. However, the chancellor himself had already done work for his natal town. He had had the parish church of his childhood renovated and enlarged. Besides, Autun was already equipped with numerous churches and abbeys that helped the poor. This was not the case in Beaune, which had no charitable establishments. Moreover, Nicolas Rolin had solid family ties in the wine capital of Burgundy: members of both his mother's and his father's families held important positions there. "*Ultimately, Beaune was chosen [over Autun], the last place where Rolin's mother had lived. It was in this fortified town that there was the most misery and the most need for aid; of 465 households, only 27 had enough to eat,*" notes the historian Herta-Florence Pridat in a biography of the chancellor. She also notes that at first Rolin thought of Chalon-sur-Saône, not far from the seigneury of Authume, but was unsuccessful: "*He could not come to an agreement with the clergy of the town, who probably did not want to allow Rolin to place his hospital directly under the control of the pope. The plot of land where Rolin had planned to build his hospital in Chalon was his private property and was directly next to a convent.*"

Guigone also had family ties in Beaune. One of her cousins was the dean of the collegiate church of Notre-Dame; another owned the seignury of Coraboeuf, a nearby fief. This agreement between the chancellor and his wife may have been very important in carrying out this shared undertaking.

Force of Character

Guigone's involvement in the preparation of this project goes far beyond the simple material aspect. It was she who oversaw the interior organization of the hospital, a task she carried out meticulously. She gathered opinions about the rules of different religious communities with hospitals; she requested and received pontifical support to further her research. A bull from Pope Eugene IV authorized her to enter any convent she wished to visit, "*to stay there one full day for any reason, to share the sisters' food, as well as to discuss any permitted and honest subject with them (...) Better equipped than she had hoped, Guigone could pass through the strictest gates and have edifying conversations with the sisters, who were exceptionally excused from their vow of silence in her presence,*" report M-T Berthier and J-T Sweeney.

The foundation of the Hôtel-Dieu was unquestionably the great event of Guigone de Salins' existence. After her husband's death in Autun in 1462, she would spend a great deal of time assuring that it was running smoothly. She had an office on the upper floor of the grand gallery and lived near Notre Dame de Beaune. But her position caused a family quarrel. Jean Rolin, the eldest son of Nicolas and Marie de Landes (his second wife), wanted to succeed his father at the head of the Hôtel-Dieu and change its rules. His spiritual authority as cardinal of Autun gave him a strong argument.

Often described as discreet and reserved, Guigone would show an unanticipated force of character. Her determination to maintain her command of the establishment would prove triumphant: in 1468, the parliament of Paris would hand down a judgment in her favor after six years of proceedings. The decision confirmed that the Rolin widow had the full and entire right to manage the Hôtel-Dieu of Beaune. Her position as co-founder was legally affirmed.

By Guigone's death almost 19 years after the first patients arrived, the institution had tripled the number of nuns. She spent her last days in Beaune wearing a nun's habit, and in 1470 she was buried in the chancel of the chapel in the Hôtel-Dieu.

The salt harvest, circa 1501, by Jean De Cubas (16th century).

Right page: *A view of Salins by Adam Frans Van der Meulen (1632-1690).*

A Grain of Salt in the Wine

The current image of the Hospices de Beaune is intimately associated with wine. The media coverage of the famous auction that is held there every November is largely responsible. Hasty reasoning would suggest that the choice of Beaune, aside from family ties, had sprung from a wish on Rolin's part to link his work to vineyards and wine, all the more so because of its paramount religious symbolism in Christianity. The economic reality might give the same idea: at Rolin's time, the vineyards already gave wines that brought merchants from Flanders and northern Italy.

However, none of this is accurate. Nicolas Rolin did not plan to have vineyards linked to the Hôtel-Dieu. Historian Hannelore Pepke-Durix insists on this point in a publication on the origins of winegrowing at the Hospices. "Given the current situation, the absence of vineyards in the initial endowment of the Hôtel-Dieu by Nicolas Rolin is striking at first." The historian explains this situation through Rolin's hidden intentions, or at least the intentions that those who study him today have revealed. The chancellor's actions are consistent with his need for aristocratic recognition. Rolin had a more "noble" way to finance his work. Here again a modern man may be surprised: his revenues from salt assured the development of the Hôtel-Dieu, salt mined just over sixty miles away, in Salins-les-Bains (in the Jura) and therefore within the duchy of Burgundy. "*Financing his work with revenue from the great salt mine of Salins was not a neutral choice as it placed the founder under the jurisdiction of the duke, which would also provide powerful support for the foundation,*" continues Hannelore Pepke-Durix.

Salt was a precious commodity in the Middle Ages as a preservative for meat and fish as well as being indispensable to human and animal nourishment. It was the object of intense trade between producing regions and those that had no local sources. As a shrewd businessman, Nicolas Rolin regularly increased his participation in the salt mines of Salins, which was the most profitable investment of the era. He made significant sums of money. His wife Guigone had also inherited an income from the same mines from her father, lord of the town of Salins.

Nevertheless, the couple did not disdain wine: the register of the governor of the Hôtel-Dieu show that in 1460, the door of a cellar where the chancellor stocked wine was repaired. As for Guigone de Salins, she sold or donated wine from her own vineyards to the institution.

The village of Meursault and its vineyards. The Hospices produces seven different cuvees in this appellation.

Its First Vineyards

However, few years would pass before the Hôtel-Dieu acquired its first vineyards. In December 1457, a certain Guillemette, widow of Humbert the Glassblower, donated to Beaune six ouvrees (a quarter of a hectare) in the Beaumont-le-Franc vineyard. The donations and acquisitions would continue and grow at a steady rate over the following decades. Hannelore Pepke-Durix calculates that at the turn of the century the Hôtel-Dieu had a minimum of more than five hectares: mostly vineyards in the commune of Beaune but also some nearby parcels in Echevronne, Pernand-Vergelesses, and Gigny. A policy of acquiring and managing land seems even to have been put in place in the same century. A winemaking hospital was born. In 1497, a significant plot (20 ouvrees or about 0.8 hectares) was purchased in the Cent Vignes vineyard, today a premier cru, on the lower slopes of Beaune. It cost the institution 350 francs. "*But the Hôtel-Dieu occasionally sold parcels, such as two ouvrees in the En Champlong vineyard of Chorey that were sold in 1503 to a man from Beaune named Guillaume Belin for a price of four francs,*" writes Hannelore Pepke-Durix. It is worth noting the great difference in value from one vineyard to another. While one, located on the slopes of Beaune, was bought for 17 francs per ouvree, another, on the flatland, was estimated at just 2 francs per *ouvree*. The respective qualities of different *terroirs* were clearly commonly recognized already at the time.

And yet there is no trace of a vineyard coming from Nicolas Rolin. The chancellor did not dub an estate that was destined for exceptional renown…. Could he have suspected that some day barrels and bottles would disseminate his coat of arms and that of his wife around the world? Certainly not. He would surely be surprised at the current importance of wine to the image and the direction of the hospital. Ironically, a function he had not anticipated does the most to assure his renown today…. The moral of Rolin's story might be: only history can decide the legacy of a mere mortal, no matter how powerful he may be.

NICOLAS ROLIN, FIRST WINEGROWER OF THE HOSPICES DE BEAUNE?

From his youth, Nicolas Rolin was the head of a wine estate with vineyards inherited from both his father and his mother. The Rolin family counted among its assets several of the most coveted vineyard sites of the Côte de Beaune: Cailleret and Taille-pieds in Volnay (both premier crus today), Goutte d'Or in Meursault, etc. Rolin's father owned a house in Volnay with a press and a curtil (a courtyard for gardening or agricultural use). But this does not mean that the chancellor was a winemaker. These vineyards were above all investments, among many others, on which the owners made a profit. They were entrusted to local winemakers, so it is very likely that Nicolas Rolin's knowledge of viticulture and vinification remained purely theoretical. Quite busy in his role as chancellor, Rolin had to look after both the internal and external affairs of Burgundy and spent a great deal of time riding all over the vast duchy, from the Mâconnais to Flanders. He once went two years without seeing the vineyards of Burgundy, quite a long time not to follow the work in the vines and cellar…

Madonna with the Chancellor Rolin by Jan Van Eyck

Madonna with the Chancellor Rolin
by Jan Van Eyck (1390-1441).

This famous painting by Jan Van Eyck (1376-1441), covered with hundreds of minuscule details, is a gold mine of information on Nicolas Rolin. The Burgundian chancellor commissioned the work from the Belgian artist. It has the double interest of being both a portrait and a landscape, all confined to a small space (66 cm x 62 cm). The work, signed by the most famous artist of the period, reveals the image that the statesman wished his contemporaries to see of himself. It would also help to secure him a place in history. The artist's vision of the man and the revelations of infrared imagery are equally eloquent.

The foreground shows the Virgin with the infant Jesus on her lap blessing the chancellor, who kneels on a prie-dieu. There is a great realism in Van Eyck's depiction of him. Rolin has an austere face, his features seemingly unembellished by the painter's brush. The imperfections in his cap haircut (the fashion in the early 15th century) were notably left uncorrected. We can therefore assume that this is a precise representation of Rolin's physical appearance. This solemn private scene in a Romanesque loggia and the benediction (etymologically "to speak well of") have a perfect symmetry. The plump Christ child holds a symbol of his double power, the earthly and the heavenly, represented by a globe topped by a richly ornamented cross. This face-to-face meeting clearly places Rolin on a higher level than the average mortal. As if to emphasize this point, the bridge in the background seems to link Christ to the chancellor.

The particularly efficient perspective and the contrasting colors lead the eye to the landscape that makes up the background. Just below, it takes the viewer away from the heavenly world to regain temporal realities. This picture within the picture opens new horizons. It shows a city and its river. To the right are churches, piazzas, and many houses; to the left is a village with an abbey and a path out to the countryside. Further off, hillsides are covered with forests and vineyards.

A multitude of people performing everyday activities appears before us. People are going to church, heading out to the fields, chatting on stoops, etc. On the bridge are people on foot and knights on horseback. There are water-mills along the river and boats loaded with merchandise on the shores. In short, the painting shows a serene and prosperous city on the morning of a new day. Did this landscape really exist? The spire on the right is certainly that of the Cathedral of Utrecht, and in the middle must be the Arch Bridge of Liège. The Cathedral of Saint

Gudula in Brussels may also appear in the painting. And the vineyards on the hillsides are obviously a reference to Burgundy. Van Eyck composed an imaginary city using various elements borrowed from throughout the duchy of Philip the Good. Remember, Burgundy stretched into Flanders and the Netherlands at the time. This serene activity is depicted as a result of the chancellor's able governance.

A more thorough political reading is sometimes argued: the elements of the drama that set the scene for Rolin's ascension fifteen years earlier are said to be represented here. While arguing for redress for the murder of John the Fearless before the court of France, Rolin earned the prestige that would make him Philip the Good's confidant. Philip's father, John, had fallen in an ambush by the French dauphin's men in 1419. The reference to this event is based on the presence of a landing stage with a tower (to the left of the bridge), which may represent the structure in Montereau (in the Yonne) on which John the Fearless was attacked. In his argument Rolin requested that a requiem mass be said daily in Notre Dame of Montereau and that a monastery be founded nearby. Indeed, a monastery also appears in the painting. As for the people on the bridge, everyone is going from left to right. Perhaps they are all going to attend the requiem mass in the cathedral on the other bank of the river? The cross in the middle of the bridge could also be a reference to the Treaty of Arras of September 21, 1435, in which Nicolas Rolin was an active participant. The document ratified by Duke Philip the Good and King Charles VII celebrated the rapprochement of France and Burgundy. On this occasion, a cross was erected on this same bridge of Montereau.

This analysis would explain the presence of two watchmen in the middle, between the foreground and the background. They might symbolize the king of France (Charles VII) and the duke of Burgundy (Philip the Good), reconciled. It was an important political event at the time, as it would promote a French victory over the English in the Hundred Years' War. Nicolas Rolin is therefore shown at the peak of his art and his influence.

An infrared imaging analysis of the painting brought further revelations: in his sketch of Rolin, Van Eyck put a coin purse with the duke's seal on the chancellor's belt, but this detail did not appear in the final version. The chancellor may have requested this modification fearing that the object would be taken as an allusion to his considerable fortune. The same analysis also showed that Christ originally had his right hand down (it blesses Rolin in the final painting).

Both what is shown and what is hidden in this painting suggest a man who is sure of himself, even arrogant, striving for greater prestige through artistic patronage. However, it is also possible to see a purely spiritual significance: Rolin is simply shown in meditation before Christ and the Virgin. He conveys his hope for salvation and his aspiration to eternal life. Contemporaries would have seen no moral conflict in the way the prosperous Flemish world associated riches, materialism, and a taste for luxury with spirituality and devotion. In paintings of the era, everyday household objects become symbols of the mystery of the evangelical message. The theology of Saint Augustine and Saint Thomas Aquinas, who saw in the tangible world a reflection of the spiritual world, were planted in the minds of the people.

The painting was conserved in the church of Notre-Dame-du-Châtel in Autun until the French Revolution, when the church was destroyed, then was transferred to the Louvre in 1800. Rolin's house (now a museum) was right next to this church. While staying in his house, he attended matins services there, and in 1434 he obtained a special dispensation from the pope to celebrate mass in the first glow of sunlight. Rolin could thus devote himself to his demanding political functions starting early in the morning.

Aside from its formal interest, the work is significant to art history for the technique used: it is one of the first known oil paintings. This innovation, perfected by Van Eyck thanks to the use of turpentine, proved to be more effective in rendering textures and was generally easier to work with. "It was called the secret of the Flemish" and allowed the creation of minuscule details (on this painting some details measure under a millimeter). All that was left for Van Eyck to do was to give free reign to his virtuosity...

The Vineyards and the *vignerons*

WITH EACH VINTAGE, A NEW PAGE IS TURNED IN THE EPIC STORY OF THE HOSPICES DE BEAUNE. IT HAS BEEN THIS WAY FOR SIX CENTURIES.... THOSE WHO WRITE THE CHAPTERS ARE THE *VIGNERONS*, OR WINEGROWERS. ABOUT TWENTY MEN LED BY A SUPERVISOR. THEY HAVE BOTH THE PRIVILEGE AND THE WEIGHTY RESPONSIBILITY OF BRINGING TO LIFE AND PROMOTING A JEWEL IN THE HISTORICAL AND CULTURAL HERITAGE OF BURGUNDY: 60 HECTARES, MOSTLY CLASSIFIED PREMIER OR GRAND CRU.

An Artisan and Much More

His feet planted firmly in the vineyards, his hands never far from a good bottle of wine, and his good humor ready to welcome visitors to the cellar, the *vigneron* is the embodiment of Burgundy as a wine region. He works the vineyards, vinifies the grapes, ages the wine in casks, and markets the bottles that carry his "signature." To put it simply, the *vigneron* personifies the wine.

In an era when wine appellations are as much a cultural treasure as a product of the earth, the *vigneron* is much more than an artisan. He is the bearer of a thousand-year-old history, the benevolent spokesman, entrusted with ancestral expertise. With wine overexposed in the media, there are those who have become true stars in the world of gastronomy and, more widely, of the good life. This is the type of *vigneron* who travels to the United States, Japan, England, etc. to present his craft and his wines. For those who are already well known, "selling" does not require any commercial effort. Far from it. All they need to do is to divide their harvest by the number of clients: prestigious restaurants, loyal clients, wine merchants, importers, etc. Their wines are rare; very rare and sometimes very expensive. These estates are generally in the Côte de Beaune, the Côte de Nuits, and Chablis. They have the most coveted appellations, of course: Gevrey-Chambertin, Vosne-Romanée, Meursault, Puligny-Montrachet, etc. Parcels that are truly a part of the French historical heritage. For example, the famous Clos de Vougeot is the size of a single château of the Médoc (50 hectares), yet it is divided among no less than 80 different owners. That is the power of Burgundy, which thus makes up a sort of limitless "game" for connoisseurs. These *vignerons* knew just how to capitalize on the subdivision of the vineyards into such small appellations. It is not unusual for an estate to sell ten or even fifteen different appellations.

Double previous page:
A statue of Guigone de Salins, co-founder of the Hôtel-Dieu, in the courtyard of the retirement home at the Hospices.

Left page:
The cliff of Vergisson (seen from the cliff of Solutré) in the heart of the Pouilly-Fuissé appellation. The Hospices de Beaune owns a vineyard of 1.4 hectares here.

An Immutable Profession?

Of all words in the French language, "*terroir*" is unquestionably the most revered by Burgundians. But contrary to the common idea that the world of wine is immutable, these professionals are at the forefront of innovation in their field. The latest techniques of their trade are no secret to them. Not one of them can seriously claim that he or she (women are slowly gaining a presence in the trade) works like his or her father did.

These *vignerons* get top billing: they are the ones who appear regularly in magazines and guides. This elite would never let the world forget that the 3,500 Burgundian wine estates are mostly run by simple artisans, men and women with the soul of a small farmer, proud of their craft, eager to develop their estates and to run them as best they can. Most are family estates, passed from one generation to the next. Some of them belong to a cooperative winery, where they pool their ample resources. They generally make a good or a very good living, but they are not sheltered from the hazards of economic circumstances. They often make trips to show their wines at expositions, tastings in wine shops, etc.

These men and women also embody all the diversity – some would say complexity – of Burgundy.

In this abundance of professional winegrowers in Burgundy, twenty-two share a special destiny: they are the *vignerons* of the Hospices de Beaune, each in charge of about 2.5 hectares of the famous estate. Their names are unknown to most connoisseurs of Burgundy; they remain in the shadows of the prestigious Hospices and the cuvees they create. But it was not always that way. Until the end of the 19th century, each cuvee bore the name of its *vigneron*. In 1889, the direction of the Hospices decided to name the products after its benefactors. Today, the public tasting on the weekend of the auction is the only time it is possible to put a face on the wines: the *vignerons* stand by their barrels, serving samples of the year's product.

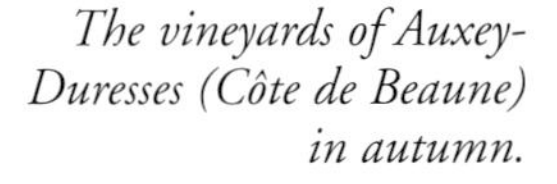

The vineyards of Auxey-Duresses (Côte de Beaune) in autumn.

VIGNERONS WITH A MISSION

They are twenty-two plus a conductor: the director of the estate. The wines he creates must be excellent, the very image of Burgundy, a reference among the many wines produced throughout the region.... "It's true, we are invested with a sort of mission, in which I deeply believe, so we have to go all out. The Hospices serves as an engine for Burgundy, and if the engine doesn't pull the train doesn't move," exclaimed André Porcheret in the magazine *Bourgogne Aujourd'hui* in 1996, when he already had been with the Hospices for about fifteen vintages.

The supervisor is a key player who must have many qualities: he must be a leader, an experienced agronomist, an able winemaker, and also a seasoned marketer. At the head of Burgundy's flagship estate, the supervisor is always under scrutiny from Burgundian professionals and outside observers. Journalists, importers, restaurateurs, etc., all come to Beaune in November for the auction, the premier event of the wine world which follows the harvest. So much attention has its risks, and certain supervisors must have left their post earlier than planned....

But the risk is worth it. To have 60 hectares of mostly premier crus and grand crus placed under your supervision is a rare opportunity in Burgundy. A few months after his arrival in 2001, Roland Masse, the current supervisor, revealed the appeal of the position for him: "I wanted to get to know a new assortment of appellations, and the wine estate of the Hospices has one of the best in Burgundy." He had just left a prestigious estate in the Côte de Nuits, Bertagna, which is notably present in the famous Clos de Vougeot. The historic and cultural aspects of the Hospices were secondary to him: "I think it took me a while to notice it," he admitted.

ONE HUNDRED AND SIXTY PARCELS

It is above all a passionate professional and a devoted admirer of Burgundy who runs the estate of the Hospices. The jovial, debonair allure of Roland Masse is no facade. Equipped with a solid education as an enologist (he has a national diploma), he knows all about the various chemical changes that take place throughout vinification. In the vineyards, he knows inside and out which rootstocks are best adapted to each type of terrain; and the estate's vineyards have a wide range of soil types. With no less than 160 different parcels, all the nuances of the clayey limestone *terroirs* of Burgundy are represented in the vineyards of the Hospices.

Roland Masse, supervisor of the estate of the Hospices de Beaune since 2000.

These are just a few examples of what the supervisor must master in order to draw the best out of his vines. So when Masse speaks passionately, he's not patting himself on the back as he sees connoisseurs and journalists from around the world flock to the Hospices; he is thrilled to talk about these *terroirs*. This word that sounds so hackneyed when others say it takes on its full depth and mystery when coming from his mouth.

When he first arrived, Masse made his priority clear: to have an optimal and meticulous knowledge of the vineyards of the Hospices. "That is what's important to get better quality grapes," he explains. He put in place a systematic

The vineyards stretch over the hill of Corton. The Hospices produce six different cuvees here, both red and white.

Right page:
A bottle of Meursault, cuvee "Humblot," served at the press tasting the Saturday before the auction.

computerized system to track the parcels. The treatments, the volume harvested, the age of the vines, etc. Each vineyard has an i.d. card. Analyses of the leaves and the soils revealed the shortcomings and assets of each fragment of the mosaic that makes up the vineyards. The final report: the vineyards of the Hospices have it all. "Considering that vines will manage with very little, there's no need to add anything," Masse believes. As a result, the estate has hardly used any fertilizers in the last decade.

Quantity and Quality

Mastering the fertility and the vigor of vines has been one of the great crusades of wine professionals for about fifteen years now since vineyards did not escape the excesses of post-war agriculture. The catchword of the day was "yield." *Vignerons* fertilized and chose vines that would guarantee the most ample harvest year in and year out, and phytosanitary products used preventively to protect against disease completed the arsenal. What was a challenge fifty years ago is a reality today: vineyards can produce great quantities with great regularity. But while some crops can take these attempts to increase production without showing much ill effect, vines are different. When it comes to wine, quality and quantity do not mix well. A vine cannot ripen too much fruit every year. And without good fruit, healthy and ripe, there is no good wine…. It is up to men to tame the plant, and *vignerons* who are concerned about quality and the expression of the *terroir* apply themselves to the task with great conviction. The supervisor of the Hospices de Beaune shares this concern with many of his colleagues. "Wine is made in the vineyard" is the adage of the perceptive *vigneron* and has spread like wildfire among the avant-garde.

The wine estate of the Hospices de Beaune is one of the pioneers of the "new" viticulture that turned its back on productivism. Since 2006, the Hospices have even adopted the most radical form of this viticulture: organics (see inset).

"I believe the system is almost maxed out. Chemical molecules are not innocuous; they have a significant effect on vigor. The vines are doped and kept in a perfectly sanitary state, which stimulates growth. And when a plant is more vigorous, it is also more susceptible to disease. It's a vicious cycle," Masse asserts. To these agronomical considerations, he adds others: "The estate is highly regarded and belongs to a hospital. It's hard to imagine that tomorrow an analysis of the wines of the Hospices would reveal a strong presence of pesticides…. It's up to us to set an example, to move away from chemicals."

Hospices

ORGANICS AND WINE

Organics and wine: the combination may seem incongruous to the general public. Wine enjoys an image as a natural product. As for vines, they are thought to be a robust, perennial plant. And yet a vine cannot yield healthy grapes without careful, constant human intervention. Vineyards especially need to be protected from insects, diseases, and fungus. Who hasn't heard of mildew, oidium, or botrytis (grey rot)? These scourges can ruin a harvest. The conventional approach to viticulture uses phytosanitary treatments created by modern chemistry. This is the most widespread method of protecting vines. But those who follow organic viticulture have chosen to banish all synthetic products; they believe that letting foreign molecules loose in an environment that is not naturally equipped to assimilate them is risky. The latest studies on the subject indicate that they have a solid argument. Instead, they treat mainly with sulfur and "Bordeaux mixture" (a solution of copper sulfate and calcium hydroxide). The ranks of "disciples" are growing and becoming increasingly structured. Regulations for organic agriculture were defined on a European scale in 1991. To obtain certification and the right to put the "AB" logo (short for agriculture biologique *or organic agriculture) on their labels, organic producers submit to a strict list of rules and inspections several times a year. If they pass the inspections (and after a three-year conversion period), they are permitted to use the AB logo. At the moment, the certification applies only to the grapes. No definition of organic vinification has yet been validated. This is currently a major bone of contention in the milieu.*

A bunch of Chardonnay grapes, the variety that gives the great white wines of Burgundy.

Working the Soil

The conversion to organics is a step toward a more environmentally friendly viticulture. The Hospices started down this path in the early 1990s, when they turned to *lutte raisonnee* in an attempt to reduce the use of chemical treatments. The supervisor at the time was André Porcheret, who had a significant influence on the recent life of the estate. From a modest family with seven children, Porcheret, a stocky man with mischievous eyes, could not deny his origins: he would always speak with a Burgundian accent, rolling his Rs. He began by learning the trade of barrel-making in Nuits-Saint-Georges and started working for the negociant (see inset) Clerget. The work was hard, but he had one ambition: to know wine. He was passionate about enology. After a few years, the young man became director of *elevage* (the maturation period between vinification and bottling) and purchasing, a position he filled for twenty-four years. The year 1977 marked a turning point in his career: the Hospices de Beaune had experienced the tumultuous vintage of 1976 and asked for his help. André Porcheret then became the supervisor of the famous "winemaking hospital." One of his first decisions was to forbid weed killers. Instead of applying an herbicide, they would have to work the land: plowing, earthing-up (partially covering the vines with earth to protect them from winter frosts), and de-earthing. The man was resolute and uncompromising. He imposed his methods, in the form of precise, dated directives. He announced his credo loud and clear: "A vineyard, especially a vineyard of the Hospices de Beaune, must be perfectly cared for. I am also very demanding when it comes to yields."

André Porcheret (in 1997), charismatic supervisor of the Hospices de Beaune, where he vinified about twenty vintages.

In 1988 began a five-year interlude during which André Porcheret would learn an even more radical approach to viticulture. A new challenge appeared, and Porcheret temporarily left the estate of the Hospices. Lalou Bize-Leroy, part owner of the Domaine de la Romanée-Conti, an estate of unequaled prestige, appealed to him. This energetic woman had just acquired the Domaine Charles Noëllat in Vosne-Romanée. A fervent believer in organics, she gave Porcheret a clear mission: to establish biodynamic viticulture for the estate's twelve hectares of vineyards. So he experimented with the rarefied, even controversial, vineyard management technique. This philosophy is based on the principal that terrestrial life and planetary life are related: what is on Earth is just a reflection of what is happening in the cosmos. The timing of work is dictated by the cycles of the moon. Vegetal, animal, and mineral preparations are sprayed on the vines. These substances (silica, horsetail, nettles, etc.) are diluted in water, sometimes evoking the principals of homeopathy.

Winter work in the vineyards. Left: The vines earthed up for the coming winter. Earthing-up promotes the health of both the soil and the vine. Right: Pruning prepares the vine for the next harvest.

Developed by the Austrian Rudolf Steiner (1861-1925), biodynamics sometimes surpasses rationality. But what does it matter; the essential is that it has proven itself as a viable alternative to conventional viticulture. It is nonetheless difficult to master, especially in years when diseases are particularly virulent. André Porcheret would have this bitter experience in 1993, when mildew, a dreadful, cryptic disease, was widespread. The vineyards of Lalou Bize-Leroy were a sad sight, and the harvest was historically small. Relations between the manager and Madame Leroy became strained. He accused her of being obstinate. Seeing the damage in the vineyards, André Porcheret had proposed in vain to intervene with convential methods. "We'd lost the equivalent of 100 barrels of wine (about 30,000 bottles) in a few days," remembers Porcheret. "We are entitled to work organically but not to lose a harvest."

Absolute Power

At the same time, the Hospices de Beaune was parting ways from Roger Coussy. The successor to André Porcheret was an impeccable worker but a feeble marketer. Rigor, rigidity; he could not adapt to the public relations demands of his post. His relations with both his team and the direction of the hospital were chaotic. "Hardly a sociable man," one *vigneron* remembers. The situation quickly became uneasy, both internally and externally. "It was a period when the Hospices considered it a given that negociants would buy their wines," analyzed Christophe Tupinier, chief editor of the magazine *Bourgogne Aujourd'hui*, a few years later. The 1993 vintage would cement the resentment: a sulfiting (the addition of sulfur dioxide to protect the wines from oxidation) a few days before the auction made the tasting particularly difficult. This incident was the straw that broke the camel's back: Roger Coussy had to leave. The affair left a mark, and André Boisseaux, CEO of the negociant Patriarche (Beaune), the number one buyer of the Hospices wines, had to get involved.

In the cellar of the Hospices. The elevage *of the wines is carried out entirely in oak barrels.*

"This all just got blown out of proportion. The wines were very good. Errors were made at the time of the tasting, in November 1993. People made a big deal about it but it wasn't the end of the world. The supervisor thought it was best, to protect his wines, to add a bit of sulfur dioxide. It should have been done the day after the auction. It wasn't an issue of quality. The Hospices have very good vineyards, very well cared for. They manage to make good wine. A bottle from the Hospices is indisputably good," he argued the following year.

But for the direction of the Hospices, it was time to bring back someone trustworthy. In late 1993, in the courtyard of the Domaine Leroy, Porcheret saw Antoine Jacquet, director of the hospital, approaching. Jacquet asked him to come back to his old position at the estate of the Hospices.

So André Porcheret was now back at the helm of the famous estate, and with absolute power.... The year 1994 was quite eventful for the Hospices. Over the summer, significant investments approved by the administrative council were finalized. A new winery and cellar were unveiled. The problems of space and temperature control in the old buildings in the center of town were resolved. Porcheret now had the tools appropriate to the ambitions of the Hospices. Success was on his side. The year the bearded supervisor returned also saw a reversal in the trends at the wine auction. In November, after four consecutive years of falling prices, the 1994 edition concluded with a 53% increase.

Newly planted vines. Some will live for more than 80 years.

The Virtue of Observation

But back to the vineyards. It was out of the question for André Porcheret to throw his twenty-two *vignerons* into the adventure of biodynamics. It was also out of the question to return to a method of viticulture that brought out the heavy artillery at the least threat. At the same time, another approach was starting to gain steam: it was called "lutte raisonnée." The principal was to act at the right time, with the right products and the right tools. The objective was to reduce substantially the number and the volume of treatments. The team was trained in this method, which demands above all an effort of observation and close monitoring of the vineyards. Porcheret justified this shift: "The *vignerons* are trained to identify distinctly the damage caused by fungus, parasites, etc. They only treat if the tolerated limit is exceeded. It seems intelligent to me to work this way – better for the environment and the soil, and therefore also for the wines – than to treat systematically. Don't forget that we still intervene whenever necessary. If a chemical treatment must be done to save the harvest, we'll do it, choosing the least harmful products. That is where our approach is different from biodynamics, which is much more intransigent..."

Roland Masse began his tenure with the same philosophy. He understood his predecessor's decision all the better since in 1993 he had experienced the same misadventure as Porcheret. That year, Masse had decided to experiment with organics at the Domaine Bertagna, and it left a bitter memory. In 2006, however, he decided to overcome his fears. "After an experience like that, you have to have faith," he observes. But in the meantime, organics had made some progress. New tools were at his disposition: "elicitors," substances that stimulate the plant's natural defense reaction. These products, from vegetal or micro-organic bases, incite the vine to activate its reactions to threats. Many different products were on the market. For Masse, they minimized the risk of converting to organics. "I believe in this," the supervisor said. "This is a way to care for the plant that corresponds with the logic of what I want to do."

Right page:
A roof of the Hôtel-Dieu (the Saint Louis room), with the vineyards of Beaune in the background.

Converting to Organics

Starting in 2006, and working gradually over three years, the entire estate was converted to organics. The first two vintages proceeded without any real difficulty, but the new method was undeniably more restrictive than conventional viticulture. Stéphane Murat, a young *vigneron* recently hired by the Hospices, can attest to this: "The products have to be applied at the best possible moment. All it takes is a little bit of rain after a treatment, and the work becomes completely useless."

The final year of the conversion, 2008, did not reassure the *vignerons*. Throughout the summer, the sky lavished its resources, both the good and the bad, with great generosity. The weather in Burgundy constantly shifted from sun to rain, wind, and drastic temperature changes, never stabilizing. One week the conditions would favor oidium, then the next mildew would threaten. Many of the vineyards were in a piteous state by the end of the summer. The situation made tongues wag all over Burgundy. "It's inadmissible to see an estate like the Hospices in this condition," people fumed. The supervisor even had to handle a minor revolt from some of the *vignerons*. The dissenters supported a point of view that Masse himself had once advocated: it's better to use a few well-placed chemical treatments than to multiply the organic treatments and still be unsure of the outcome. The losses were weighty: only 544 barrels of wine would be auctioned off that year, a volume comparable to the 2003 harvest, a historically meager year because of the heat wave that summer. The estate could potentially produce 40% more. One example of the meagerness of 2008: only ten barrels of the grand cru Mazis-Chambertin were produced, compared to twenty-four in 2005. At the average price fetched per barrel for this cuvee, the loss of profits was nearly 300,000€!

Arriving in Meursault, capital of the great white wines of the Côte de Beaune.

It was a difficult time for Roland Masse: "All the estates that had converted from chemical to organic were experiencing a delicate phase. The vineyards were in shock, having to give up chemical protection. Unfortunately, when the 2008 vintage came along, there was a lot of damage. Once that bridge was crossed, things went better. In 2008, vineyards that had already been converted to organics for a number of years didn't have any more problems than others." Even less, in fact, since in that vintage many chemically treated vineyards finished their cycle in an unenviable state. That year's experience was painful and sometimes incomplete (conventional treatments had to be used), but the organic approach was not called into question.

A "Public Service" Estate

Supervisor of the Hospices de Beaune: the position is not comparable to any other in Burgundy. Solid shoulders are not overmuch to carry such responsibility. His mission is eminently collective. The estate's format and its renown intertwine it with the life of many Burgundians. The vineyards of the Hospices have the particularity of being acquired entirely from donations. Benefactors have bequeathed all or part of their holdings over the centuries, legacies that must yield a profit for the common good. In short, it is a public service wine estate. Woe to the man who will not prove equal to this noble mission! Especially since Burgundy's vineyards are truly her pride and joy, causing jealousy and drama. No *vigneron* would not be delighted to expand his property a bit, but such opportunities are rare. Burgundy, with less than 30,000 hectares, is a small region in terms

of surface, and potential buyers are numerous. Each one keeps his ears open for any morsel of vineyard news, which is passed from one *vigneron* to another as they run into owners of neighboring parcels while they prune, treat, plow, trim, etc. A *vigneron* with no heir who will retire soon? A troubled succession? Investors who want out? Whether solid or baseless, information spreads quickly. The better placed the vineyard – that is, the greater its potential to produce the best cuvees of the appellation – the more excited people get. Each individual has his own ideas about the qualitative potential of the possible prey and of the positive impact such vineyards could have on his own line of wines....

It is easier to measure the singularity of the estate of the Hospices de Beaune in terms of the frenzy that occasionally strikes the region when a vineyard is up for sale. Not only does the Hospices have an exceptional total surface of vineyards (60 hectares), but the parcels are also located on some of Burgundy's best *terroirs*. Signboards with Nicolas Rolin's coat of arms are scattered throughout the region, from Gevrey-Chambertin to Chassagne-Montrachet and including Pommard, Meursault, Aloxe-Corton, etc.

While there is a heavy media presence for the annual auction, it is also the moment when members of the trade begin to judge the new vintage. The cellars are open for them to taste the wines of the recent harvest. Journalists squeeze in under the arches where the new barrels are sleeping. Before the wine is even finished, the supervisor's work is examined and critiqued. Antoine Jacquet, director of the hospital of the Hospices de Beaune since 1988, describes the frame of mind necessary for the supervisor of the estate: "When it comes down to it, he's serving a greater cause. He has to realize that the institution and the event will always surpass him. He must listen to everyone's advice openly and attentively. It's a position where you can't worry too much about criticism and you have to accept that the whole thing is very irrational and emotional." "The Hospices is constantly under scrutiny; if something is wrong they won't miss it...," remembers André Porcheret. And he should know. His arrival in 1977 and his later return transpired against a background of psychodrama. At the time, the 1976 vintage was in the eye of the storm. Part of the harvest had turned: during the aging, acetic acid bacteria had developed in certain barrels. Simply put, these cuvees were turning into vinegar. In a typical estate this sort of occurrence would remain secret – other properties had the same issue in 1976 – but at the Hospices, the slightest problem inevitably becomes public knowledge. A combination of circumstances led to this enological accident. The wines were a bit acidic and thus conducive to bacterial growth. Moreover, construction had forced the supervisor, André Masson, to stock part of the harvest in buildings that were too hot. But it is undoubtedly the singular way that the Hospices worked that struck a heavy blow to its production: at that time, the buyers of the previous vintage brought the empty barrels back to the Hospices. This permitted the estate to keep part of the next harvest in used barrels (the rest was aged in new barrels). When the barrels were received, the personnel steamed them – a common practice to sanitize wine barrels. But this year of heat and drought changed everything. "The negociants were returning the barrels up to just fifteen days before the harvest. In 1976, the harvest was early and, if you ask me, they must have rushed a bit. The bacteria just had to start up again," Porcheret analyzes.

100% New Wood

In light of the turn of events, the Hospices relinquished part of the revenue generated by the 1976 auction: the turned wines were distilled. These events would cost André Masson his job, and he would find solace in his family vineyards in Aloxe-Corton. Today he still remembers this episode as a particularly painful moment in his career. "I worried myself sick," he remembers. This trauma would also have a significant influence on the Hospices' policies about barrels. It was now out of the question to reuse returned barrels. The rule of 100% new wood would remain for many years. In principle, it is still in effect. "I don't want to take any risks with the barrels," Roland Masse firmly declares. His position has its pros and cons.

A new barrel. All barrels of the Hospices de Beaune are replaced each year.

A barrel is not a neutral container; it reveals the qualities of a great wine. The wood brings greater complexity; its porosity allows a gentle oxidation; aside from the famous "oaky" tones it imparts (vanilla, hazelnut, roasted notes, toast, etc.), the barrel provides favorable conditions for the wine to liberate its own aromas. It also has an effect on the very structure of the wine: under the influence of this oxidation-reduction reaction, the tannins polymerize (the molecules combine), their texture softens, and they develop a silkier mouthfeel. But a barrel that is not properly used can also have negative effects. A wine that is not structured enough to "digest" a large proportion of new wood will become irreparably distorted; at worst, it can become drying. Moreover, barrels can have a homogenizing effect: a wine that is dominated by wood shows the character of its *elevage* rather than of its *terroir*.

These criticisms are sometimes applied to the wines of the Hospices in weak vintages or with regard to entry-level appellations. Roland Masse has taken on this obstacle. His work is to select the most "discreet" possible wood sources and barrel-makers. He has also punched a few holes in the doctrine of 100% new wood. In 2006, five cuvees (one white and four reds) aged in second-passage barrels were put up for sale for the first time. These barrels had been used the previous year to age their "reserve particulière" wines (see inset). The practice was repeated in the following years. In 2008, the estate had an innovative new "zebra" barrel created with alternating staves of new and used wood. This barrel was used for the Auxey-Duresses "Cuvée Boillot."

The oak influence also mellows out in the second phase of *elevage*. This stage occurs in the cellars of the negociants, as a significant part of the aging period falls to them. They collect their purchases a few weeks after the auction, in December or January. The negociants generally vary their approach with different cuvees: "Some wines stay in new wood, but most are put in other barrels that will mark the wine less," explains Albéric Bichot, CEO of the negociant Albert Bichot (Beaune), a principal buyer the last few years.

LA RÉSERVE PARTICULIÈRE

A word of advice: if by some misfortune you end up hospitalized in Beaune, it is best to be there during the holiday season. That way you will have the chance to try a glass of the Hospices wine at meals (except if the doctor forbids it, of course…). A portion of the wines produced by the estate of the Hospices is not sold at the auction: the reserve particulière *or special reserve. The percent of the production set aside in the estate's cellars varies with each vintage. The institution can thus regulate the offer it puts up for auction. A few barrels of the more abundant cuvees are generally reserved. Less often, an entire cuvee is held back from the auction. That is the case, for example, with the Saint-Romain Blanc (Côte de Beaune). This wine is from vineyards that have only been worked by the estate for a short time, and the cuvee has never been in the auction catalog. The* réserve particulière *provides a glimpse of each vintage and gives a hint as to how it will age. But most of it nevertheless leaves the cellar. The wines are served at receptions organized by the institution, the hospital personnel receive a few bottles at the end of the year, and a few more bottles are available for purchase in the gift shop at the Hôtel-Dieu.*

The Modern School

André Masson, André Porcheret, Roger Coussy, Roland Masse…. These four men have vinified the last fifty vintages for the Hospices. All, that is, except one: not on their list of achievements is 1978, the year before Porcheret, who had learned about wine by working with it, had been named supervisor. He had succeeded Masson, an agronomical engineer who held a national diploma in enology. Masson had all the experience necessary for the responsibilities of the job. Few people had such a level of wine education at the time, least of all Porcheret. Undoubtedly still shaken up by the misadventure of 1976, the administration had searched for someone up on the latest enological technology. They recruited a certain Guy Accad, a young enologist fresh out of the University of Montpellier. Accad has only one vintage at the Hospices to boast of, and yet thirty years later no one has forgotten his name….

Accad is considered the father of what is called the "modern" school of enology, which was popular in Burgundy in the 1980s and '90s. The vineyards were emerging from unexceptional vintages; the vineyard management, as seen previously, favored high yields above all. The grapes weren't ripe enough and the wines lacked body. Over the next few decades, methods and philosophies would be reevaluated. Guy Accad was the first to make a change. His method can easily be summed up: make the most of the fruit before it ferments. To achieve this, the grapes' natural propensity to begin fermentation once in vat must be staved off. Two methods are available to winemakers: keeping the grapes cold and sulfuring. The grapes can be kept cold by controlling the temperature of the vats. Sulfur is an antiseptic and an antioxidant used in enology since Antiquity; in heavy doses, it extinguishes the ardor of the yeasts responsible for fermentation. Accad would use sulfur for another of its properties: as a solvent. The winemaker's task is to draw the noblest substances from the grape skin into the juice; this is what happens naturally while the wine is in vats. The grape juice and then the wine are enriched by the famous polyphenols that give the cuvee its structure, aromas, and even its color (the juice of most wine grapes is colorless). Sulfur encourages this phenomenon.

Guy Accad became famous for his "sulfited pre-fermentation maceration." He was one of the most sought-after consultants of the '80s and into the early '90s. His method allowed winemakers to leave their wines to macerate seven, ten, or even fifteen days longer to maximize color and concentration. Wines made under Accad's guidance had some success in tastings and with the specialized press. They also caused controversy: they lacked typicity, they didn't always age harmoniously, etc. The Accad method would fall out of fashion. At least, its most extreme version would. This period reassured wise *vignerons* and reminded others that wine is made in the vineyard. No trick can replace the assets of a good, healthy, well-built grape. Once fruit like this is in the vat, there is no need to readjust it to get a great wine. The Accad experience would not be repeated at the Hospices de Beaune. "These miracle cures may have helped, but they went too far," André Porcheret concludes today.

The Controversy Over the 1997 Vintage

The Hospices would see heated debates again. Almost twenty years later, the estate found itself once again at the center of an enological controversy. André Porcheret confirmed to an American journalist from the *Wine Spectator* that he intervened significantly in the winemaking of the 1997 vintage. Come cuvees were chaptalized (sugar was added before fermentation started in order to raise the alcohol level of the wine), a practice that is both ancestral and legal. Here is what Henri Jayer, a famous Burgundian *vigneron* widely known for the outstanding quality of his wines, had to say about it: "Used only when necessary, in moderation and with respect for the demands of the vintage, it can be very beneficial. In effect, when done in several steps, it can significantly lengthen the fermentation period, which favors better extraction of color, aromas, and various natural components of the grape. We also know that the wine of Burgundy reveals it assets the most delicately with an alcohol level between twelve and fourteen percent."

But Porcheret also acknowledged having acidified some wines while they were in vat. Like hundreds of others, he added a dose of tartaric acid to re-equilibrate wines that were a bit flabby, another practice that was legal. The episode caused quite an uproar since the two practices, though legal independently, may not both be used on the same "product." The national press got wind of it, and the image of the Hospices was stained. Porcheret did not let it rattle him, and with the *vignerons'* association of the Côte d'Or he composed a rebuttal (many domaines have done the same). He was not afraid of getting his hands dirty; quite the contrary. "I like a good fight," he declares. To him, the two interventions were indeed applied to chemically different "products." The must (the grape juice before fermentation) was chaptalized and the wines were acidified. The controversy would eventually die down, and the Hospices was no worse for the wear. The homogeneity of the 1997 vintage was uncertain: in some vineyards the maturation suddenly climbed at the end of the growing cycle, causing the acidity in the grapes to drop drastically, while in other, later-maturing parcels the vines struggled to produce grapes with sufficient sugar.

The Hand of Man

The vineyard: it is here that quality is determined. The vine is an astonishingly robust and long-lived plant, but it needs the hand of man to give the best of itself. Left to its own devices, a vineyard will produce nothing of any value. Pruning is one of the most important times of year: in the winter, the *vigneron* prepares each individual vine for the next harvest. It requires close observation and judgment. The *vigneron* must choose the branch that will give the best the new vintage has to offer, both in quality and in quantity. Later, in May, comes the debudding, when the *vigneron* must eliminate any excess shoots that would use precious nutriments needed for the main shoots. Extra vegetation can also prevent good ventilation for the future bunches of grapes and can promote the development of diseases.

Debudding is a painstaking process that sometimes demands certain precautions...

These are just two examples of the vineyard work that the *vignerons* of the Hospices must complete each year. But who are these *vignerons*? On the surface, nothing distinguishes them from their counterparts at other wineries. Their involvement with the famous estate began in a very ordinary manner: they replied to an ad. Stéphane Murat was the last to join the team. He has officially been a *vigneron* for the Hospices de Beaune since January 1st, 2008. One interview with the supervisor and then another with the director of the hospital would insure his destiny. This young man,

Stéphane Murat: the newest vigneron *of the Hospices.*

only 26 years old, was entrusted with three of the estate's jewels: two cuvees of the grand cru Clos de la Roche (Morey-Saint-Denis) and one of Mazis-Chambertin (Gevrey-Chambertin). Both of these vineyards are located in the Côte de Nuits, which produces the greatest red Burgundies.

Stéphane's enthusiasm is still palpable. "I'm very proud to be working for one of the best-known estates in the world. I used to go to wine tastings with my father on weekends, but I never imagined I'd pass over to the other side," he admits. And yet it's been a long time since wine held any secret for him, and wine has been his profession for quite a while too. His father is at the helm of an estate with about ten hectares in the Hautes-Côtes de Nuits, which is a regional appellation and therefore at the bottom of the hierarchy of Burgundy. Yields there are almost double that of a grand cru, and harvesting is done by machine. Stéphane Murat discovered another universe with the Hospices: the "haute couture" viticulture Burgundy's grand crus. All treatments in the vineyards are carefully restricted to what is necessary given the vines' reactions to climatic conditions. Each parcel, with its own unique geology, soil, exposition, type of vine, etc., reacts differently. The differences are obviously reflected in the prices of the final bottles. A bottle of Bourgogne Hautes-Côtes de Nuits costs around 10€, while a grand cru goes for about five times as much. A bottle of Mazis-Chambertin, for example, is worth about 70€ at the time of the auction in November.

Autonomous Work

The Murat family domaine is one of many thousands of such estates in Burgundy. For these winemakers who produce basic Burgundy, to manage more than two hectares of a grand cru (just 2% of the total vineyard surface of the region) is quite simply unimaginable, especially knowing that such wines are surrounded by a media frenzy and with the entire profession watching. "It's a heavy responsibility, and the first vintage was very stressful, right up until the harvest," Stéphane confesses. "I have to get results. It would be different if I were my own boss." Indeed, that first vintage was not easy for the new arrival. Diseases were rampant. The young *vigneron* remembers several weekends spent treating since the weather had left no other opportunity. Luckily, his colleagues were more reassuring than the climate. Murat counts his integration into the team as very gratifying; he was pleasantly surprised by the welcome shown by his new colleagues. "I was given a lot of advice," he notes. They always took advantage of opportunities to exchange ideas. As soon as he was hired, in January, he had a chance to get to know everyone better during an annual team outing: a day in the vineyards, with winery visits, tastings, and a meal. The calm period in the vineyards in early spring is another occasion when the *vignerons* of the Hospices hold a festive group dinner.

Thanks to the Hospices de Beaune, Stéphane Murat has started professional life in a way he had never dreamt of. He works under a seasoned supervisor but still has a certain freedom in organizing his work. The job description of a *vigneron* for the Hospices includes specific tasks for each time of year, but he can choose how best to achieve his goals. The supervisor monitors the work, provides advice, and establishes the general path to be taken. During critical periods Roland Masse is a bit more involved, providing recommendations for treatments, and the *vignerons* in turn submit a form showing that the work was duly accomplished. Mase sums it up: "To be a *vigneron* for the Hospices, you have to be a self-motivator and be autonomous. That's one of the main points we look for when we're hiring."

All told, the work of a *vigneron* is about thirty hours per week on average, although vineyard work obviously varies a great deal with the seasons.

The *vigneron*'s autonomy also allows him to do other work on the side. The possibility is even more enticing since each of them is required by the Hospices to own his own tractor and equipment; the requirement is costly, but the hospital provides a stipend for tools. As a result, many of them also own and work their own vineyards. One of them has earned the nickname "the Man of the Two Hospices": Daniel Gossot is in charge of two wines in Beaune – "Hugues et Louis Bétault" and one of the flagship wines, named "Nicolas Rolin" for the founder of the Hôtel-Dieu – and since 1989 he has also managed the vineyards of the "Hospices d'Allerey-sur-Saône." This small village in the Saône-et-Loire, about twenty kilometers (almost 12.5 miles) southwest of the wine capital of Burgundy, was given an estate of five hectares (in the Beaune and Savigny-les-Beaune appellations). Daniel Gossot oversees the vineyard work and the vinification under the metayage (sharecropping) system. A large part of the fruit produced is sold off to negociants, who then vinify and sell the wine.

Daniel Gossot, one of the most experienced vignerons *of the Hospices. He is responsible for two cuvees of Beaune.*

A Second Job

Stéphane Murat's second job is a family affair: his father is passing the estate over to his two sons little by little. Already in charge of three hectares in 2008, Murat added two more hectares to his estate in 2009. "Knowing that I would gradually be taking over more and more vineyards, I needed a job that would give me some freedom. The Hospices is ideal," he comments. As his own property grows, he plans to hire help to manage the increased workload. But his priority is clear: to take good care of the vines entrusted to him by the Hospices de Beaune. In 2008, this job accounted for 60% of his earnings. "If in the future the total workload gets to be too much, I would give up some of my own vineyards in order to continue to work at the Hospices," he hints. For this young *vigneron*, the institute is a springboard with a safety net. It is also much more. His experience at the Hospices has already led him to rethink certain practices: his family domaine practiced *lutte raisonnee*, but Murat discovered organics through Roland Masse. He added organic products to the treatments already used, which will further serve him when more synthetic molecules will be removed from the market (a reevaluation of the health risks associated with these products should assure their elimination). His method for evaluating the optimal harvesting date has also evolved.

Dominique Cornin, who is in charge of the Pouilly-Fuissé "Françoise Poisard," gives a similar account. Also running his own estate (Domaine de Lalande), he highlights the influence of the two supervisors he has worked with at the Hospices on his own career path. "André Porcheret and Roland Masse taught me that when a grape is ripe you have to harvest it. It's pointless to try to get 14% potential alcohol content. In my wines, I look for equilibrium and finesse above all else," he explains. Today Dominique Cornin's wines are widely recognized for their quality, while in 1993 when he left his village's cooperative winery he was a complete unknown (Chaintré).

A Family Connection

Yann Colette, another young *vigneron* on the team, discovered the establishment gradually over time. As an adolescent he wandered through vineyards belonging to the Hospices that his uncle, Laurent Dechaume, managed. "Every year I came for a weekend during the harvest. It was hard work, of course, but at the end of the day we sang, we danced, and we ate well. The ambiance was great. When the harvest was over I was always eager for the next year," he remembers. Later, he would occasionally help out his uncle with work in the vineyards. When it came time to choose a career, Yann Colette chose a professional school in viticulture and enology. Like many *vignerons* of his generation, he did internships abroad: first in Switzerland, then in South Africa. Back in Burgundy in 2000, he completed a project for an estate in Santenay (Côte de Beaune). Upon learning from his uncle that a *vigneron* at the Hospices would soon retire, Yann carefully put together his job application as he waited for the official announcement of an opening. Motivated, well organized, and prepared, the young man went in search of the materials necessary for the work he would have to do if he were hired. He also started looking for a house with dependencies for his tools in a local village. Everything was ready for him to start right away. Yann Colette convinced the supervisor and the director of the hospital that he was the right man for the job. He soon took over the Meursault-Genevrières "Philippe le Bon" and the Beaune "Rousseau-Deslandes." Like the others, he also set about to create his own estate.

Dominique Cornin in his vineyards in Pouilly-Fuissé. He is the only vigneron *from the Mâconnais at the Hospices.*

Le Clos de Avaux in Beaune. The Hospices has almost 2 hectares of vineyards here.

This family connection, from uncle to nephew, echoed the career path of Daniel Gossot twenty years earlier. From a farming family a few miles from Beaune, Daniel had an uncle who was a *vigneron* for the Hospices. As an adolescent in 1969, Daniel began working the harvest every year. He would later work as a *vigneron* for a historic winery in Beaune: Bouchard Père & Fils. Finally, when his uncle retired in 1978, he joined the team at the Hospices. "There was a certain prestige about the Hospices. They paid well, and the work was less restrictive than on my parents' farm," he points out. But getting assimilated into the team wasn't as easy as it is today. Unlike most of his colleagues at that time, Daniel Gossot did not have his own estate on the side. That was his handicap: respect was proportional to the total vineyard surface you owned. "In meetings, I could never have my say. The old men decided everything. They told me, 'Count yourself lucky to be here. Do your work and keep your mouth shut.' A *vigneron* who owned a significant parcel in Corton (Author's note: a grand cru of the Côte de Beaune); he was someone."

Yann Colette, vigneron *with the Hospices since 2000, in the vineyards of Beaune (Les Montrevenots).*

 A *Vigneron* in His Vineyard

Laurent Dechaume, who was in charge of the Pommard "Dames de la Charité" and the Auxey-Duresses "Boillot" confirms the difficulty of starting out at the Hospices in the early 1980s. "It took a year for one of my colleagues even to shake my hand. You had to find your niche!" he remembers. "I was just a hired *vigneron* arriving among people who had a lot of property. But I have to say that things went very well with some of them. For me, it was a step up in society. The day I became a *vigneron* for the Hospices was one of the greatest of my life." Nevertheless, Laurent Dechaume wasn't exactly a beginner. Following in the footsteps of his father and grandfather, he had previously managed the vineyards of the Coste-Caumartin estate in Pommard.

At that time, the status of a *vigneron* for the Hospices was different from what it is today. Vineyards belonging to the hospital were often entrusted to professionals who were already well established at their own family estates. Sometimes the job was passed from father to son. "They are not just *vignerons* for the Hospices, but also owners. Managing a *vigneron* who is in the habit of managing his own employees is not a simple matter! So I set periods for the different tasks in the vineyards.... I try to give structure," Porcheret commented. This was a great challenge for Porcheret. When he arrived in 1977 some *vignerons* had much larger vineyard surfaces to work while others handled small surfaces, and the vineyards could be in more or less prestigious appellations, so their pay also varied a great deal. The *vignerons'* pay was directly determined by the auction: he received 25% of the price his cuvee fetched. "The differences in pay were enormous; some of them made practically three times what others did," Porcheret remembers. In the particularly prosperous years of the late 1980s, the *vignerons* had very substantial paychecks. So much so that he remembers some of them making more than the director of the hospital.... At the same time, the less scrupulous *vignerons* had their personnel work the vineyards. "They didn't go into the vineyards themselves very often, and yet they were the ones making the money," one *vigneron* still remembers indignantly today. "I had to try repeatedly just for a chance to meet with some of them," Porcheret confirms. So the supervisor decided to even out their responsibilities: from then on, each worker managed the same surface of vineyards, down to a few tenths of a hectare. Later, he insisted that all major work be done by the *vigneron* himself. "We wanted guys who needed work, who would go work the vines themselves." The new principals of viticulture adopted by the Hospices were also more demanding: "You have to go to the vineyards even if there's nothing to be done there," Porcheret liked to say.

There was much complaining from the team; the former bigwigs were not pleased. In the end, almost the entire team would be renewed between 1976 and 1990: some quit or retired, and others were fired. In fact, the legal status of the *vignerons* at the Hospices changed entirely during that period: where they used to rent the vineyards, they were now employees of the Hospices. Their salaries still fluctuated depending on the results of the auction, but a salary cap was established as well as a floor. There was no longer any gain from individual cuvees either; since 1997, the profits from all cuvees are totaled and each winemaker is compensated according to the vineyard surface he works. But one variable is still left to the supervisor's discretion: the quality bonus. "To earn it, the *vigneron* must complete all of the tasks set out." Roland Masse is particularly concerned with the vineyard work from May through July, the so-called "green" work during the vegetative development of the vine. These are the tasks that guarantee quality and control the quantity of the harvest, work that is well known to many successive generations of Burgundian *vignerons*.

The *vignerons*' earnings are complemented by the equipment stipend mentioned earlier. They work with their own tractors, but upkeep is paid through this extra, tax-free revenue. Products necessary for treatments are also provided by the Hospices.

The *vigneron*'s responsibilities also include recruiting his own team of harvesters. The growers for the Hospices often work together in groups of two or three and take

Laurent Dechaume, vigneron *of the Hospices. He is responsible for one of the most prestigious premiers crus of Pommard : Les Epenots.*

The village of Pommard, just a few miles from Beaune, between its two vineyard slopes.

turns harvesting each other's vineyards, according to the supervisor's harvesting schedule. Their mission is completed when they deliver the grapes. This is another aspect that has changed recently: until the late 1970s, they were responsible for vinification too. "They filled the vats, they punched down the cap (the mass formed as the grape solids float to the top of the vat), they racked the wines (transferred them, leaving the sediment behind) and put them in barrels according to my instructions. I have good memories of that. I got to know people," remembers André Masson. Today, the supervisor has a team in the winery and cellars ; during the harvest, seasonal workers are hired to handle the reception and sorting of the grapes.

In the Elite

Though he is not prone to exaggeration, Roland Masse doesn't hesitate to say, "The estate is a reference point in how to work vineyards." So what more can the supervisor and his growers do to enhance the Hospices de Beaune? The directors of the estate have very high expectations: the measures taken in the vineyards are no more and no less than those of the most elite estates of Burgundy. And quality is costly.

A view of the vineyards of the Corton-Charlemagne appellation. This cross originally sat in the courtyard of the Hospices.

Take the example of green harvesting, which has gradually worked its way onto the *vignerons*' calendar over the last twenty years. It involves removing any surplus grapes in July if yields promise to be too high despite concerted efforts. Here again, the Hospices de Beaune was a pioneer, as it first employed the technique in 1983. Green harvesting requires costly labor and reduces the ultimate profit. It did not go unnoticed when it was first introduced, and people were very critical. Laurent Déchaume remembers how difficult it was to get people to accept the practice: "Doing all that work only to remove some of the bunches later and not get any wine from them just didn't seem logical to the *vignerons*." Roland Masse also advocated this method, but he was counting on organics and rigorous uphill work to dispense of in the future.

The mayor of Beaune, Alain Suguenot, reproached the negociants in 2004 for not taking these special efforts into account. "Certain cuvees go for 1,500-2,000€ per barrel, which given the constraints of our expenses means no profit," points out Roland Masse. In addition to the prestigious cuvees, the estate also has entry-level village appellations: Pernand-Vergelesses, Monthelie, Auxey-Duresses. The supervisor estimates that one eighth of the estate's production is barely profitable, if at all.

The formula is ultimately no different for the Hospices than for other estates. On one hand are the prestigious wines that are consistently in demand the world over; their prices can reach irrational levels. On the other hand are wines that are expensive to produce and which are in direct competition with other wine regions. Obviously not all the wines produced by the Hospices de Beaune are destined for the auction. This sums up the issue for the estate of the Hospices for the coming years. Its elitist position must absolutely be reinforced.

In order to do this, the Hospices has to put its best *terroirs* in the spotlight. This policy was formed in recent years. In 2007 a new cuvee appeared in the catalog: the Corton "Baronne du Baÿ" from the Clos du Roi vineyard, one of the finest in the appellation. The grapes of this famous walled parcel had previously been blended into the Corton "Docteur Peste" along with four other parcels. Roland Masse decided to make the change after observing the vineyards: "We had the potential to make a really good wine from these superb vines. They were just 30% of the "Docteur Peste" cuvee and were lost in the mix. Isolating them was a way to propose a very nice Corton without penalizing the original cuvee," explains the supervisor.

At the same time, the Hospices stopped directly working a hectare and a half in Savigny-les-Beaune. The lowest-quality parcels of each cuvee from that appellation were removed from the Hospices' production and entrusted to an employment center for disabled workers. Previously, the Hospices could sell the product of a total of six hectares of vineyards in Savigny. There is less to sell at auction now, but the three cuvees are still in the catalog and their quality is more consistent than ever. History and economic interests have thus been preserved, and the attraction for buyers has doubled.

The northern vineyards of Pommard at sunset. Tomorrow morning, the very first rays of sun will waken the vineyards.

With the various vineyards donated to the Hospices, a cuvee can sometimes combine several *terroirs* that are quite different; and in Burgundy, *terroir* is king. With grapes maturing at different times in each area, the reaction to the threat of disease can vary a great deal from one parcel to the next, complicating the supervisor's job. At the time of the harvest, these differences count, so making the crucial decision of when to harvest is not easy.

A Monument Under Construction

The estate has thus seen a number of changes over the last few years. Moreover, a 42nd cuvee was introduced with the 2008 vintage, a premier cru Pommard that was baptized "Dom Goblet" for the last monk responsible for the finances of the Clos de Vougeot. Here again a particularly high-quality *terroir* has been isolated, a change that distresses some purists who find it sacrilegious to change anything about the wines. Roland Masse has very definite ideas on the matter: "If we have the possibility to improve quality, we have to do it," he serenely declares. His predecessor also felt strongly about it: "There is so much work in trying to improve quality. First by selecting the best parcels, including in the smaller appellations. I would like, in the future, for the catalog to include only the very best of Auxey-Duresses, the very best of Beaune, the very best of Volnay…," judged André Porcheret in 1996.

So why wasn't it done earlier? At the Hospices, history and heritage are omnipresent. A donation comes with obligations. For instance, the Cyrot-Chaudron gift, one of the most significant contemporary donations to the Hospices, gave birth to four cuvees. Suzanne Chuadron's will contained specific conditions: "Furthermore, I prohibit the Hospices de Beaune to sell any of the vineyards that we donated in 1979 for at least thirty years from the date of my death; and I require that all wines produced from those vineyards be sold entirely at the auction under the cuvee name of Cyrot-Chaudron, providing that the quality so permits." Since Suzanne Chaudron passed away in 1990, the Cyrot-Chaudron cuvees therefore cannot be changed before 2020.

With deep local roots, the wines of the Hospices de Beaune are collective works. The estate that gives them life is a perpetual atelier of Burgundian viticultural prowess. Just as medieval cathedrals were built by many workmen over several decades, generations of *vignerons* have pooled their knowledge to get the best out of the vineyards of the Hospices. Today, the men of the 21st century are contributing to the prosperity and evolution of a priceless institution nearly six hundred years old. With each vintage, the story continues…

The Pommard "Cyrot-Chaudron," one of four cuvees born of Suzanne Chaudron's donation of 1979.

Market day in Beaune, in the shadow of the roofs of the Hôtel-Dieu.

Where Do the Estate's Profits Go?

The estate and the wines of the Hospices de Beaune are designed to serve a hospital, a fact that is sometimes eclipsed by the media frenzy that surrounds them. "People tend to see our estate and our hospital as separate even though they are, in fact, one single, cohesive institution. The revenue from the estate goes to help the hospital achieve its purpose of assuring care. This income can help us double, sometimes even triple, our capacity to reinvest: we buy equipment, have construction done, etc. For us, it's logical that the estate should bring us the most money possible," explains Antoine Jacquet, director of the hospital.

The Hospices Civils de Beaune holds about 500 beds and covers surgery, pediatrics, intensive care, voice therapy, and medium-stay care. It has a maternity ward, an emergency medical center, and an intensive care unit. The hospital also manages three assisted-living homes for the elderly. It has more than 750 employees, and about 1,000 meals are served there each day.

The revenue from the estate allows the hospital of Beaune to insure much higher quality care than other local institutions can. In a world where the cost of health care is constantly rising, this advantage prevents (or puts off) certain restructurings that have touched other hospitals.

Beaune: A City Blessed by the Gods

Locals like to say that Beaune is encircled like a barrel by her ramparts and bastions. It's true that everything here reminds you that this town made her fortune from wine. Every shop window has a vine leaf, a miniature press, or a poster of the slopes striped with rows of vines. Located 40 kilometers (about 25 miles) south of Dijon, this town with 22,000 inhabitants could have remained a provincial town like so many others in France. But it had another destiny. Beaune is a name that is exported the world over, and for many people it is synonymous with luxury and pleasure. The vineyards cover 580 hectares, of which 320 are premier crus. The old city touts itself as the heart of Burgundy's wine country.

In addition to being the wine capital, Beaune has a very important history. The parliamentary capital of the duchy of Burgundy in the 15th century, the city has retained a medieval character and draws many tourists year in and year out.

Situated on the axis joining northern Europe to Mediterranean Europe, Beaune also enjoys an enviable geographic position. Three events regulate the cultural life here: the Festival of Suspense Films (previously held in Cognac) in the spring, the International Baroque and Classical Music Festival in July, and of course the unrivaled auction in November.

A label of the cuvee made from vineyards presented to Marshall Pétain in 1942. The vineyards were later confiscated when France was liberated.

Hemingway and the Hospices de Beaune

Ernest Hemingway is one of the most famous enthusiasts of the Hospices de Beaune. The author praised the wines of the Hospices many times in his books. In 1925, he drove from Lyons to Dijon. In a letter to the poet Ezra Pound, he recounts his stops along the way in the vineyards of Burgundy and the wines he tasted there. He describes a meal accompanied by a 1918 wine of the Hospices de Beaune: "And 1918 was one of the best years since 1896. But why discuss technicalities; there has never been a bad wine from the Hospices de Beaune." A note written for his book Torrents of Spring also mentions his taste for the production of the Hospices. The future Nobel prize winner (in 1954) tells that he drank a 1919 wine of the Hospices de Beaune with a rabbit stew.

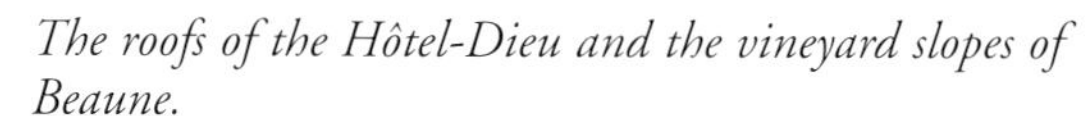

The roofs of the Hôtel-Dieu and the vineyard slopes of Beaune.

The Solemn Affair of the Clos Pétain

It was one of the darkest pages in the history of the estate. In 1942, a delegation of notables from Beaune went to Vichy to present Maréchal Pétain with the title to a plot in the Hospices' "Dames Hospitalières" parcel of the Les Teurons vineyard. Local authorities had devised the initiative and the administrative council of the Hospices had consented. "By all accounts, it is the most charming and pleasant parcel," Pétain replied. The Hospices continued to work the vines, and the wine was bottled with a special label: Clos du Maréchal Pétain. After the war, Pétain's belongings were confiscated and the vineyard was reintegrated into the estate. This story was forgotten until Georges Chevaillier, a doctor at the Hospices with an avid interest in history, discovered in the archives in 1990.

The Vintage

Tamed and guided by the hand of man, the vines are wearing their summer colors. Lined up in neat rows on the slope, they bear the promise of a new harvest. But the vignerons are watching the sky, worried; until the morning of the harvest, nothing is sure. Finally, on a September day, the aroma of new wines will start to permeate the air. This is the story of the birth of a new vintage at the Hospices de Beaune.

Double previous page:
The historic heart of the grand cru vineyards of Corton. Their boundaries were the cause of a long legal battle.

Left page:
A vine in early May. The plant is taking flight toward a new vintage.

Behind this wall, a vineyard of the Volnay cuvee "Général Muteau."

A World in 50 Grams

The second half of August. France has not yet emerged from its summer torpor. Soon people will be gearing up for back-to-school, reflecting on the tourist season, or talking about the first slight drops in temperature as autumn approaches. The ambiance of vacation coming to an end. The A6 highway that hugs the slope of vineyards between Beaune and Savigny is packed with vacationers coming back north through the Rhône Valley. Cars, trailers, and campers with license plates from all over northern Europe line up. Out the window, the passengers glimpse the green rows of vines stretching over the ochre background of the clayey soil. The vines, too, have begun the last leg of their journey. The trip began in April, when tiny cottony buds appeared on the vine, and it will end one September day when a harvester passes through. His back bent and often aching, he will take the bunch of grapes in one hand, and the clippers in his other will make a resounding metallic click. The final moment of vineyard work. The climate, the soil, the plant, and all the treatments done by the *vigneron* throughout the year come down to these bunches of grapes, six to eight per vine if all is well. About fifty grams each, and each carrying the i.d. of the *terroir* that gave them birth and watched them grow. They are no heavier at the Hospices de Beaune than at neighboring estates (luckily, since that would not be a sign of quality). Nothing looks as much like a grape as another grape, even if it comes from one of Burgundy's most famous estates. But what makes up these bunches cannot be weighed on a scale: they contain a rich and unique history that goes back hundreds of years. Their "sap" will go into the Pommard cuvee "Dames de la Charité," the Volnay Santenots "Jehan de Massol,"

the Meursault "Philippe le Bon," etc., cuvees that wear the coat of arms of Nicolas Rolin and Guigone de Salins. And the wines will be sold on a November day when the whole town is in the spotlight and celebrating.

But the excitement surrounding the third Sunday of November is still far off. The sky is clear and the heat of summer still hangs in the air. Mid-August is past and there's not a soul in the vineyards. The die has already been cast.... But it hasn't landed yet, and nothing can predict what fate has in store. For the *vignerons* this is the waiting period, and their only hope is that the weather will hold, or at least that the storms in the southeast will stay there, over the plain of Bresse. Sometimes the clouds send hail that can irreparably damage the fruit, which is more fragile than ever as its skin softens. Luckily that sort of calamity is the exception, or at least is very localized, at this time of year. This is also the period when winegrowers are on vacation, often fifteen days later than the rest of the country. A vacation that is a lot like one last deep breath before the final sprint.

The Northern Limits

Though the *vignerons* may have gone away, their thoughts are still with their vines. They listen to the weather report or call close friends who stayed in the area. The question, imbued with worry, is inevitable: "What's the weather like there?" And it's not just small talk....

Making wine in Burgundy is a challenge every time. That's the first thing that is remarked upon whenever winegrowers from New World wine regions (South Africa, Australia, California, etc.) discover Burgundy. In these "exotic" countries, eight or nine years out of ten the weather is predictable: hot and dry. In Burgundy, each vintage brings surprises. "The major difference from California is obviously the climate. Each year is different," confirmed Joe Wender, an American and a co-owner of the negociant Camille Giroud (Beaune) in a column in Bourgogne Aujourd'hui. Located in a semi-continental zone, Burgundy is subject to a number of climatic influences. Rude continental winters can give way to Mediterranean summers. Other times there is hardly a hot day all year. In the worst cases, oceanic disturbances file through the vineyards. Not many vineyards are further north than Burgundy, and especially not those that produce red wines, which is the greater part of the production of the Hospices de Beaune (but not in all of Burgundy, contrary to common perception). That is the strength and the weakness of Burgundy. "The great wines are produced at the northern limit of grape cultivation," believes Denis Dubourdieu of Bordeaux, one of the world's most reputed enologists. Only in these areas does the vine find the ideal conditions that allow its grapes to ripen slowly. This allows the fruit to develop aromatic complexity while also keeping its balance between sugar and acidity. Each year, the producers are on pins and needles as they wait...

The vineyards of Pernand-Vergelesses (Côte de Beaune) under the snow.

A winter sight in the vineyards: branches being burned after pruning.

Which Way is the Wind Blowing?

So this is why a Burgundian *vigneron* is constantly watching the sky. The most astute among them are especially interested in the direction of the wind. Tell me which way it's blowing, and I'll tell you how the vintage will be; that is the formula so often used in Burgundy. If the wind is coming from the west, the oceanic influence will soon arrive. In other words, rain and humidity aren't far off, which could also lower temperatures significantly. Vines don't like that kind of weather. If the wind is coming from the south, danger! Storms will come with it and bring along their violent, destructive phenomena (heavy rains, hail, etc.) and the mugginess that encourages sporophytic diseases like mildew, oidium, and botrytis. These fungi attack both the leaves and the grapes. In short, the entire harvest could be spoiled. On the first day of the harvest, a *vigneron* often uses this simple reasoning to explain to his team, seriously and efficiently, the difference between the good grapes and the bad: "Only take the grapes you'd want to eat!" In a great vintage the bunches are perfectly healthy (except in the production of dessert wines). Sporophytic diseases can cause aromas that detract from the purity of the wine's character.

The sight of a scorching summer: 2003. A suffering bunch of Pinot Noir grapes that is lost for the harvest.

Taking a sample for analysis and tasting. This is one way to track the progress of fermentation.

The only wind that is welcome news to a *vigneron* comes from the north or the east. These dry, cold winds also favor a lot of light, which are both conditions conducive for the grapes to ripen slowly and therefore develop more complexity. Many vintages have been improved, or simply saved from some difficulty, by these beneficial winds. It is quite astonishing that the Burgundians haven't openly dedicated a cult to them the way they honor their patron saint, Saint Vincent, every year on January 22nd.

The last decade has provided a few spectacular examples of "Aeolian salvation." In 2004, for instance, a series of storms came through the region in rapid succession throughout July and August, sometimes bringing hail with them. These conditions caused a particularly virulent attack of oidium, and morale among *vignerons* couldn't have been worse. In late August, they evoked the sad harvest of 1984, exactly twenty years before. This year is still known as the most recent "catastrophe" vintage in Burgundy. Rot was already spreading quickly when the fruit had just begun to ripen, just as it had in '84. But in 2004 a miracle happened. Almost precisely as August ended and September began, the north wind cleared the sky, bringing a sturdy, intense light with it that would last throughout the month. The botrytis was completely stopped in its tracks. Widely known as "grey rot," this fungus is the age-old enemy of quality in wine, especially for reds. With the new wind sweeping through the vineyards, the botrytis dried out and began to look like dust on the shriveled berries. Infected grapes readily fall off the vine, making it easier for the harvesters to collect only the healthy fruit. This "dry" rot is less likely to affect the flavor of the wine. Another positive consequence came in the long-term: the winds caused evaporation in the bloated grapes, which quickly became more concentrated. Their sugar level climbed. In the end, 2004 was not a legendary vintage – July and August had been too hard on the vines to allow great aging wines to be made – but it will always have an honorable mention for its respectable whites. The quality of the reds would have had to be more consistent to make long-aging wines.

Water Soluble

The same climatic phenomenon of the end of the growing season has given magnificent red and white wines, but only when the plants are not handicapped by a difficult summer. The 1999 vintage is the perfect example. That year, the wines had unusually expressive, complex aromatics. From the very first tastings, a wonderful silkiness appeared on the palate. And yet the harvest had been abundant, a characteristic that does not generally go hand in hand with quality. A few years before, the same personality was found in the 1996s, but with a more austere and vivacious profile. The 2002s were also similar, much less expressive than the '99s but with an equilibrium and structure that will delight connoisseurs for many years to come, or at least those who are patient enough to wait for them. More recently the 2007 vintage enjoyed what could be called a Burgundian version of an Indian summer. The recovery was only partial, though. A particularly hot spring (especially April) hurried the development of the vines, throwing off their growing cycle. In mid-May, the first flowers were already popping up on the Chardonnay of the Côte de Beaune; normally flowering doesn't occur until around June 15th. Given that the grapes are completely ripe about 100 days after full flowering, the clippers and sorting tables were already in action in late August, three weeks or even a month earlier than the average period of the harvest. When all was said and done, the latest-ripening *terroirs* fared the best that year, taking full advantage of the return of the good weather. Hypothetically, if there had been a normal spring, 2007 would have been an almost identical copy of 2004. The threat of catastrophe loomed even larger in 2007… but, luckily, there was dry weather during the harvest. Nothing is worse for a *vigneron* than having to bring in water along with his grapes. His entire year's work is water soluble! In 2007, after the weather improved, a wind of euphoria also swept through the cellars. Cuvees were finishing their fermentation and these new babies, born after a chaotic gestation, made their parents very happy. They lacked a little depth, of course, but they were fruity and pleasant, perfect for drinking young. They were just the thing for a certain clientele that had grown weary of the powerful, concentrated wines that had defined the 1990s.

Autumn light over the Côte de Beaune.

2005: The Vintage of Great Acclaim

With the exception of the famous 2003 vintage – dry, very sunny and very hot, which inspired a litany of superlatives – great vintages are those in which the *vignerons* have the least say. "Everything came off like a dream, with the minimum of interventions," many of them said of 2005. "All you had to do was put the grapes in the vat. We could have left for a three-week vacation; the wine would have done just as well on its own." A professional *vigneron* is always attentive to, and even anxious about, any comments that clients, journalists, or even importers may make about their wines. But in tastings of the 2005s, even the most laudatory comments could hardly strike this sensitive chord. All the credit for this enological bounty went to Mother Nature, and they all knew it. More practically, the vintage sold very quickly. With the extravagant praise from the press helping, cellars emptied out incredibly fast. The reaction from the media had all the more impact since the vintage had been a great success in all of France's wine regions. Bordeaux especially,

with its sales of futures (starting the spring after the harvest), quickly drew a lot of attention from journalists and critics.

Left page:
The vine: a plant that is particularly sensitive to its environment.

In short, the producers didn't have to add much. But how can you help elaborating further on 2005. Concentration, balance, purity, and aromatic intensity all joined forces long enough to create this magical season. Add to that the finesse of the tannins, the persistence and the length on the palate. The dream profile of a Burgundy from a great vintage. Each generation sees at least one in the span of a career, but rarely more than two or three.... Better not let it slip by! In a year like this the vines find ideal conditions for perfectly formed grapes at every step of their cycle. The thick-skinned berries are rich in polyphenols that are easily extracted during the maceration (for the reds), but they also have plenty of sugar, all without giving up their good acidity. These grapes please the eye before they even hit the palate. In 2005, some producers put away their sorting tables altogether, while others just used them to pull out leaves or verjuice (unripe "second generation" grapes) collected by careless harvesters. The absence of endemic diseases on the vines was a double blessing, as they not only put the quantitative potential of the harvest seriously at risk but can also mar the quality of the fruit. For instance, the effect of oidium on white wines is apparent from an odor that resembles leeks, potatoes, mold, etc. Luckily, these unpleasant odors are only found in years when the fungus proliferates.

When Vines Suffer

The perfect conditions for vines are easily summarized: a little water, sun, and no extreme heat. Limited water to prevent dilution, of course; but also so that the vine, seeing this necessity strictly rationed (along with the nitrogen it carries) stocks its production in its grapes. Otherwise, it is more inclined to build up its foliage through an advanced point in its cycle. "The vine must suffer to give its best," tells an old adage, and this philosophy has largely been confirmed by the most recent viticultural research. An excess of vigor does not make great wines. "Grapes from a vigorous vine have very little sugar and high acidity, lack color, and have astringent tannins and aromas that are more leafy than fruity. (...) To get high-quality grapes, it's not enough to limit yields; also, and above all, you have to control the vine's vigor so its growth stops at the moment of veraison, at the very beginning of maturation," confirms Bordeaux's enologist Denis Dubourdieu.

If there hasn't already been a severe drought earlier in the cycle, the vine must be weaned off water in the month preceding the harvest. The products of photosynthesis (sugars, aromas, and color) and nutriments drawn from the soil will fortify the fruit more effectively. The importance and necessity of sun for all plants to develop goes without saying. Leaves are, after all, just the solar panels of the vegetal world.

Sun, yes, but without too much heat, especially since the Burgundian varietals, which adapted to a northern climate, are not accustomed to heat. High temperatures make the acidity in the grapes drop quickly, and without acidity certain aromas disappear. Moreover, a wine that lacks acidity seems flabby and tired. Its capacity to age is also diminished, especially in whites, which cannot compensate for this deficit with pronounced tannins.

Leaves collect sun. But that's not all: they also serve as lungs. When it is very hot, the plant stops breathing, a simple defense reflex that helps protect it from getting scorched. Evapotranspiration, a process in which the vine drains water, comes to a halt. An apnea until conditions become less hostile. During this time, the maturation process is blocked and the grape temporarily becomes an orphan.

The 100-Meter Hurdles

None of this happened in 2005, the reference point of the decade. From the first buds opening their leaves to the last bunches being snipped off the vines, conditions were ideal for the grapes to ripen. There was just one moment of apprehension in mid-August, when a drought had set in. The youngest vines, with less developed root systems, started to turn yellow and drop their leaves. But a spell of storms in September eased everyone's nerves.

If the vine's vegetative cycle were compared to an athletic feat, it would have to be the 100-meter hurdles. The beginning of the cycle is punctuated by important stages, like obstacles to be overcome. First, the bud break: the risk here is not excessive heat but rather frosts. If the thermometer falls below freezing for too long, the fragile little leaves won't develop any further. They will become brown and dry on the branch, and the vegetative growth will have to start anew, belatedly, to overcome this setback. This is not lethal to the quality of the vintage (aside from the delay in the evolution of the vines), but the potential production is diminished. This was the case in 2003, a year that produced all the extremes. The blisteringly hot summer made everyone forget that on April 11th in the Côte de Beaune, the vines that had been launched by a sunny, early spring were caught by surprise in mid-revival by an unexpected frost. In the end, the heat wave in August and this spring frost led to a historically meager harvest.

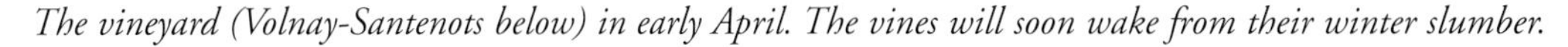

The vineyard (Volnay-Santenots below) in early April. The vines will soon wake from their winter slumber.

Flowering: An Important Step

The flowers have ceded their place to burgeoning grapes (mid-June).

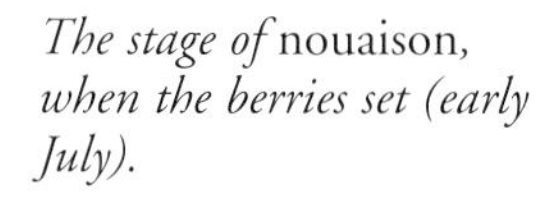

The stage of nouaison, *when the berries set (early July).*

About fifty days after bud break the energetic vine has crowned itself with a mane of brilliant green. Under the sun, the well-spaced leaves sway in the wind, giving off silver glints. They keep watch over the glistening branches with their yellow pistils. Delicate aromas reminiscent of a mild honeysuckle delight attentive noses. The vines are flowering, and the date of the harvest can now be predicted quite accurately: just count 100 days more to find out when the grapes will be fully ripe. The flowering also largely determines the volume of wine that will be produced. If the weather is chilly and rainy, the pollination of the flowers will be meager or won't happen at all. The bunches will have fewer or smaller berries. This phenomenon is known as coulure (when there is no pollination) or millerandage (poor pollination). In the case of millerandage, the vine's vigor is naturally restricted, which is good for the future crop!

The obstacles in this race must be handled one by one, under the best possible conditions to attain the "perfect" wine. But nothing is sure until the last hurdle has been cleared, because it may be the one that causes the fall. In 2005, the vines blithely avoided all these pitfalls. That is how great vintages are: the vineyard seems to be running the race of a lifetime, like it's on the starting line at the Olympic finals. Once the faultless performance is done, the gold isn't far off.... But it's still August, and there are still hurdles to clear. Anyone who can say on which step of the podium this vintage will stand is quite crafty.

T Minus 30 Days: The Nuances of Colors

The heat of summer hangs over Burgundy. In this second half of August, the vineyards are quiet and empty. The rows of vines, left to themselves, are a pleasure to see. Bunches of Pinot Noir grapes draw the eye. At last the varietal is beginning to earn its name, as the skin of the fruit grows black – noir – and for the first time becomes easily distinguishable from the foliage and shoots around it. The pigment is the result of a molecule called anthocyan. Thirty days before the harvest, the vine is midway through the stage of veraison. Each bunch displays numerous hues, and you can see that some of them have berries that are already a deep blue while others are still entirely green.

Only thirty more days until they all fall into step. Then the bunches will have all the colors of fully ripe fruit laden with sugar: black with blue or even purple glints for the Pinot Noir; slightly translucent gold for the Chardonnay.

The véraison, *when the grapes change color late July.*

The grapes have begun their final approach to maturity. This is the phase that allows the vigilant eye of Roland Masse, supervisor of the estate of the Hospices de Beaune, to hone the date of the harvest. "The full flowering gives a pretty precise idea of the timing of the harvest by counting about one hundred days. The mid-veraison lets you calculate more precisely: the harvest will be thirty days later." Even very different climatic conditions can only marginally change this term. The countdown has begun.

T Minus 13 Days: A Recurring Question

"So when do you start?" Starting at least two weeks before the harvest, this is the question that every *vigneron* hears at least twice a day. Professionals get restless, showing how nervous the men of the wine world can be during this period. The question also draws the interest of observers or simple passersby. Beaune, the wine capital of Burgundy, lives to the rhythm of the vine. Even stores and supermarkets are stocked for the occasion: family-size packs of canned vegetables, fruit compotes, and fromage blanc have appeared on the shelves. In a few days, there will be a whole team of harvesters to feed.

But for the moment that bustle of activity seems far off. In the vineyards morale is wanting. A low grey sky has appeared over the slopes. It has been raining almost nonstop since the small hours of the morning. It is as if the summer wanted to end just the way it was all along: without any stable weather. Beautiful summer days were followed by grey periods. No anticyclone stayed in France for very long this year. The climate of Burgundy regularly had oceanic tones, which is clearly not typical in the region. Summers are generally dry and hot. The Morvan prevents the area from getting much rain. This mountainous, wooded massif lying just west of the winegrowing zone dries the air driven by Atlantic depressions. A walk though the vineyards on a summer day in Burgundy usually promises an intense sun beating down and oppressive heat: everything a vine loves. The angle of the slopes also adds to the effect, like a beach chair that exposes the vines to the very first rays of sun.

These are the main elements of the climate of Burgundy. Quietly waiting, the winery seems particularly sober, the pale glow of a few neon lights doing nothing to cheer the atmosphere. But what is most disturbing cannot be seen, but rather heard. The building sounds hollow. It is hard to imagine that in under two weeks it will be a center of intense activity with dozens of people working in shifts until late at night. And yet the team that receives and sorts the grapes is almost complete. Are they predicting sun tomorrow? They need it now and until the harvest in order to have a good vintage.

T Minus 8 Days: The Pre-Harvest Meeting

Eleven o'clock on a Thursday morning. A small cloudburst distressed Roland Masse in the early morning hours. But there were just a few passing drops; the week is supposed to begin sunny with a bit of a chill. The supervisor can greet his troops with his habitual joviality before the great wooden door of the winery. The estate's *vignerons* have been asked to attend a traditional pre-harvest meeting. His troops plus a few more: the members of the committee for the legacy of the Hospices are also in attendance. This committee is charged with overseeing the proper management of the property of the institution. Their presence brings a note of solemnity to the gathering.

Even if the sunlight has assuaged them, hearts are not light. And it's not because of the formalities of the business at hand. The uncertainty of the vintage is far from resolved. But the day of the harvest is fast approaching; it is no longer just a mental image. It has a date, a schedule, a deadline. This is the information that Masse is communicating to his team today. It is also an opportunity to remind them of certain guidelines that will ensure optimal conditions for the harvest. "Don't squeeze the grapes into the crates or leave them in the sun," begins the list. This is of course to help the grapes arrive at the winery as unblemished as possible. In wine as in haute cuisine, excellence is possible only with raw ingredients of the highest quality. But unlike chefs, *vignerons* don't get a second chance: the work of an entire year is at risk. They all know that "forgetting" these logical precautions is not an option. So it is surprising to see the *vignerons* for the Hospices de Beaune, these seasoned professionals, getting a reminder. "I'm responsible for twenty-two *vignerons*, each with his own personality, way of working, etc. It's never a wasted effort to go over the basics," justifies the supervisor.

Roland Masse (second row, far left) and his assistant, Sébastien Lecomte (first row, yellow shirt) surrounded by the Hospices' team of vignerons.

"Respect habitual rotations" is the second point. Harvesting is teamwork. Once the grapes are in the crates, the cutters hand over the reins to the sorters. Just a short trip to a truck or a trailer hitched to a tractor. "If my team of sorters is in place at nine am but the first crates don't arrive until ten, I have an organization problem," Masse notes. And one last thing: the *vignerons* are asked to separate out grapes from vines that are under six years old for the reds and under four years for the whites. The fruit from these young vines are kept aside and not included in the auction. The first grapes worthy of the appellation are from a vine's third vintage. But in practice, the Hospices doesn't consider their fruit at that age worthy of a *terroir* wine. The *vignerons* call them "the plants," a vague but common name for these trainees. They will have to become hardened to earn the right to use the name of that noble species of the vegetable kingdom: vines. If their health permits, these "plants" may someday be venerable octogenarians, like the elders of the estate…

T Minus 5 Days: Tasting the Grapes

Roland Masse, supervisor of the estate of the Hospices de Beaune, and Anthony Hanson, head of Christie's wine department.

Left page:
A bunch of Pinot Noir grapes, the variety that gives the great red wines of Burgundy.

Roland Masse welcomes Anthony Hanson, director of Christie's wine department. The famous London institution has been in charge of the auction since 2005. This lanky man with salt and pepper hair is here to inquire about the vintage. He has not come out of courtesy; Hanson is hurrying to prepare the auction catalog. He will also need to inform all the potential clients about this year's wines. Rather than give a long speech, the estate supervisor brings him to the vineyards to see the grapes for himself. It's a tour he's given regularly and increasingly often over the last few weeks. This is also his own primary task in the period leading up to the harvest: keeping a very close eye on the development of the grapes, both in terms of their maturation and of their health. At this advanced stage in the cycle of the vine, the fruit is unusually sensitive to climatic conditions. Masse remembers one past experience: beautiful golden grapes that he saw on a Friday, with the promise of an excellent wine. A storm and a weekend later, the beautiful bunches had turned brown. They were overripe. All that was left to do was to note what damage had already been done and harvest what could still be salvaged as quickly as possible.

This situation could have recurred for the whites in 2006. The harvest schedule was changed at the last minute. The Chardonnays had to be harvested right away; they were gaining a degree of sugar every three days, almost three times faster than usual. It is imperative to collect ripe grapes in order to make a great wine, but harvesting when they are overripe is also an error. As the berries gradually increase their sugar content, they lose acidity. If too much acidity is lost, the equilibrium is thrown off; the wine loses its vivacity, length, and aromatic freshness. Its ability to age is also diminished.

But there is more to it than just a visual exam: Roland Masse also tastes the grapes. Their balance, the thickness of their skins, and the texture of the seeds are all crucial information.

This presence and knowledge of the vineyards is the heart of the work of a winegrower in any region the world over. It may be even more essential in Burgundy than elsewhere, though, because the vineyards here are a patchwork of *terroirs*. "At the beginning of flowering, if I want to see the first buds open, I know which parcel to look in. It's the same thing with diseases: if I know the conditions are favorable to oidium and I want to see the first cases, again I know where I'm most likely to find them," Masse declares. His predecessor, André Porcheret, had the same philosophy back in 1997: "You have to be in the vineyards regularly, even if there's nothing to be done there, just to see and understand. I would be unable to vinify a wine without knowing the vineyards it came from."

The visit has confirmed a few fears. August was ambiguous, rather chilly and humid. The consequences were twofold: the veraison was slow, which made it hard for the final phase of maturation to get off the ground. This climate thus favored sporophytic diseases (fungi), especially mildew, which has made producers break into nervous sweats over the last few days. Some areas were even hit by hailstorms. This vintage will not be smooth sailing.

T Minus 3 Days: The North Wind Returns

Morale has improved over the last few days. The last grey day is already a distant memory; almost two weeks have passed without a single cloud in the sky. The familiar scenario is playing out: the north wind has cleared the sky and dried the land. It arrived like a squadron of water bombers over a forest in flames: a savior. Days are sunny and beautiful, and the weather is cool, not exceeding 20°C (68°F) during the day and happily dropping below 10°C (50°F) at night. Under these conditions, the rot that appeared a while ago cannot develop any further; in fact, it is drying out. This cool weather maintains high levels of acidity, so Roland Masse has pushed back the harvest to start three days later than he had predicted at the finish of veraison. It is better to let the grapes make the most of the Septmber sun. There's no hurry.

Until now, the sugars have slowly been concentrating in the berries, mainly as water evaporated. The process seems to be accelerating lately. Samples taken from various spots around the vineyards of the estate are pressed, and the juice is analyzed to determine the fruit's state of maturity. Most samples have a potential alcohol level around 12-13%, meaning that the grapes are ripe: not only are they rich in sugar, but the substances (polyphenols) present in the skins can easily be extracted during the fermentation.

The moment has come to harvest in the vineyards of Beaune (Les Bressandes).

Zero Hour: Clippers in Hand

Let the harvest begin! The slopes are mottled with the white of the vehicles that have brought the first teams of harvesters to the vineyards. Looking more closely at the rows of vines, we see the backs, usually bent, bustling along. A bold sun illuminates this long-awaited day. Long awaited and feared. Masse has consulted the weather report even more anxiously than on previous days. Luckily, it is reassuring. The sky promises a successful operation; as for the grapes, he remains skeptical, knowing he can only wait and see. What should you expect of a vintage that blew hot and cold throughout the season? The answer will only come when the last pieces of the puzzle are put in place, gradually, as each load of grapes arrives

A bunch of ripe Chardonnay grapes.

on the sorting table; then the first juice will be analyzed, and the feeling of the first tannins (for the reds) on the palate will start to paint a picture; finally the outlines of the full image will appear in about two weeks, when the fermentation finishes.

The first grapes arrive… in a refrigerated truck. They are from the farthest vineyard from Beaune: Pouilly-Fuissé. The vineyard is more specifically in the commune of Chaintré, at the extreme south of the wine-producing part of Burgundy. There are three parcels here that go into the cuvee "Françoise Poisard." Since the varietal, Chardonnay, and the altitude here are almost identical to those of the Côte de Beaune, the fruit ripens first because of this more southern latitude. These crates of grapes therefore had to travel about one hundred kilometers (62 miles) before being unloaded at the winery. Then they are taken to the sorting table, even if whites are rarely sorted; their skins don't macerate with the juice as for red wines, so a few rotten berries won't affect the quality of a white. In fact, they can bring an extra level of aromatic complexity and presence on the palate. This year, though, Roland Masse has decided to be particularly selective. The vineyards in Pouilly-Fuissé were hit by hail, and a few damaged berries could give a "dry" flavor. Other grapes were attacked by oidium and show the characteristic whitish film. These will also have to be removed…. Only after this has been done can the healthiest bunches go to the press.

Pressing and Racking the Whites

Pressing is an essential step in vinifying white wines. Only during this process are all the components of the grape extracted into the must (juice), because unlike red wines, white wines have the skins definitively removed. The estate of the Hospices de Beaune uses pneumatic presses in which a sort of balloon is inflated under the force of compressed air. "This sort of machine allows a long, gentle pressing, but above all it can be adapted to the type of grape," Masse explains.

The winery is packed; the harvest is in full swing.

Right page:
At the sorting table: any grapes that are unripe or tainted by rot are removed.

The resulting juice is left to settle in a vat for 24-48 hours. The heavy sediment falls to the bottom of the vat and is removed.

T Plus 1 Day: At Cruising Speed

The harvest reaches its real cruising speed when the first Pinot Noir from the Côte de Beaune arrives. The earliest-ripening *terroir*s of Volnay and Beaune are harvested; piles of crates appear at the winery as trucks and tractors rotate through. Everything is weighed on arrival. With each delivery, a plaque indicates the appellation, the cuvee, and the name of the vineyard to assure traceability. Teams are busy over three sorting tables. The grapes show midnight blue hues, a sign of advanced maturity. The few rosy bunches are removed – neon lights over the tables allow the sorters to distinguish them – and finish their journey in a bin with those attacked by rot. Sorting is not too hard this year since it was a "dry rot": the affected berries are grey and shriveled, and they easily fall off their stems. The ones that pass the test continue their voyage to the vats. A conveyor like an escalator brings them to the destemmer, a machine with a cylinder in which a system of spiral arms rotates, separating the berries from the stems. By removing the stems, the *vigneron* avoids extracting green, bitter tannins or simply adding off flavors to the wine if the stem isn't entirely healthy. Finally, a series of pipes brings the berries to the vats.

The tone is set for the rest of the operation; the harvest beats out a rhythm of four to five cuvees gathered per day.

Hand Harvesting and Sorting

The wine estate of the Hospices de Beaune practices hand harvesting; about twenty harvesters are hard at work each day in the estate's vineyards. This may seem obvious, but given the technical advances in machine harvesting, many estates now use this alternative. One of the advantages of hand harvesting is that the grapes remain whole, with a minimum of damage. They are transported in small crates to avoid crushing the fruit on the bottom. If the juice ran it would quickly oxidize, tainting the quality of the must. "The goal is for the grapes to arrive at the winery in the same condition they were in on the vine," Masse attests.

T Plus 5 Days: Rigorous Sorting

"You'd think we were in Rungis!" exclaims Roland Masse, referring to the gargantuan wholesale food market outside Paris. A wall of pallets stretches towards the canopy of the winery at the Hospices. A fleet of forklifts adds to the bustling atmosphere. Volnay, Pommard, Savigny, Meursault… the grapes are coming in from all over the region. Some crates boast beautiful, healthy bunches with a deep, brilliant color. You permit yourself to taste one or two of the sweet, juicy berries. Others, however, are marred by hail (which especially affected the Santenots vineyard in Volnay) and sporophytic diseases. Damaged fruit is easy prey for these fungi. They are a pitiful sight. "Practically every year we say that the vintage is different in each parcel, but I think it's particularly true this year," Masse observes. The rigorous sorting that is necessary for some cuvees slows the process, which is why the crates are accumulating…. In the vineyards, however, Masse has picked up the pace. All the grapes are now ready to be cut. The best vineyards are the priority. It is important to know to harvest what's ready. Some of the whites have sugar levels approaching 14% potential alcohol. Even the Bâtard-Montrachet, a grand cru white that systematically fetches the highest bids at the November auction, has easily reached this threshold. Concentrations this high were beyond hope two weeks before the harvest. The favorable weather is responsible, of course, but only in part. Mother Nature is not the only one to have played a part. If the estate of the Hospices managed to achieve such levels of maturity this year, it is also because of the strictly controlled yields. Each vine was trimmed back to give no more than seven or eight bunches. A vine with too many bunches could not have properly ripened all its fruit this year. The months of effort from the *vignerons* are now paying off. But nothing is sure yet. Until 9pm tonight the sorting tables will be in action…

The work of sorting can last late into the evening.

Left:
A crate of grapes arriving at the winery. In the background is the Philip the Good Hospital, a modern version of the Hospices Civils de Beaune.

The plaques identifying the provenance of the grapes.

Macerating the Reds

Maceration is a period of four to five days when the grape skins soak in the juice (which is almost clear), before fermentation has started. The must is kept at a low temperature (15°C, or 59°F) to keep the yeasts from activating. The vats at the Hospices de Beaune are equipped with a thermoregulation system in which hot or cold water can be circulated to warm or cool them. During this period, the *vigneron* uses the protective and antiseptic virtues of sulfur dioxide (SO_2) to prevent the must from deteriorating. The sulfur also has solvent properties that helps extract the components of the skins (especially the color) into the must. Even before fermentation begins, a first exchange occurs in the vats between the juice and the grape solids.

T Plus 6 Days: The First Fermentations

The Burgundians have been making wine for at least 2,000 years. And yet *vignerons* are still finding ways to improve their methods! This morning a technician from the sorting table manufacturer came to make a few adjustments. For the first time, the Hospices de Beaune is equipped with a vibrating table: before reaching the conveyor belt, the grapes pass over a sifter that oscillates vigorously, controlled by an electric motor. There are two advantages to this system: dried berries that could give off flavors to the wine fall through the cracks, and any extra humidity in the bunch will fall (it is also sometimes called a draining table). The stainless steel tubes that make up the sifter were set too close together, according to Masse's preference, letting the dried grapes pass. The technician increases the spacing.

A few feet away in the winery are the first signs of fermentation. Subtle bubbles of carbonic gas are starting to rise to the surface of the juice. In a few hours it will look like the vats are gently boiling. The control board that regulates the temperatures through probes installed in each vat show values above 20°C (68°F). They rarely go above 30-32°C (86-90°F) at the peak of fermentation since the yeasts could die at higher temperatures. During this active period of vinification, the components of the wine are determined: color, body, alcohol, acidity, glycerol, etc. The art of the *vigneron* is to draw out the best of the grapes' potential, letting the famous polyphenols pass from the skins into the juice. For the moment it is just a sweet liquid, warm and almost colorless.

This year, nature needed a little encouragement. The weather is cool, and the natural yeasts on the grape skins and in the winery are having a hard time stirring themselves to action. So Masse has decided to use selected yeasts (bought dried, in packets) to seed these first vats.

Putting the whole bunches into the vat.

The Tasting

Man's sensory organs – his eyes, nose, and mouth – are veritable tools to *vignerons*. "Tasting is not a light matter. We spend a lot of time tasting, and sometimes it's no picnic," Masse remarks. The must of the white wines is tasted first, during pressing, in order to judge the quality of the juice and possibly to stop pressing if it is not satisfactory. For the reds there is a similar tasting when the skins are pressed after vatting. The must is regularly tasted during maceration too to evaluate its purity and look for any possible faults. Once fermentation has started, the exercise is much harder. The commotion going on makes sensorial analysis a very delicate matter. Only after fermentation can the *vigneron* get a final idea of his work. "Then you can appreciate what you've made. This tasting can also help determine how it's best to age the wine," concludes the supervisor.

T Plus 9 Days: Whole Bunches

Stéphane Murat, the newest *vigneron* at the Hospices, brings in the grapes from the Mazis-Chambertin and Clos de la Roche grand cru vineyards. The harvest is looking meager. The vines suffered, but the fruit looks good, a nice dark color and suitably healthy. The sorters won't have to work too hard on this lot. Masse even opts for a tailor-made vinification: half of the grapes will remain on their stems.

This crop is healthy enough for a partial "whole-bunch" vinification, in which half of the bunches are put directly into the vats without being destemmed. These grapes arrive in the vats just as they were on the vine. The absence of destemming induces a different sort of vinification: fermentation begins inside the grapes. It is an intracellular fermentation. The berries progressively distil their juice, and the fermentation tends to take longer. Wines that are made principally through whole-bunch vinification are easily identified: the nose shows spicy and floral notes, often reminiscent of rose petals.

Punching Down the Cap and Pumping Over

Punching down the cap and pumping over are two vinification techniques common during fermentation. Pumping over is generally done when the yeasts begin their work and consists of pumping the must from the bottom of the vat and progressively pouring it onto the cap formed by the grape skins, pulp, and seeds. This process aerates the must so that the yeasts can evolve in a favorable oxygenated atmosphere and may be carried out up to three times a day. Over the course of fermentation, it is replaced by punching down the cap. The cap, a mass of grape solids pushed to the top by effects of fermentation, is broken up and pushed down into the must, where the alcohol plays a solvent role, helping certain elements pass from the skins into the wine. This practice is typically Burgundian since it is specifically adapted to Pinot Noir.

T Plus 10 Days: The Harvest Comes to a Close

A feeling of nostalgia, and also of fatigue, hovers in the air this afternoon. The ambiance at the sorting tables is less studious. The harvest is coming to a close. The last bunches have been cut. In about fourteen days, all of the forty-four cuvees will have seen the light of day: "I keep the wines in vat for about two weeks: five days of maceration, eight days of fermentation, and two days of post-fermentation maceration," Masse explains.

The cap formed by the grape solids is regularly punched down into the juice to extract the polyphenols.

Of the reds, the Auxey-Duresses "Boillot" cuvee brings up the rear. This well-exposed *terroir* with good drainage managed to keep its fruit in an almost perfect state of health. The sorters didn't need to spend much time on this one. Of the whites, the final harvesting was done in Saint-Romain, in some of the highest-placed vineyards of the Côte de Beaune. The cooler temperatures here delay ripening. The vineyards rarely vary by more than 300-400 meters (about 980-1310 feet) in altitude, but this parameter is also one of the many characteristics of Burgundian *terroirs*. The cuvee that is born here is not sold at the auction in November, but is rather added to the "réserve particulière" (see "The *Vignerons*").

The Meursault wines, also white, were cut last week and are now fermenting. If you get close to the barrels you can hear the yeasts bubbling away. Jean-Jacques Blondel, the oldest member of the team in the cellar at the Hospices de

The cuvee named for the founder is progressing in a stainless steel vat.

Beaune, is bustling about. He is carefully noting each barrel's density in sugar, which lowers gradually as alcohol is formed, in order to assure that the fermentations are proceeding properly.

In ten days the Hospices has wrapped up the harvest of about sixty hectares of vineyards, a relatively short period that has been getting even shorter over the last ten years. "I don't know if it's an effect of global warming, but the vines tend to ripen in a shorter and shorter window," Masse observes. The effects of increasingly rigorous vine management may also have an effect on yields: a vine has an easier time ripening six or seven bunches of grapes than ten.

The Fermentation of the Whites

In Burgundy, the great white wines ferment in oak barrels. The barrels are not filled all the way because the bubbling of the fermentation can build pressure until the bung (stopper) pops out and some of the contents spill over. This phase of transforming the sugar can last anywhere from ten days to two months, depending on the activity of the yeast, the temperature of the cellar, and the quality of the fruit. Halfway through the process, the *vigneron* stirs up the lees that have fallen to the bottom of the barrel with a pole called the "dodine." This process, known as batonnage, makes the wine more round and full-bodied. It also stimulates the yeasts by bringing in oxygen.

T Plus 20 Days: 544 Barrels

The grapes are only a memory now. The yeast has transformed the sugar in the fruit into alcohol. The cap formed by the solids of the grapes has finally fallen back into the juice. A dark, gassy liquid has appeared: the wine has arrived. Until this point it was just a project, a sample, an analysis laid out on the letterhead of an enology lab. Now it is finally showing its face.... Or rather, we can finally make it out. It is still fuzzy, full of lees and carbonic gas. In short, it bears the marks of the clamor that saw it coming. Four days ago already, the first vats started to cool down.

Today the floor of the winery is covered with a web of pipes; crenellated and light red, they snake over the floor tiles. They run from the press to the vats or from the vats to grates, where they disappear into the floor. At the ends of the pipes, in the cellar one floor down, a man monitors the wine flowing into the barrels. He is equipped with a lamp on a headband to help him track how full each barrel is. This de-vatting is the first opportunity to evaluate the vintage. The verdict is not expected yet, given the state of the vines in early September. The least ripe cuvee has a potential alcohol of 12.2%, while the most ripe is at 14.3%. But the mark of the vintage lies in its high acidity: "all the cuvees are above 6 grams of acidity per liter, compared to 4.5-5 grams most years." This is the stamp of a year with no real heat waves, when *vignerons* were rewarded for patience and a cool head.

Roland Masse will soon be able to announce how many barrels will be up for auction, a figure eagerly awaited at Christie's in order to prepare the auction. This year is also marked by a particularly small crop due to the sorting and climatic conditions. Five hundred forty-four barrels will be for sale this November, or 35-40% less than the estate's potential total. But that won't stop the cellar from welcoming the numerous wine professionals and journalists who come to taste the wines of the new vintage. One more harvest in the long history of the Hospices de Beaune...

Transferring the white wines into barrel.

de Beaune

The Event

IN BEAUNE, PASSIONS EMERGE AND ESCALATE ON A FIXED DATE: THE THIRD SUNDAY IN NOVEMBER. THE WINES OF THE HOSPICES DE BEAUNE ARE SIMULTANEOUSLY PLACED IN THE SPOTLIGHT OF THE AUCTION AND IN FRONT OF THE CAMERAS. THESE EMBLEMATIC CUVEES ARE SOLD FOR THE PROFIT OF THE CITY HOSPITAL. HISTORY, GOOD DEEDS, FAT WALLETS, AND CELEBRITIES HAPPILY COEXIST FOR ONE WEEKEND. IT'S AN INCONGRUOUS MIX. THE PEACEFUL WINE CAPITAL OF BURGUNDY SUDDENLY TAKES ON THE APPEAL OF A GAUL VILLAGE IN A COMIC STRIP...

A GAME, THE STAKES

For a few days now, everyone is talking about les Halles of Beaune, the covered marketplace that is also used for festivals and expositions. The murmur slides over the shining cobblestones, reverberates from the glazed roof tiles, and runs through the streets. As the November weekend approaches, houses and businesses are abuzz with figures, and the buzz is loudest in the plush sitting rooms of the local negociants. People are making bets, disapproving, analyzing: the most sensible among them are content to express what they are hoping for. A drop? An increase? 10, 15, 20, 50%.... From the mayor, Alain Suguenot, in the local paper to the simple shopper in the street, an entire city of 22,000 inhabitants discovers – or rediscovers, every year when autumn rolls around – its gift for divination. The little people also chatter about the celebrity who will preside over the auction. Is he big enough to follow in the footsteps of Catherine Deneuve, Barbara Hendricks, Lino Ventura, Mstislav Rostropovitch, and so many others who have sat in the place of honor in the gallery at the wine auction of the Hospices de Beaune?

Left page:
Actresses Alice Taglioni and Fanny Ardant on the platform of the 2006 wine auction.

The wine negociants, and a few of their clients, have taken their places in the covered marketplace of Beaune. The auction has begun.

"The bidding is open," proclaims local newspaper Le Bien Public, but it makes no attempt to read the future in the… grape leaves. Elsewhere, people profess to associate their destiny and honor to the vagaries of a soccer game, a ball on a roulette wheel, or the outcome of a horse race; in Beaune it is the auction at the Hospices that loosens tongues, makes people tremble or gloat, excites or enrages them. Of course, the historic Burgundian town doesn't unfurl the expertly orchestrated pomp of Monaco or the southern exuberance of Marseille, but it does get a thrill each year at the end of November from this guessing game. The city prepares itself to live, for one afternoon, at the rhythm of the auctioneer's gavel and according to the moods of bidders from France, America, England, or Japan. All the way to the Palais des Congrès, a multipurpose facility where producers and negociants have set up their stands for the General Exposition of the Wines of Burgundy, all eyes are on the temporary auction house. There's no doubt about it, the estate and the auction of the Hospices de Beaune are out of the ordinary, a mix of media circus, political stakes, and economic interests, with a small dose of folklore. It has a long heritage and, above all, a prestigious history. One of those cocktails that sometimes detonate.

The Wheels of the Mechanism

Nevertheless, the situation rarely leaves room for hesitation. In Beaune, no change in the wine market, no downward trend, not even the smallest deviation will pass unnoticed. In a micro-market where international demand has a dominant role, the health of the world economy can force prices up or down. But it is a rare year when suppositions do not figure in conversations. The dollar has dropped, a government has decided to raise taxes on wine, the vintage was particularly stingy, a conflict is worsening in the Middle East, etc. "The result of the auction of the Hospices draws on many constituents that have different effects, sometimes

Three Miss France winners: Maréva Georges, Linda Hardy, and Sonia Rolland lead the 2007 auction, watched by Richard Berry.

conflicting. In the end, the factors with the strongest influence determine the outcome," judges Denis Duveau, adjunct director of the Federation of Negociants of Burgundy. In the mechanics of the auction, important wheels are left in the shadows. "Irrational, unpredictable, elusive," you sometimes hear. Only an eye trained to follow the evolution of the wine world can hope to decipher its workings. On the face of things, it is a theater ruled by a relatively simple code of drama: the unity of time, place, and action. But behind the scenes you see the full extent of the intrigue. The actors sometimes move their pawns before the curtain is even up. "I told the press I expected a 15% increase, just to give things a push," admitted Alain Suguenot, the mayor of Beaune, in 1997 in a confidential conversation with Pierre-Henri Gagey, a representative of the negociants of Burgundy. It was the night before the auction, and the following Sunday the counters would show + 47%! So apparently the bidders didn't need any "encouragement" that year.... The anecdote illustrates how drastically the auction can veer away from expectations. Some people have given up on finding any logic in it. And yet understanding the mechanisms at work is a fascinating exercise.

1994 was the vintage when confidence was restored at the Hospices.

Historic Names

But who are the players? Essentially they are locally well-known names: more than 80% of the bidders are negociants based in or near Beaune. The list of the top buyers is relatively consistent from one year to the next. In 2008, for the twelfth year in a row, Albert Bichot, a Beaune negociant founded in 1831, came in first. In the best vintages, Bichot snaps up twenty percent of the lots and spends about 800,000€ in the course of the afternoon. Another very active buyer is Corton-André, a negociant based in Aloxe-Corton that is best known for its flagship labels Reine Pédauque and Pierre André. On the third step of the podium is Patriarche Père et Fils, one of the major organizers of the auction since the Second World War (see inset concerning André Boisseaux). The names of other historic local houses fill out the ranks: Joseph Drouhin, Bouchard Père et Fils, Louis Latour, Louis Jadot, Chanson Père et Fils. Add Boisset (Nuits-Saint-Georges), Michel Picard (Chassagne-Montrachet) and Labouré-Roi (Nuits-Saint-Georges) and all the heavyweights of the business are included. The list is rounded out with some smaller houses, or those that buy less consistently at the auction: Lucien Lemoine, Béjot, Champy, Demessey, Roux Père et Fils, etc.

"They all have a stake in the auction; they all have a good reason to be there," observes Denis Duveau. This unflagging annual presence in the closed marketplace deserves further examination into its origins. Business has an important role, of course, as it is the raison d'être of these wineries. Despite the charitable nature of the event, it would be naïve to shrug off the commercial dimension of the auction. The wines of the Hospices de Beaune only represent a tiny part of the total profits of these companies (a maximum of 2-3% for the biggest buyers), but they do contribute to their activity. At the same time, they bring essentially no risk. As soon as they are purchased, the wines are sold. Most acquisitions at the auction fulfill orders already placed with the negociants by importers, restaurateurs, high-volume retailers, airlines, individuals (alone or collectively), or even companies outside the wine business.

Top: *The plaques of Beaune's negociant firms. They are the principal buyers of the Hospices wines.*

Louis-Fabrice Latour, CEO of Louis Latour, confirms: "The buyers are also there to do business. The margins are smaller than on other transactions and the Hospices de Beaune represents almost nothing in the total volume of the winery, but I do earn my living partly from these wines. We spend about 100,000€ each year. It's purely practical. I don't do any elaborate calculations before going to the auction, but you have to be careful because the wines can fetch very high prices."

An Escape Through the Cellar

Charity? Absolutely. "At the same time, I'm doing a good deed. That's in the back of the minds of everyone who participates in the auction," Latour continues. Emotional? Undeniably. The attachment of the negociants to the auction is indisputable, whether for the entire range of wines from the Hospices de Beaune or for one cuvee in particular. Frédéric Drouhin, who runs the eponymous family estate, is the principal or the exclusive buyer of the cuvee that carries his grandfather's name. He relates the origins of the wine: "Maurice Drouhin was a liaison officer in the Resistance during the Second World War. One day, he found out from a friend that the Gestapo had surrounded his house and cellar. He had already planned ahead and walled up one of the doors to the cellar, so he broke it down and escaped to the Hospices. The nuns hid him there for six months. After the war (author's note: December 23, 1947), he donated two and a half hectares of vineyards to the Hospices de Beaune. He also decided to dedicate one day of every week to them." Maurice Drouhin's attachment hadn't waited for the ordeals of war: as early as 1925 he joined the administrative council, and from 1941 to 1955 he was the vice-president. On the event of his death in the early 1960s, the cuvee that bears his name (a Beaune premier cru) appeared in the auction catalog for the first time.

Maurice Drouhin receiving the French Legion of Honor, surrounded by the nuns of the Hôtel-Dieu. He was one of the great leaders in the life of the Hospices de Beaune in the mid-20th century.

Louis-Fabrice Latour also remembers his grandparents' generation: "My grandfather, Louis Noël, began every day at the Hospices. He and my great-uncle Jean devoted a considerable part of their life to it. Public interests were very important to their generation. Their Catholic convictions also played a major role in their commitment." In Louis-Noël and Jean Latour's shared office in the rue des Tonneliers in Beaune, which is still just as they had it, an engraving representing the 1934 auction bears witness to their story. As a mark of reciprocity, the conference room in the modern hospital (unveiled by Georges Pompidou in 1971) carries the name of Jean Latour. "Our generation has taken a step back from running the hospital, but that wasn't historically the case," Latour concludes. This may also have closed the chapter of a certain paternalism in the management. The employees of the negociants also have access to the hospital.

The negociant André Boisseaux congratulated by Carole Bouquet (1989). He was an important figure in the history of the auction.

At Patriarche Père et Fils, the management pays especially close attention to the Clos de la Roche cuvee "Georges Kritter." This grand cru carries the name of the cousin and right-hand man of André Boisseaux, the symbolic director of the estate, who passed away in 1998. Since he had no children, Georges Kritter left all his property to the Hospices to go towards the purchase of a vineyard. His wish became a reality in 1991, when the institution acquired a parcel in this red grand cru of Morey-Saint-Denis (Côte de Nuits).

At the headquarters of the negociant Bichot, the grand staircase that leads up to the second floor is lined with family portraits. The paintings portray, notably, the faces of a hospital nun, Agathe Moyne, and a surgeon, Etienne Morelot, who presided over the Hôtel-Dieu at the end of the 18th and the beginning of the 19th centuries. The Volnay Premier Cru "Blondeau" and Beaune Premier Cru "Rousseau-Deslandes" cuvees carry the names of donors related to the Bichot family. And when they send out the 2009 company holiday cards, they will bear a photo of Nicolas Rolin's ledger – listing his property, the rules of his domain, etc. – and his estate in Chappey (in the Saône et Loire). The document was purchased during an auction a few months ago by a member of the family.

Benoît Goujon's attachment to the Hospices de Beaune comes from a more painful experience. Seized by cancer in 1984, he went to the hospital of Beaune for a diagnosis. When he took over the direction of Corton-André in 2003, the negociant was already deeply involved in the auction. But he had to decide whether or not to follow his predecessors' example. Along with the new shareholders, he quickly decided to continue the policy already in place. The special presentations put on for visitors to the display cellars at Reine Pédauque in the center of Beaune were continued. These cellars welcome almost a thousand people over the course of the weekend.

ANDRÉ BOISSEAUX: "PATRIARCHE" OF THE AUCTION

A long love story joined André Boisseaux, CEO of the negociant Patriarche (Beaune), to the wine auction of the Hospices de Beaune. The affair began one Sunday in November, 1933. Alfred Boisseaux, director of the family estate "Boisseaux-Estivant," was not able to attend the auction due to a fractured heel. So his son André, just 24 years old, was sent to represent the firm. André had tasted the wines the night before, and the Meursaults in particular had grabbed his attention. The next day he put his trust in his own taste and, caught up in the excitement of the auction, bought all the lots of Meursault. Back home, the young man walked through the door fearing that his fervor would anger his father. Upon hearing about the purchases the father looked at his son for a long time before delivering a terse: "Good"....

This experience deeply marked André Boisseaux. When the magazine Bourgogne Aujourd'hui asked him, in 1994, what was his favorite wine, he replied: "A Meursault-Charmes from the Hospices de Beaune, vintage... 1933!"

Later, in 1941, Boisseaux acquired the negociant Patriarche and developed a habit of buying the first lot up for sale. In 50 years, he would only interrupt this tradition twice.

Benoît Goujon, director of the negociant firm Corton André. He is one of the main buyers at the auction today.

The twenty percent or so of buyers who do not represent negociants are individuals, connoisseurs, or collectors. Their arrival at the auction is quite recent. This is an adventure that we will have to recount in more detail on the following pages…

One Single Seller

Facing these bidders is one single seller: the Hospices Civiles de Beaune, public hospital. The hospital is represented by the president of its administrative council: Alain Suguenot, who has been mayor of Beaune since 1995. The institution puts into play the product of the more than sixty hectares of its wine estate. It expects to bring in substantial revenue to fund its investments. The old Beaune establishment has offered up its wines this way for almost 150 years, a relatively recent development considering that the estate has existed for almost five centuries. Until the French Revolution, and depending on the year, the wines of the Hospices were sold unofficially, on friendly terms, but most of the production was probably consumed "internally." The manager of the estate noted in 1789: "I've had the wines mixed with Gamay, half and half, and had them served at the Dames de la Charité [a charity run by nuns] starting on May 1st."

A procedure of official submission would later be put in place. In 1794, for example, noticed were posted around the town announcing that the crop was up for sale. On fixed dates, the negociants dropped off

Alain Suguenot, mayor of Beaune, with actresses Sandrine Kiberlain and Anouk Aimé. They are on either side of Lord Sterling of Plaistow, president of the company P&O Ferries (1998).

envelopes at the sale with their best offers. The highest price got the lot, provided that it respected the minimum established by the administration. If that price wasn't attained, the sale was rescheduled.

The first attempt at a public auction came in 1825. Lacking in publicity, the event was a bitter failure. In the middle of the previous century, a number of sales at a loss caused by a series of poor vintages filled the cellars of the Hôtel-Dieu to the brim. Seeing the urgency of the situation, the treasurer of the Hospices, Joseph Pétasse, decided to take up his pilgrim's staff: he traveled to different regions of France and also to Belgium, Holland, and Germany, where the reputation of Burgundy's wines was already established. The treasurer was also a poet and always found the right words to win people over. The operation was a success: from then on the name of the Hospices de Beaune was synonymous with greatness and high quality. In less than two years, Pétasse dispensed of the entire stock of the Hospices! He then concluded that conditions were ripe once more for an auction. Upon returning from his pilgrimages he proudly went to the administration: "Gentlemen, you can start holding auctions again starting this year. There is no longer any need for us to take any trouble; the clientele is established, our wines are known, and the connoisseurs will now come to us!" The year 1859 marked the true beginning of the auction, and the event took on its annual rhythm.

Barrels of the cuvee "Nicolas Rolin" in the cellars of the Hospices.

But what exactly does the Hospices sell? A total of forty-four cuvees, divided by lots of one to nine pièces (this is the name used in Burgundy for 228-liter barrels, or about 300 bottles). The wines have only been sleeping in the cellars of the institution for a few weeks; they are mere babes. This wine is not drinkable, but rather needs more time and care before it finds its way to a table, where it will bring joy to those gathered there.

Jumping Forward 150 Years

But in Beaune, one event can hide many others. To understand the auction is to venture off the beaten path, like that which leads one Friday night to the orange grove at the Château de Beaune. About sixty journalists and wine professionals are gathered. They are astonished, overwhelmed, enthusiastic. An 1846 Meursault Premier Cru Charmes has just been poured, and an amber glow lights up the tables. Each of them quickly brings his glass to his nose, and the comments start flowing: "This just bowls me over, it smells like pineapple and candied fruit. What great complexity!" Then the wine seduces the palate: "The balance is superb, and it still has a stunning freshness." This Meursault, made by men who didn't yet have electricity, seems indestructible. Today is November 17, 2006, 160 years after this wine was born. Some of the people gathered today think of the *vignerons* who gave it life, men of whom all traces are lost. This Meursault, however, still has a dazzling vigor and generosity. And these happy few will find more sensory revelations today: the Beaune Vigne de l'Enfant Jésus 1865, the Volnay Caillerets

Tastings Meursault Charmes 1846 at Bouchard Père et Fils the weekend of the auction.

"Former cuvee Carnot" 1929, the Montrachet 1939, etc. All of these wines carry the signature of the negociant Bouchard Père et Fils. What is the relation to the auction? Technically, there is none. It's just that this is the Friday before the famous event, a date traditionally chosen by Bouchard Père et Fils to host a tasting dinner. They often take the opportunity to mark a special occasion: in 2006, it was the 275th birthday of the negociant, the following year it was the 100th year of production of the cuvee "Beaune du Château," etc. But the date was not randomly chosen. Journalists and other important personalities of the world of wine are in town for the auction at the Hospices de Beaune; it is the perfect time for them to get to know the winery, its history, and its wines a little better. Bouchard has the necessary stock for many more auctions to come: about 5,000 bottles from the 19th century are waiting in its cellars…

Tastings other old vintages at Bouchard Père et Fils the weekend of the auction.

The Theory of the Three Circles

It is the invisible dimension of the auction, inaccessible and unsuspected by the general public. All great festivals have behind-the-scenes proceedings. The auction of the Hospices also has an unofficial program that helps raise expectations for the cuvees of the Hospices. Aside from the events for insiders, a number of diversions have latched on, involving a broader audience: the entire region is caught up in the celebration. The Trois Glorieuses, or "Three Glories," held on this third weekend of November. One of these is the auction of the Hospices de Beaune. The auction is preceded, on Saturday night, by a chapter of the famous brotherhood of the Chevaliers du Tastevin (see inset), a festive soiree at the Château du Clos de Vougeot that assembles almost a thousand guests. On Monday morning, Meursault takes over the reins: a few miles south of Beaune, this village that is known for its great white wines holds its famous Paulée (see inset). "You have to distinguish three circles," analyses an employee at the tourist center in Beaune. "The first, reserved for specialists and involving the negociant business, has an economic importance. The second, which is social and sophisticated, sprang up in the thirties (author's note: during that period, regionalism was in fashion and tourism began to include folklore and gastronomy). It includes the brotherhood chapters and other ceremonies, like the Paulée in Meursault, which you sometimes have to reserve a year in advance. Finally there's the third circle, the one open to the general public, which developed in the sixties: it encompasses tastings at wineries, street shows, and uncorking contests that bring the town to life during the weekend of the auction. These three circles draw toward and away from each other, but they never intersect."

The auction is therefore more or less a major event, carefully prepared by the wineries of the region. It is the apogee of the calendar. While the men who make wine live for the harvest, those who work in commerce and communication are already thinking of the third weekend of November. At Bichot, the biggest buyer at the auction, the directors definitely wanted it to be this way. Albéric Bichot, CEO, remembers the period in the late 1990s that propelled the negociant to the forefront of the scene of Beaune: "In 1998, after the death of its CEO, André Boisseaux, Patriarche wanted to be less present. It bought 30% of the lots, so the cards had to be re-dealt. Everyone wondered what was going to happen…. In the end, things naturally fell into place. Our decision was to make that weekend the event of the year, a time to receive our biggest clients, international journalists, etc. Ever since, we've organized a weekend of celebrations, Burgundian-style." In other words, conviviality, good meals, and good wines. Once things were in motion, the company's salespeople began to approach potential buyers. Their clientele is a very eclectic group: the Intercontinental Hotel in Berlin, the Plaza in New York, Aoyagi in Tokyo, one of Japan's most renowned restaurants …. They rub elbows with the best-known names in high-volume distribution in France.

"Once people are here, they discover the Hospices. They get into the mood and think, why not buy a barrel or more…. Now they come back as a matter of course. Some of them reserve each year for the next. For them, having the wines of the Hospices de Beaune in their cellars is the memory of a great weekend in Burgundy," theorizes Albéric Bichot. A snowball effect was set off. This weekend event is no product of chance. "Clients came to us because they saw that we were a major buyer. That gave them confidence." The negociant doesn't hide that it attracted some of its colleagues' clients this way.

These buyers will not leave without tasting the wines produced or aged by the house. "It makes sense. Our buyers at the auction are also clients. We make sure they stay in the bosom of the company," concludes Albéric Bichot. That is what's called killing two birds with one stone.

LA CONFRÉRIE DES CHEVALIERS DU TASTEVIN

"Quality wines like ours should bring joy and optimism. Enough complaining! If our cellars are full we must empty them – and invite our friends to help. Let's bring back our old Bacchic brotherhoods. To ward off ill fortune we shall borrow Rabelais's lust for life and his good humor, we shall emulate Molière's joyous philosophy and good sense…." These are the words attributed to Georges Faiveley and Camille Rodier as they signed the birth certificate of the Confrérie du Tastevin. The declaration was imprinted with voluntarism and dynamism that rejected the melancholy of the era. It was 1934, and the economic depression had hit hard in Burgundy. Surrounded by friends, the two men solemnly swore to fight for the great wines of France in general and for those of Burgundy in particular. Thus was born the most famous Bacchic brotherhood. It would make its home in the Château du Clos de Vougeot. Each year the members organize chapters and meals to which they invite celebrities, men of state, or industrialists. On the menu: good wines, drinking songs, the traditional ban bourguignon, jokes…. All in evening dress but increasingly relaxed as the evening wears on. The group also organizes a wine tasting contest: le tastevinage. Created in 1950, its goal is to select wines. Twice a year, in the spring and the fall, enologists, restaurant owners, negociants, vignerons, brokers, and amateur connoisseurs convene to taste the samples that have been submitted. The wines selected have the right to use the group's seal on their label. "This way the general public, which may need help choosing, is drawn to these wines," explains Louis-Marc Chevignard. Many wine societies have sprung up after the Confrérie du Tastevin: la Cousinerie de Bourgogne, la Confrérie des Trois Ceps, le Baillage de Pommard…. They all help maintain the Burgundian reputation for optimism and gaiety. Their members have known for a long time that wine is never as good as when it is shared….

www.tastevin-bourgogne.com

A chapter of the brotherhood of the Chevaliers du Tastevin. Good humor and good wine…

LA PAULÉE DE MEURSAULT

The Paulée de Meursault is one of the most unusual and convivial events of the wine world. About 6,000 wine connoisseurs and professionals from all around the world meet after the auction at the Hospices de Beaune. Tickets are hard to come by and must be reserved a year in advance. It is a banquet where each participant brings a few of the best bottles from his cellar, from Burgundy or elsewhere. Some very prestigious bottles are opened: a Château Classé from Bordeaux or a grand cru of Burgundy....

The first Paulée de Meursault was held in November, 1923. It was heir to an old tradition: the owners of an estate invited their workers to share a feast at the end of the harvest. The name of the event has also been linked to the last shovel (pelle) of grapes dumped into the press. Since its first years, this event has begun to look like a celebration between journalists and important producers rather than a country meal. Thanks to the Parisian press, it quickly established an enviable reputation.

Today, it is mostly important wine connoisseurs, collectors, and professionals who attend the event. The ambiance quickly becomes festive. The luncheon lasts through the entire afternoon. And it is not unusual for the day to end, quite late, in the cellars of a local winemaker.

Since 1932, a prize for the best "work of wit" (most often literary) is awarded during the festivities. It is paid "in liquid" since it consists of one hundred bottles of Meursault! It has notably gone to Colette (novelist), Henri Vincenot (author, painter, and sculptor), Jean-François Deniau (diplomat and novelist), Françoise Chandernagor (novelist), Pierre Schoendoerffer (film screenwriter and director and war veteran), Max Gallo (writer, historian, and politician), Erik Orsenna (politician and novelist)...

The day after the auction: the Paulée de Meursault.

At the "Confessional"

After fifteen years, the event is a well-oiled machine at Bichot. The clients pay their own travel expenses, but once they arrive the company takes over. There are about 100-120 people. On Saturday, the meals are in Nuits-Saint-Georges at the winery Lupé-Cholet (author's note: a satellite of Bichot). In the evening, some of them also attend the chapter of the brotherhood of the Chevaliers du Tastevin. But on the big day, everyone meets at exactly 11:00am in one of Beaune's best restaurants. Some of them just arrived from tasting or re-tasting in the cellars of the Hospices. Most of them already went one or two days before.

At noon on Sunday, Bichot reserves the entire restaurant "Loiseau des Vignes," one of a group run by Bernard Loiseau, the Michelin three-star chef who passed away in 2003. The team at the restaurant has set up the dining room specially for them. "We have a good time, and the ambiance is great," Bichot brags. During this banquet a strange ceremony takes place. Albéric Bichot installs what he calls his "confessional"…. He settles himself into a corner of the room and receives each client, one by one. "They tell me which cuvees they liked. I note everything and try to compile it all. We establish a bidding cap and I have them sign a purchase order. Then it's up to me not to screw it up." All of these beautiful people then head for the closed marketplace of Beaune at 2:00pm to make their wishes reality. Just a few cobblestone streets later….

At Corton André too, planning for the Hospices campaign begins well ahead of time. Starting in the summer, they send information to their clients and ask if they will be present at the next auction. Finally, mirroring the organization at Bichot, between 60 and 80 people are received each year by the estate with the famous château adorned with colored tiles. At least a dozen nationalities are represented. Some clients are legitimately collectors of the wines of the Hospices de Beaune. Not a marriage or a birth is celebrated without one or a few of the cuvees. The estate also boasts some prestigious clients from the world of gastronomy: Le Grand Véfour (Paris), l'Oustau de Baumanière (Les Baux de Provence).

The principal buyer at the auction for about fifteen years: Albéric Bichot, CEO of the negociant firm Albert Bichot (center). At left, the enologist Alain Serveau.

The approach is a bit different at the negociant Joseph Drouhin. Here the ambiance of the weekend is more subdued. "Our marketing strategy is not organized around the auction at the Hospices de Beaune. We receive importers throughout the year. The Hospices is not the motivating event," Frédéric Drouhin is quick to clarify. Here we want to present, above all else, the face of a traditional Burgundian winery: 80% of our wines are exported and distributed only in the networks that do the most for the brand (restaurants, boutique wine shops, etc.). "We contact our clients and importers and explain how the vintage is turning out, what the style of the wines will be, and what prices to expect. We confirm our impressions after tastings before the auction. Then we tell our customers what cuvees we did or didn't like, which ones we're interested in buying, and in what price range. Finally we ask if they want to follow us. Nine times out of ten, they do, and they decide on a number of barrels," reports the CEO. The demand varies from one year to the next since they may want to put away wines from the vintage of a birthday or another special occasion. Some of them also want to purchase whites in addition to the famous "house" cuvee: the Beaune "Maurice Drouhin."

Strong Symbolism

For many participants, the weekend lasts through Monday, when the famous Paulée is held a few miles away in Meursault. Guests with a bottle in hand also fill the Drouhin cellars in the center of the old town of Beaune. About sixty of these "friends" of the winery are gathered, mostly foreign but with a few winemakers from Burgundy or other French wine regions. While Drouhin is well respected, this weekend is nevertheless an uncommon occurrence. The doors are opened only rarely to groups with reservations. "Most of the people we receive are French, and a lot of very loyal Belgians, in groups of about twenty people. They take the opportunity to come see us and spend a nice weekend in Burgundy," explains Frédéric Drouhin.

This approach echoes the one at Latour. The auction is above all an opportunity to create or cement relationships with clients. "We invite clients who are prestigious or to mark a new relationship. They taste our wines, then we propose that they participate in the auction. These aren't regular invitations, even if certain

buyers do return. We also receive quite a few journalists. Some participate in the meeting of the Chevaliers du Tastevin at the Clos de Vougeot, etc.," clarifies Louis-Fabrice Latour. "We don't have a strategy for the Hospices with annual contacts and so on."

Nevertheless, over this one weekend, public relations and marketing mix as they rarely do. "I remember receiving the owner of Unilever (second in consumer goods worldwide); he bought a barrel at the auction. We also received the owner of a large Japanese group, Asahi Beer (author's note: producer of one of the most widely consumed Japanese beers and distributor of numerous alcoholic beverages). He bought a barrel of Corton and another of Clos de la Roche. It was in the papers. It was a way to demonstrate, symbolically, that Burgundy is important to them," Latour specifies.

To Be There or Not to Be There

Left page:
The vineyards of Beaune in October. The Côte d'Or or "Golden Slope" deserves its name....

One figure shows the magnitude of the influence of the auction: in 2008, about fifty journalists rushed to the Burgundian town to relate the event to a very large audience, which is surprising for an auction reserved for the trade! The Burgundians have shown themselves over the years to be very eloquent communicators. Local negociants were preoccupied with the impact of the auction very early on. In 1900, the president of the wine and spirits union of Beaune, Albert Morot, alerted his "honored brothers." Buyers were hardly hurrying to the auction. His letter was stamped "Confidential." "The fear that there will not be enough buyers to absorb the large quantities at the Hospices has moved a number of our fellow citizens, and we are concerned that selling some or all of the lots at a loss might dishonor all of the products of Burgundy." The letter proposed a preliminary meeting of the owners of all the negociants to discuss what measures should be taken to protect the interests of them all. "We will tell you our intentions and you will do the same; it should be simple to come to an agreement," he concluded.

Jean-Paul Golin, photographer.

Asking a local negociant if he will be present at the auction seems incongruous. Missing out on an edition is hard to imagine. "Inconceivable," Louis-Fabrice Latour instantly adds. "We're a medium-volume buyer, but we always have been and always will be there." Part of the reputation of the negociants is at stake on the third Sunday of November. "If a negociant doesn't buy," notes Denis Santiard, former CEO of Corton André, "people in the trade will definitely wonder what's going on." Each one has to play a part; it is a question of honor and respectability. Frédéric Drouhin remembers the 1998 auction. That year, the bidding went quite high. "The moment came when the cuvee Maurice Drouhin was on the block. I let it go by and didn't buy the first lot. I immediately heard the murmuring around the room: what's happening at Drouhin? Everyone was looking at me. Then they asked: were you sleeping or something?"

Right from the start, the auction was a very singular moment in local life. A text from 1896 published in the monthly l'Illustration describes the ambiance. "I looked over the shoulder of one of Beaune's biggest negociants and read, next to the names of the cuvees: vinous, very clean, a bit off, a bit flabby, fruity, good character, unfinished, short, no length on the palate, etc. Friday and Saturday are spent tasting, and you can already pick out the likely buyers. M----, a Parisian restaurateur, tasted the Beaune cuvee "Trapet-Bard" three times; P----, the king of fine foods, spent a long time chatting with Latour-Porcheray of Meursault. Then comes the Sunday of the auction. In the morning you can already feel the excitement that invigorates Beaune. Every train arriving from Nuits-Saint-Georges and Dijon, or from Meursault, Chalon-

A ritual: tasting from barrel in the days before the auction, in the old cellars of the Hospices in the mid-1980s.

sur-Saône, and Mâcon brings those who are involved and those who are just curious. On the narrow little train track that runs from Pommard to Beaune, extra trips had to be organized. Storage rooms and hotel courtyards are full of horsecarts from the villages. The Café de la Concorde and the Café du Balcon are packed with a noisy clientele.

"People are already crowding into the first courtyard of the Hospices where a display of chrysanthemums has been set up to draw them in. The tousled flowers go very well with the architecture of the monument, with its intricate wood- and ironwork on the roofs and galleries and the elegant wrought iron of the old well. In the second courtyard, in front of the entrance to the cellar where the tasting will continue until noon, is gathered everyone from Beaune or nearby who is known to be price-conscious and concerned about the quality of the new wines."

On reading this account, regulars of the auction today will say, "nothing new under the sun…."

Already in 1934, the negociant Bichot proudly announced that it was "buyer of twenty-one great wines of the Hospices de Beaune in 1915, 1916, 1918, 1919, and 1920." In 2008 Albéric Bichot boasted of no less than 107 years' presence at the auction and a first purchase in 1876. The estate never fails to remind you that it tops the list of buyers. In recent years, a press release has been sent out just after the auction: "Albert Bichot, top buyer at the 148th auction of the Hospices de Beaune."

This event is decidedly a communication tool with multiple functions. Bichot became seriously involved just as it opened a new page in the history of the company. Living somewhat in the shadow of other famous negociants that enjoyed a more established public image, Bichot made some changes during the '90s. For this estate, the Hospices de Beaune was the perfect way to proclaim its new ambitions and move up in the hierarchy.

The signs reflected by the event don't lie. While the auction of the Hospices is undoubtedly a moment of charity, it is nevertheless a prestigious "ceremony." The important men of the town meet and see each other there. The rows are dotted with hats and fur coats. In the room, each person has reference points; places are the same from one year to the next. They are based on the volume of purchases in previous years. The heavyweights are in the first rows, while occasional buyers are in the back…

Examining the Results

Such a great vehicle for a message cannot be ignored. "It's the first worldwide spotlight on the vintage. And it's in Beaune! Not in Bordeaux, not in Napa Valley, not in Sydney…. The first time people talk about the vintage, it's in Beaune. We can't lose this media spotlight," insists Frédéric Drouhin. Before finding its way to newspaper columns or screens, the results of the auction are a wave that spreads through the vineyards. It can be interpreted in different ways. In Burgundy there are two distinct professional categories: negociants and *vignerons*. Neither can survive without the other. Basically, the negociants buy and commercialize a large part of the wines or grapes produced by the growers. The growers' goal is to sell their product at the best price possible. The negociant looks for the best wines and the lowest prices. The law of supply and demand is at work here. So the Hospices auction doesn't escape extensive

The entrance to the Clos des Avaux vineyard in Beaune.

commentary. Its role in the local economy has been debated countless times. Should it be taken as a true indicator, even an initiator, of the general direction of the trade between viticulture (sometimes called the "property") and the negociants? Or does it, more modestly, reveal the mood at a given moment?

If the clients of the negociants show less interest in the wines of the Hospices than in the previous year, arms won't rise quite so easily over the heads of the crowd during the auction. "Wine is a festive gourmet product, especially the cuvees of the Hospices. People buy less wine when they don't feel like celebrating," Duveau believes. The progressive decreases of the early 1990s, marked by the first Gulf War, amply confirmed this.

The Pendulum

The prices of the Hospices wines unquestionably change with the economic climate. In fact, they exaggerate the variations. The history of the auction is punctuated by spectacular swings of the pendulum: -42.5% in 1965, +79% in 1985. These are just two examples of the most drastic changes. Researching the recent history of the auction is sure to make you dizzy. In the 1970s there were several staggering drops and increases. While the average selling price per barrel at the beginning of the decade was 3,805 francs (580€, or about today), by the end of the decade it was 13,891 francs (2,117€). France did see a period of strong inflation (about 10% yearly) that accounts for the bulk of the change, but at the same time the average prices of Hospices wines gained no less than 365% in ten years! The 1980s finally beat the records for the highest market prices and sales figures with a constant currency (balanced by inflation). The 1985 auction would set a record for the average price per barrel, at 44,856 francs (6,868€). Four years later, the 1989 auction would set a new sales record: just over 29 million francs (4,420,731€, thanks to a higher number of barrels sold. The 228-liter barrels of Corton-Charlemagne sold for 300,000 francs, or 150 euros per bottle. Things collapsed over the following years: -25.2% in 1990, -29.6% in 1991, -23.1% in 1992, and -21.3% in 1993. The record set in 1989 would not be broken until the triple-zero vintage: the 2000 auction ended with more than 34 million francs (5.3 million euros, or 7.8 million dollars) in sales.

François Curiel (Christie's) is poised to bring down his gavel.

An Undeniable Gauge

The Hospices auction continues to find its way into conversations between the two groups long after the gavel signals the last sale. "If the Hospices de Beaune wines sell well, it is inevitably reflected in the prices of other wines. All the winemakers benefit. How many times have we waited for the auction to establish certain prices? It is an undeniable economic gauge," declared André Boisseaux a few weeks before participating in one of its recent editions.

With few exceptions, the Hospices prices are an exaggerated reflection of the tendency of the market, sometimes drastically amplifying either drops or increases. The average prices fetched have always followed the

In 2008 it took more than 5,000€ on average to acquire one of these 228-liter barrels (about 300 bottles).

trends of the regional market. The negociants declare it in unison, and their sales figures prove them right. The trends go hand in hand, always keeping in sight of each other. There is nothing shocking in that. The nature of the product is the same: Burgundy wine sold in bulk. The strengths and weaknesses of the vintage, in both quality and quantity, are comparable.

There is a strong temptation to exploit the numbers from the Hospices auction when the tendency favors one side or the other. "Yes, we use them in our business dealings. I've said to *vignerons*, 'Oh, but there was a 20% drop at the Hospices. Prices will have to go down this year!'" admits Louis-Fabrice Latour. In the other camp, the same reasoning is used when prices rise. Whenever the tendency is strong, there are efforts to cut this game short. "It's not the increase that worries me but rather the interpretation of the increase. You have to learn to put things in perspective. This increase is a barometer that indicates atmospheric pressure…. A barometer has never moved a cloud," declares Marc Jambon, president of the Interprofessional Office of the Wines of Burgundy, a group created for the very purpose of uniting *vignerons* and negociants, in 1997.

The auction of the Hospices also has to deal with a historic heritage. This third weekend in November coincides with the General Exposition of the Wines of Burgundy. This show, started by *vignerons*, joined the program of festivities in the late 19th century. The goal was to present the wines of the new vintage in the main square of Beaune, the wine capital of Burgundy and home to many wineries. A dual public of professionals and amateurs now squeezes into the aisles of the Palais des Congrès exposition center over the entire weekend, but the event is attended mainly by wine merchants who serve as intermediaries between the growers and the negociants and by negociants themselves. To say that the auction establishes going prices is wrong: the prices of the Hospices wines are well above regular bulk wine prices. And yet to deny that it has an impact would also be wrong.

Auctioneer for the Hospices until 2005, Master Herry has a slightly different interpretation. "The Hospices auction doesn't react according to the viti-viniculture market. Here, you're on the international stage; you see the same phenomena as for a high-end real estate sale or for art."

The Repercussions for the Clients

Let's talk about the international market. After spreading across the vineyards, the wave of the auction reaches the market. The origins of the buyers at the auction are a result of the diverse countries that import the wines of Burgundy. Once dominated by two major destinations – England and the United States – shipments now go to every corner of the world: Japan, Scandinavia, Australia, Russia, Brazil, Italy, etc. China appeared in the "top 15" markets for the first time in 2008. "During the auction we receive people of a dozen different nationalities. If you look back twenty years, there were no Japanese, Russians, etc. But the English and Americans were better represented," reports Frédéric Drouhin. For the negociant's sales network, the image projected by the auction provides fodder for explication and pedagogy. While the Burgundian negociants may want their suppliers to see a drop, they certainly do not want this message to get out to their clients. The old adage for all types of business, "don't buy during a drop," also applies to the wine trade.

The event draws an international clientele.

"It's not the message within Burgundy that worries me, but rather the signals sent out to the world. When there is a drop at the auction, I get faxes saying, 'The prices at the Hospices de Beaune have dropped, so your prices are going to drop!' In 2008, for example, I got messages like that from England and Canada," complains Benoit Goujon.

And as soon as an increase is seen, clients may worry about possible repercussions. The higher and more drastic the increase, the stronger the media impact is: it leads the public to believe, rightly or not, that Burgundy's best wines are exorbitantly costly. As prestigious, rare, and unrivaled as Burgundian wine may be, there has been ample proof over the last few years that versatile consumers will forego a product that, in their opinion, has become too expensive. So with each surge, Burgundy risks losing buyers. Even an inexpert economist would warn a producer

Until 2004, Master Herry, auctioneer in Beaune, wielded the gavel. On his right Antoine Jacquet, director of the institution, follows the auction.

against such a strong and brutal price increase, a collateral prejudice as damaging as it is only partly founded. In reality, only part of the price shifts in bulk wine sales determine the final price of a bottle of wine sold by a negociant. The variations are tempered.

"I try not to say anything rash to the journalists, to remain moderate," Benoit Goujon reasons. "I don't crow that we've won if prices have dropped, and I don't lament the catastrophe if they've increased." But these extreme reversals nevertheless leave their mark on the Burgundians, and when the auction starts heading out of control, there is fear of ramifications. After the increase of 1997, Christophe Tupinier, editor-in-chief of the magazine Bourgogne Aujourd'hui worried aloud: "All the conditions for the prices at the Hospices to plummet are there. Just as in 1989 the increase is drastic, and just as in 1989 there has been a series of good vintages in Burgundy." The collapse came a few years later, in the early 2000s.

The rise and fall of prices at the Hospices regularly cause the traders to knit their brows. "The 1993 auction (author's note: -21.3%) provided excellent evidence of the Burgundians' inconsistency in their pricing policies. In today's world, where the gradual evolution of prices is a common notion, you have to wonder if these practices are normal and if they can last very long," wondered Bertrand Devillard. More than fifteen years later, the results are unquestionable: they can last…

And the Influence of the Vintage?

Connoisseurs of vintages in Burgundy have plenty to confuse them. The 2007 vintage sold for more than the 2006 or even the 2005; where is the logic? You have to be skeptical when you see that 1997 showed a 47% hike over 1996. Caution was also advisable when the 1994 vintage sold at much higher prices than the 1993. And what can be said about the significant drop that marked 1990 compared to 1989, despite the fact that these were two of the best vintages of the last thirty years. To chart the prices fetched at the Hospices in each vintage would be to get thoroughly lost. It would be inaccurate, however, to say that the vintage doesn't have at least a secondary role. The trends in the evolution of the auction since 1961 are instructive: the peaks correspond to great vintages – 1999, 1989, 1985, and 1978. "You realize that when prices per barrel hover around the average, only a great vintage can incite a progression," analyzes Denis Duveau. The value of the vintage will therefore push the auction to one or the other side of the average. "The vintage gives an appeal to the products. When everyone is smiling in the vineyards, and Burgundy is more beautiful than ever, that shows in the media coverage. Everyone is positive. When the auction comes, this combination of elements is a supporting factor for prices."

Nevertheless, certain great vintages remain in the shadows since they don't fall at the right moment. Recently, the superb 2005, which arrived after a four-year crisis in the market, could legitimately claim injustice. "Cycles of 5-7 years often play a role in the wine business," Duveau analyzes. Looking at the graph, you see a striking example of this between 1989 and 1999: two peaks and in the middle, a valley. In two five-year periods, the Hospices had drawn a splendid sine curve. The auction functioned as an oscillating machine, and that can shock people. If the prices at the Hospices were representative of charity pure and simple they would demonstrate a constant progression, a straight line always rising. "Charity is giving what you have. When you have less, you may give a bit less. When you have plenty but you fear for the future, you may still give a bit less," Duveau reasons.

The millennium effect was just one of many factors that affected the prices of the Hospices wines.

To be exact, the good vibrations of the late 1990s lasted through 2000. Against all expectations, the curve didn't peak in 1999 but the year after. The 1999 vintage had its thunder stolen: though generous in both quality and quantity, this last vintage of the millennium has reason to be jealous of its younger sibling. An unexpected increase occurred in 2000. A exceptional external factor upended the predictions: the "millennium" effect. Buyers wanted those three zeros on the label…

Wines Out of the Ordinary

Inextricably associated with Burgundy, the wines of this Beaune institution are nevertheless out of the ordinary. Few estates enjoy such unprompted fame. Yes, the price evolutions of the cuvees of the Hospices follow paths that are parallel, or nearly, to those of Burgundian production as a whole; but they aren't navigating the same waters.... Negociants pay 2.8 times more on average for the wines of the Hospices than for those of the average grower (a figure calculated from ten years of data by the Syndicate of Wine Negociants of Burgundy). This is what some people call the "charity effect." This coefficient clearly adapts itself to each cuvee. For less prestigious appellations, which are also produced at the lowest cost, the figure regularly exceeds three times the average: Monthelie, Pernand-Vergelesses, and Auxey-Duresses. "Some cuvees are sold at up to four times more than the going rate," Duveau points out. The most expensive wines are favored by a lesser coefficient, closer to 1.5. In the range from 2.5 to 3 are the Beaune cuvees (the most widely represented appellation at the auction) but also the cuvees of Savigny, Pouilly-Fuissé, Meursault, etc. These numbers are tracked closely by the syndicate of negociants in order to prove to any skeptics the benevolent attentions they reserve for the Hospices.

And yet to buy a wine in bulk is to bet on the future. The wines acquired at the auction cannot be delivered or put on the market for another year and a half to two years, the time required for a great wine to complete its *elevage* and be ready for bottling. This means having to sit on stocks for at least eighteen months, an eternity in our fast-paced modern economy. The negociants therefore tend toward caution: they only buy, as discussed above, when they already have a buyer lined up. But they do sometimes outstrip the demand. "I have on occasion bought a wine that I hadn't planned to acquire. In 2008, for example, I bid on the Pommard cuvee 'Suzanne Chaudron.' It was a very good wine, but I had no client. When I like a wine, I know I'll be able to sell it without a problem," Frédéric Drouhin attests.

In short, it is not unusual to find Hospices de Beaune wines on the price lists of Burgundian negociants. Meursault Premier Cru Charmes 2002, cuvee "Bahèzre de Lanlay": 60.10€; Clos de la Roche 1998, cuvee "Cyrot Chaudron": 110.50€. Just two examples at Latour, which lists a total of six wines produced by the institution. You find the same situation at Bichot: five or ten barrels per year will end up in the lineup of house wines.

Seeing these numbers also allows you to understand some fear or at least reticence. Buyers sometimes see the third Sunday of November approach faster than they might like. This was especially the case after the price explosion of the late 1980s. A crisis, a loss of confidence, and the economic situation was completely reversed. "The negociants went to the auction dragging their feet," remembers Sylvain Pitiot, a former *vigneron* for the Hospices.

A Share of the Prestige

The spectacular surplus accorded to the wines of the Hospices remains to be explained. The historic fame of the institution and the media-heavy nature of the auction draw back the first veil. André Porcheret, former manager of the estate, had a formula of his own to account for the generosity of the buyers: "By the barrel it's expensive, everyone realizes that, but if you had to pay for the publicity...." The media circus that surrounds the auction outdoes by far any other regional event. The entire weekend, including that Monday, television, radio, and the written press focus on the ambiance and the local mood.

1995 : Catherine Deneuve presides over the auction.

Right page:
The Salle des Pôvres or Poor Men's Hall. The morning of the auction, journalists from every corner of the world gather here for a press conference.

The purely journalistic hype reaches its climax on Sunday morning at the Hôtel-Dieu. Between the rows of beds that once welcomed the sick, and under the multicolored beams of the Salle des Pôvres (Poor Mens' Hall), a crowd gathers. Journalists from every corner of the globe have come to hear the Good Word at the Sunday mass. The mayor of Beaune, the director of the hospital, the director of the Hospices' wine estate, the president of the Interprofessional Bureau of the Wines of Burgundy and that of the Committee Uniting Burgundian Winemakers, negociants, etc, file onto the platform. All the current affairs of Burgundy are discussed here, from the economic situation to the character of the vintage, the proposed regulation reforms, etc. All with a healthy dose, obviously, of predictions and other hypotheses on how the auction will unfold just a few hours later….

Buying the wines of the Hospices is also helping yourself to part of the extraordinary prestige enjoyed by this Beaune institution, entering its gravitational field and going into orbit. The almost compulsive character of André Boisseaux's purchases over several decades made his contemporaries talk. The man bought 4,300 barrels (more than 1.2 million bottles) throughout his career. His reputation as a great "communicator" was never questioned. Boisseaux was a precursor to the athletic philanthropist. The saga of the "Kriter" sailboats piloted by the big names of racing in the 70s and 80s – Olivier de Kersauson and even Michel Malinosky – he was the sponsor. Many of his colleagues also saw Boisseaux's theatrics at the auction as promotional moves for his company and his five hundred employees. He never hid from it: "I like the Hospices de Beaune. It has considerable importance in Burgundy. We have to support it and do what we need to do to promote our wines. Without it, Burgundy would be missing something." There are those who mocked the stacks of Hospices wines that were put away for aging, or to collect dust, in the cellars of Patriarche Père et Fils. He barely acknowledged them: "For the most part, the wines are brought to our cellars and sold later. Like all expensive wines, they don't sell like hot cakes."

Fame

Every connoisseur of the wines of Burgundy will praise to the skies some of its most prestigious domaines. The richest among them devote a cult to the inaccessible Romanée-Conti. In the Côte de Nuits, Gouges, de Vogüe, Armand Rousseau, and Clos de Tart have solid historical references, etc. The whites of the Côte de Beaune and Chablis have a staggering international renown whenever they carry the names of Coche-Dury, Comtes Lafon, Raveneau, etc. But what estate in Burgundy is more quickly recognized by a broad public of connoisseurs than the Hospices de Beaune? This surplus of promotion, constantly in the public eye, is proof. The regular presence of buyers from the high-volume distribution sector also bears witness.

The grand crus of Gevrey-Chambertin. One of them, Mazis-Chambertin, gives one of the auction's most highly sought cuvees.

For them, the auction is a unique opportunity to stock up on a big name in Burgundian wine. The estates previously mentioned take care to avoid this type of association; an image that took so long to build is not to be toyed with. And then the volume of wine available at estates that often have no more than a dozen hectares do not permit any real merchandizing.

"The stamp of the Hospices de Beaune means something. Big brand names approach us when they need a wine or two for a wine show or for Christmas promotions. So they buy thirty barrels of different cuvees from the same appellation – Beaune, for example. That makes a total of 9,000 bottles, which is enough to launch national sales. In their catalogue, they list 'Beaune Premier Cru from the Hospices de Beaune.' One region will have the cuvee 'Hugues et Louis Bétault" while another has 'Nicolas Rolin,' etc. The name of the Hospices draws people to their wine department. This year (author's note: 2008), buyers came to me saying, 'I need such-and-such a bottle price in the store, so I have to buy at this much.' And we see what we can do, according to the auction. I've worked with them for ten years now. If they keep coming back it's obviously because they're finding what they need. In 2007, 34 of the 120 barrels I bought were for high-volume distribution," recounts Albéric Bichot.

The Thrill of the Auction

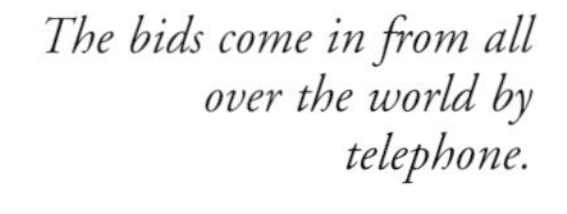

The bids come in from all over the world by telephone.

The effect of the auction must be examined. It is a sales method unique to Burgundy's various Hospices (Beaune is not the only town in the region to have such an institution). The rest of the year, the realities of local commerce are much more discreet. A context of heightened competition descends for one afternoon in the heart of Beaune. "We put people in the same room with the same objectives. The process has a bullish format. As long as the economy is functioning well and the cellars are empty, the demand is strong and it takes off like a rocket," notes Denis Duveau. The auction can sometimes look like a cock fight. Here is one scene from the 1997 edition, which was marked by one of the biggest increases in the last fifteen years:

A murmur runs around the room. Lot 24 A (24 barrels of the cuvee baptized "Dames de Flandres") has just drawn a bid of 148,000 francs. The previous record is crushed: this white grand cru fetched 140,000 francs in 1995. A cigar in his mouth, a man heavily seated on his chair digests his instructions. One hand brings a telephone to his ear; the other, permanently installed on the shoulder of his neighbor, transmits the signal to bid higher. "149,000 francs," announces the auctioneer. "150,000." Cold and determined, his only competition has raised his paddle. The battle reveals a contrast in the two men's styles: one is exuberant, while the other tends towards discretion and restraint. "So, what says the banker on the phone?" asks Paul Berbey, the auction "caller" (see inset), in an unsuccessful attempt to relax the tense crowd. Whether bluff or true prudence, the seconds of hesitation become longer as the bidding mounts. Eyes around the room are fixed on Master Herry's hovering gavel. "151,000": the bidding resumes and incredulity consumes the onlookers. The caller intervenes again: "It's time…." The reply comes quickly: "152,000." Thc final bang has comc. A ncgociant from Puligny-Montrachet (Côte de Beaune) just acquired the two barrels of this grand cru for two American clients from Dallas and New York, as well as for a local hotel and restaurant.

A Little Discipline

"There are many types of people in the room. There are the effusive ones who, with a grand gesture, wave their notebooks above their heads. Others are discreet, using a wink, a subtle movement of a pen, a nod of the head. There are even those who cluck their tongues! By force of habit, I easily see the little signs. And then I also know who will buy certain barrels," assured Paul Berbey, for more than 25 years, in the daily paper Le Bien Public.

The personalities of the protagonists and the ambiance of the auction also have an influence. "It does happen that a buyer gets carried away during the auction, out of pride," points out Denis Santiard. "I remember the difficulties one negociant had when he had just started his business. He bid high on a lot of Corton-Charlemagne. He got the lot, and he turned white…."

Albéric Bichot confirms this auction frenzy: "Personally, over the six or seven hours of the auction, I don't know where the time goes." Your entourage sometimes spices things up. "Even when we've reached the cap established before the auction, clients tell me anyway: Go ahead, raise the bid! You have to be careful because on Monday morning there can be a rude awakening. I'm afraid they'll say, 'Actually, I didn't really want it. I was supposed to buy with my mother-in-law…,'" jokes the negociant. "Anyway, it's a question of buying at the right price. If a client realizes the next day that he's going to spend more than his neighbor, he may not come back. A little basic discipline doesn't go to waste. "I don't allow anyone to raise a hand next to me. If we start outbidding each other…."

PAUL BERBEY: A JOVIAL "CALLER"

A bowtie, a twinkle in his eye, and an unmistakable Burgundian accent: Paul Berbey has made his mark on the recent history of the auction. For more than 25 years, until the early 2000s, his jokes stirred up the auction: "To buy or not to buy?" "Watch out, he's grabbing his gavel!" "Good thing we're not faint of heart." His role: "caller." It is his job to prod the buyers and make them forget for one afternoon their calculators and cell phones. A stroke of fate brought him to the auction platform: a gardener by profession, this local of Beaune was the victim of an accident on the job in 1965. Hospitalized at the Hôtel-Dieu, he was then hired as a gardener there. Jovial and endowed with a voice that carries (he sings in the chorus known as the "Joyeux Bourguignons" or Joyous Burgundians), Paul Berbey would become the auction caller in 1978.

Paul Berbey.

But let's return to the "product" itself. Though physically invisible at the auction, the wines of the Hospices have their say at the event. The consistently high quality of the estate is not in question; at least not since the psychodrama of 1993 (see the chapter "the *Vignerons*"). Supervisor Roland Masse, who arrived in 2000, has the unanimous approval of the negociants. "He's a very good winemaker," you hear in the business. A value-added "Hospices de Beaune" is recognized for its quality. Even more so since the estate is made up primarily of premier crus and grand crus, two categories that fill the top 15% in the pyramid of Burgundy's famous *terroirs*.

"The Hospices allows you to procure quality wines with the name of a well-known estate, from relatively scarce appellations: Meursault Genevrières, Mazis-Chambertin. Here we have the possibility of obtaining 25 cartons or more of a great wine. That's all the more reason to support of the Hospices de Beaune," exclaims Frédéric Drouhin.

"The Presidents' Barrel"

James Thomson, the generous buyer of the Charity Barrel in 2004 and 2008.

It's almost 4:00pm in the closed marketplace on this Sunday in November, 2008. There is a long series of commendations on the platform. Actors Jean-Pierre Marielle and Michel Blanc smile in acknowledgement. They warmly congratulate a lanky man wearing a kilt. His height and his elegance, as picturesque as they are outdated, draw everyone's attention. This Scot, as you must have guessed, does not ask as much and exudes discreet poise. He nevertheless accepts the French kisses on the cheek from Sophie Vouzelaud, first runner-up to Miss France, a young woman who has been deaf since birth. His name: James Thomson. He has just acquired the "charity barrel," also known as the "Presidents' Barrel." This is the big moment of the auction. Since 1945, the Hospices de Beaune has put up for sale one barrel for the profit of one or more charitable works.

This year, 2008, it is a barrel of the Pommard Premier Cru cuvee "Dames de la Charité" that was chosen. Jean-Pierre Marielle supports the League Against Cancer and Michel Blanc, Children of Asia, an association that comes to the aid of more than 8,000 children who are orphans or in distress in Cambodia, Laos, Vietnam, and the Philippines. Before the beginning of the auction, the two actors each took a moment to plead their respective causes. Michel Blanc even seems overcome by emotion when he speaks of his trip to Phnom Penh to visit the young girl he sponsors.

Without any further ado, the auction begins. "20,000€," cries a buyer in the third row. "35,000." The rejoinder comes almost immediately from one of the middle rows. A pause. In these moments of hesitation, one or another of these celebrities intervenes to prolong the action: "Come on, let's see a little effort," or "Thank you to those who have already come this far." "40,000€," comes the reply from the back of the room. Another pause. "Higher! Higher!" you seem to hear from the crowd with their noses pressed to the windows of the hall. "50,000!" The matter is closed. The gavel comes down, and there is a burst of applause. Our Scot can now climb the steps that separate him from the platform. The officials stand waiting for him. The photographers are already pushing to get a better shot. A joyous crowd brings charm and an air of improvisation to the scene. But

is there really any spontaneity here? Rarely. Before the auction, the negociants search for sponsors. A few days before the auction, if no one has stepped forward, they meet and "count themselves." Who wants to bid, and how much? "It's sort of like our telethon. The negociants are there to play a role. During the auction, we turn up the heat. We organize groups of two or three to bid," reveals Albéric Bichot.

The Plan is Foiled

Such an understanding was planned out in 2008. But a last-minute benefactor foiled their plans. Bichot remembers: "Louis-Fabrice Latour, Pierre-Henry Gagey, and I were bidding. We got to 50,000€. I was next to James Thomson, one of our buyers. I thought to myself that he might have an impulse just then; he's very emotional. I asked him: are you interested? Shall we? In three seconds, he said, Okay! It was the cause for the children. Since he doesn't have any children himself, I think his heart went out just then. Michel Blanc's speech was deeply moving. I translated it to him in my own way. At 50,000€, I had the lot. I saw my colleagues signaling: That's enough, we stop here!" To the great surprise of those watching, it was not the president of their syndicate who rose, as is the custom when a group of negociants is the buyer, but the man in a kilt and knee socks....

It was not a first for James Thomson. This self-made man from Edinburgh, who owns a chain of luxury hotels, had already bought the Presidents' Barrel in 2004. Having come to the auction with friends nine years earlier, he fell in love with Burgundy. A decade marked by Scotland's colors. A famous countryman of his also climbed the steps up to the platform in 2007: David Murray, owner and president of the Glasgow Rangers soccer team. He spent 65,000€ and received the thanks of Richard Berry and three former Miss France winners.

David Murray, president of the Glasgow Rangers soccer team, buyer of the Charity Barrel in 2007.

Claudie André-Deshays, the first French woman to go into outer space and the energetic president of the auction in 1996.

This scene inspired a number of memories: "When Professor Montagnier (author's note: co-discoverer of the AIDS virus) came in 1987," remembers Master Daniel Herry, "the barrel donated by the Hospices went to funding AIDS research. An unknown bid against André Boisseaux. This person was not in the section reserved for buyers. The administrative council of the Hospices and I were worried we might be doing business with a joker. I can refuse a bid, even if it is very badly received by the public. But it was very tough to refuse 600,000 francs (over 91,000€)…. When we asked him why he had done it, he said he wanted to fight this disease. He was from Luxembourg." In Beaune, people also remember the 1996 edition and the energetic Claudie André-Deshays, the first French woman to go to outer space and who later became (under her married name of Haigneré) Minister of Research. Her dynamic involvement brought in 300,000 francs (45,000€) for an association that fights for families with hospitalized children. "It's an emotional sale," explains an employee in the tourist center who is involved in promoting the event. "The media appeal of the president plays a major role and is an important factor in its success. But in the end, it's his personal involvement that is a measure of the ultimate result. This was blatantly obvious when Claudie André-Deshays came; everyone could feel that she really believed in the work she was championing."

An Electric Evening

"The current bid is 5,200€…" François Curiel, auctioneer and president of Christie's in Europe, lets his words hang in the air as he grips his gavel. The dull bang reverberates for the first time this afternoon. It is 2:45pm on November 20, 2005. Bichot has just acquired the first lot of the Beaune cuvee "Dames Hospitalières." The 145th edition of the auction has started, and with it begins a new page in history. Christie's, the famous London auction house, has just sold the first barrel of wine on behalf of the Hospices de Beaune.

To speak of evolution would be a euphemism. The reality was much more turbulent than the polite words of the press let on.

The few observers still present at the end of the 2004 edition still remember. It was past 8:00pm, usually the hour for the customary pleasantries and thanks. Time to praise the good deeds of a philanthropic event. But there was none of that. Prices had dropped an average of 30%. The city mayor, Alain Suguenot, scarcely veiling his irritation, opened fire. "This result raises a lot of questions. Economic considerations are eclipsing the charitable nature of the auction." This little sentence was pronounced before a few journalists, but it was directed at the chairs facing the famous candles of the auctioneer.

An article published the night before in Le Figaro, penned by Laure Gasparotto, had already worked people up a bit. "Last Monday, the negociants of Burgundy held their general assembly 'in order to coordinate before the auction,' in the words of their president, Louis-Fabrice Latour. After the harvest, vinification, and a few promotional trips, these wine professionals gather often throughout the month of November. Seeking an agreement, they develop an official game plan. "Last year, the auction showed a 23% increase. This year, we'd like to see things take a turn down since this would befit the rather morose situation," announced Louis-Fabrice Latour. "We hope to return to a normal basis thanks to a 30% drop in prices."

That hope would become a reality the next day, an alliance that the mayor did not appreciate. Could a "cartel" cooperate to make or undo the auction prices according to its own interests? That evening, during a dinner that traditionally brings the day to a close, the magistrate publicly shared his point of view on the issue: "He unequivocally declared that the negociants had conspired to effect a drop at the auction. That's illegal!" remembers one negociant, rather vexed.

The microphones are upstretched for the sale of the Charity Barrel.

Right page:
Until the arrival of Christie's in 2005, the auction was traditionally held "by candle."

Childhood Friends

The tête-à-tête between the most famous Burgundian institution and the buyers had turned sour. Celebrations among old acquaintances became strained. Before Christie's arrived, the identity of the bidders held no surprise or whimsy: only professionals, more specifically only the Burgundian negociants, were allowed to raise their hands. Only they bottled these wines sold in bulk. Remember that the cuvees bought on the third Sunday of November are not drinkable yet. They are from the vintage harvested just a month and a half or two months before. These wines require long months of *elevage* before bottling, care that only these estates can administer. Moreover, the aging must legally be carried out within the region of production. In the eyes of the law, the negociants guarantee expertise and origin.

But for all that, is an entente among the negociants to direct the auction according to their own interests really possible? "Impossible. That's accusing us of a forbidden practice!" the negociants exclaim in unison. In sight of the perpetual pendulum of the auction, if the negociants are pulling the strings their grip leaves something to be desired. But it would be foolish to deny the possibility of some weak attempts to come to an agreement. A scene related by Benoit Goujon provides an illustration: "Albéric (author's note: Bichot) and I were childhood friends, and he's not seated very far from me during the auction. In 2004, he said to me about one cuvee:

- You want some?
- Yes, I replied.
- A lot?
- Four barrels.
- Okay, I'll buy you the first four, then I'll take the next ones.

In the end I did buy the first four barrels, but I paid more than I had expected. Albéric raised the bid anyway. And on the next lot another buyer got involved. Albéric payed more than I did. These things can't work."

The phone calls the week of the auction don't change a thing. "Of course we call each other before the auction to see if the others have many clients or not. But I can easily have no orders on Monday and then everyone suddenly jumps into action on Friday. It's impossible to give any meaningful information about my purchases before Sunday at 2:00pm. If another negociant's client wants a certain wine and I need the same one, it'll go to whoever bids more. End of story," Goujon continues. The conditions under which he comes to the auction corroborate these remarks. His financial director is seated next to him with the clients' orders in hand. In front of him is his enologist, keeping an eye on his tasting notes. So how do you explain that certain "prognostics" made by the negociants exactly fit the outcome of the auction? Denis Duveau elucidates: "For about 150 years the negociants have come and they've bought. They know the auction well and often drive its evolution. If anyone involved knows what they're talking about, it is clearly the negociants. They have a historic understanding of all the factors, a sense of the market, and the expertise of professionals. The fact that they have a hunch shouldn't be taken as a prognostic. This debate should be diffused, everyone should be more understanding.

A Triumvirate

The virulence of Alain Suguenot's reaction was challenged by the economic arguments of the negociants. "This drop is not illogical after the numbers in 2003 (author's note: +21.4%). Our clients wouldn't understand why they would pay more for the 2004s than for the 2003s," retorts Louis-Fabrice Latour, president of the negociants' syndicate.

But the negociants' justifications would not budge the mayor of Beaune. On this highly charged night in 2004, something must have changed for Alain Suguenot. He wondered allowed whether to rethink the format of the event. The de facto monopolistic buyers should not call the shots. In the crowd, old chimeras were conjured up: opening the auction to individuals, bottling the wines at the Hospices.... But no one really believed it. After all, the collapse of 2004 was not the first.

And yet in the lethargy of late summer in 2005, rumors were spreading throughout Burgundy. Christie's, the venerable London firm, would oversee the auction. The objective: to widen its glory to an international scale and open it to individuals. In short, to extract it from the microcosm of Burgundy and Beaune; to cut the auction free from the real or imagined barometer of the local economy. With Christie's a triumvirate was established, a totally new arrangement to avoid a divorce.

An auction in the early 1950s, in the old winery of the Hospices, as seen by the artist Henry Cheffer.

Anthony Hanson (Christie's) preparing the auction catalog.

But why Christie's? "The long relationship binding Christie's to wine convinced the mayor. Ever since 1766 and its first auction, Christie's had featured wine in its catalogue. For Beaune, there was no real reason to change a formula that worked. But the year before, the interest of the Hospices had clashed with that of the local negociants, its traditional buyers. The atmosphere at the auction was gloomy. Christie's internationalized the buyers and helped bring a wider dimension to this prestigious sale," declared Anthony Hanson, manager of the wine department at Christie's. In 2005, part of the folklore of the auction passed into history. It had always been an auction "by candle," ending when two flames (wicks lit by an assistant to the auctioneer) burned out. The gavel came down as soon as the last glimmer gave way to a thin wisp of white smoke. Goodbye to the candles, but hello to bids placed by telephone or online. The auction planted its feet firmly in the 21st century.

Christie's Effect, Are You There?

The problematic of the 2005 auction and the two following editions (the invitation to tender was applicable for three years) was evident: to measure the famous "Christie's effect" expected by the mayor. After an increase in 2005 (+11%) everyone tried to ascribe the bulk of the credit to the protagonists of the auction, without detracting from the outstanding quality of the vintage. "Everyone played along. The negociants bought in large quantities. The buyers attracted by Christie's also participated," noted an amenable Alain Suguenot.

2006: The Charity Barrel has set a new record: 200,000 euros. In the hall, director Claude Lelouch films the scene.

Right page:
The auction is running smoothly under the leadership of Emmanuelle Vidal.

This premiere must have caused new situations, like the lightning-fast bidding war by telephone over a barrel of the Pommard cuvee "Dames Hospitalières." It was finally sold for 12,000€ (compared to 4,000€ the year before…) to an individual in the Middle East. Then there was the comical scene when the auctioneer momentarily reverted to auction by candle for one lot. François Curiel, much more accustomed to a gavel, pretended to fumble around awkwardly with the candles, hinting at the archaism of the process. Finally, there was a stroke of culture shock when the auctioneer, in unison with the entire hall, began singing the "Ban Bourguignon," raising his hands in the gestures that inevitably accompany this festive Burgundian cheer; they were saluting a notable bid on a cuvee of Bâtard-Montrachet….

But the premiere did not go off without a few hiccups. For example, an Indonesian man made the winning bid on eight barrels of Pommard thinking he had bought only one. He only realized his mistake after the auction when he received an invoice multiplied by eight! Aside from these anecdotes, the message to draw from these first years in the era of Christie's is not one of a total upheaval. The change engendered a certain… continuity. The negociants are still, and by far, the primary buyers. About 80-85% of the volume sold goes to one or another of these estates. For Christie's it is not a simple task. Selling so much wine as futures is new to them. Auctions run by the English firm usually involve small lots of collector's bottles from old or moderately old vintages.

But following a strong upturn in export in 2006 and 2007, the auction was showing a solid increase. With stocks at a minimum and a rather small crop, the 2007 auction ended with a significant increase of 27%. The following year, marked by a new reversal in the market, would not be so calm.

It is a little past 4:20pm on Sunday, November 16th. The figures are in the red. The mayor is having another fit of rage in the wings. "If we finish with a drop of more than 15%, I'm going to have the wine bottled at the estate," he threatens. "Requests have been made by clients of Christie's." Anthony Hanson would impassively confirm the claim.

Tasting in the cellars before the auction.

A Recurrent Issue

A recurrent issue reared its head again. In his time André Boisseaux had dredged it up. In the middle of the 1994 auction, after placing the winning bid on one lot, he officially requested that his purchase be bottled by the Hospices. He described his reasoning a few days later in the magazine Bourgogne Aujourd'hui: "The wines of the Hospices de Beaune should be bottled at the Hospices. The auction would proceed as it does now, but instead of the buyers taking the wines, they'd be left at the Hospices. They would keep them and handle the *elevage* for as long as was necessary for the wines to mature. The bottling would be done at the Hospices in a specific bottle. That's the way it should be. We should give the consumer every guarantee of authenticity. It's indisputable. You would never see the Romanée Conti or the great chateaux of Bordeaux sell their wine in bulk to any Tom, Dick, or Harry."

The negociants of Burgundy work very differently from their counterparts in Bordeaux, at least on high-end wines. In Bordeaux the negociants manage the commercialization of the great chateaux after the wines are bottled on the premises. In Burgundy, the wines are selected and purchased from the *vignerons* in bulk, then the negociants handle the *elevage* and bottle with their own labels, thus promoting their own brands. The term "umbrella brand" is sometimes used: a single negociant has a wide range of products from dozens of different appellations. The negociant's name has to be a guarantee of quality and accountability to the consumer, at least as meaningful as the famous phrase "mise en bouteille à la propriété." As for the Domaine de la Romanée-Conti, to which Boisseaux referred, it takes care of its own commercialization and therefore has no need for negociants. The same case applies to many estates in Burgundy: they would never leave it to someone else to bottle a wine with their own label. This would be inconceivable.

But in this matter, Boisseaux was a lone dissident. His associates did not see things the same way. The very next day, Bertrand Devillard, then at the head of the negociants' syndicate, took up his pen. In his letter, addressed to the institution, he expressed a "formal opposition" to Boisseaux – without naming him – and to his reasoning, "which is contrary to the historic spirit of the auction and also to the habitual practices that have built the reputation of the great negociant business of Burgundy." In the end, the submission presented by the CEO of Patriarche went unanswered.

Casus Belli

In 2008, the mayor's challenges were in vain. The expected drop came to pass, canceling out the previous year's gains (-26%). The negociants, under fire once again, took up the defensive: "Imagine, in the middle of a financial crisis, that the prices rose. That would be ridiculous! In such a situation, if

I were a journalist, I wouldn't even come any more," declared Louis-Fabrice Latour. Alain Suguenot's "proposition" was being considered more seriously than ever. It even went further than the idea presented by Boisseaux in his time. For the mayor, bottling at the Hospices would open the door for a "finished" wine sale, without passing through the negociants. "We can do without your services, at least for some of the cuvees!" That was, in effect, the message that the magistrate was sending to the negociants.

In the first row at the auction is the negociant Patriarche: Monique Boisseaux (widow of André Boisseaux), Jacques Boisseaux, CEO, and Philippe Peulson (General Manager).

All things considered, the implementation of this project would create a singular situation: a single estate would be sold, under a single label, both directly and through negociants. The two protagonists would then simultaneously be partners and competition… which would only serve to exacerbate tensions. "When a *vigneron* sells me an appellation, he is selling under his name and I am selling under mine. He doesn't sell me the name of his estate. And who's to say that the Hospices won't keep the best barrels and sell the rest to the negociants," confides Benoit Goujon.

At the end of 2008, the negociants immediately launched a broadside. "Casus belli!" The phrase was employed by many of them. They threatened to boycott the next auction if the administrative council of the Hospices decided to go through with the project. "If that's what they decide, let them fend for themselves. They'll end up drowning in stock," Latour blurted out. The covered marketplace deserted on the afternoon of the auction! The effect would be devastating….

The negociants firmly intended to keep their prerogative as the only bottlers for the wines of the Hospices. At the same time, they reproached Anthony Hanson for having added fuel to the fire. Christie's weak attempts to position itself upstream in the commerce of the Hospices fundamentally irritated these professionals. Objectively, the situation could seem astonishing. If the bottling at the Hospices were to be established, Christie's would wear two hats: auctioneer and competition to the main buyers. "The negociants are not the helpmates of Christie's, nor of the Hospices de Beaune. It would be a mistake to humiliate us. You can't insult the main economic activity of the city," Latour adds. Ultimately, bending to the raging global economic crisis, the conflicts were ironed out and the project filed away.

In 2010, the auction of the Hospices de Beaune will celebrate its 150th edition. Few events, including in the world of wine, can boast of such longevity. Will it change significantly in the coming years? Are the arrival of Christie's and the mayor's attempts to make changes the first signs of a profound evolution or just the hiccups of a turbulent period in its history? Between the constancy of old institutions and the renewal imposed by the needs of a new era, the auction of the Hospices is finding its way – sometimes painstakingly. But the key to survival is for both the buyers and the sellers to retain their interests. And they have too much in common not to get along…

The Hôtel-Dieu at night.

Right page:
A gargoyle at the entrance to the Hôtel-Dieu.

 The Magic Potion

As original and unique as it may be, the wine estate of the Hospices de Beaune does not escape the tensions that punctuate life in the vineyards. The two grand families of Burgundy – viticulture on one side and the negociants on the other – rarely have peaceable relations. At issue is the division of the revenue earned. Should the bigger part go to the producers or those who commercialize the product? This question comes up with every new vintage. The friction created by this problem has influenced the history of Burgundy's wines, leaving its mark everywhere down to the boundaries of the appellations.

The auction of the Hospices de Beaune is a story of a gavel and an impulse. But it also involves many other things: publicity and communication, flare-ups and slumps, fits of rage and gambles. Eclipsed by the folklore presented to the general public, these realities are largely unknown; it begged to be decoded. Those who know the region or have studied its history won't find any surprises. The world of Burgundian wine gladly presents an immutable image of thousand-year-old *terroirs*, festive brotherhoods, and unwavering secular traditions. But the reality is different and much more complex. The auction of the Hospices de Beaune, with all its vicissitudes, bears witness. The spread of the renown of Burgundy's wines was not a path strewn with rose petals and lined with angels sounding trumpets. It has long been fueled by the energy produced by tensions, disagreements, clashes, and gnashing of teeth. Could it be any other way in a world of wine where history, passion, emotions, and economy are so tightly entangled? And finally, how can you not think of the village of Gauls in the comic of Astérix…. A proud city buttressed by its exceptional history. A simple country town, but it swells with pride. The villagers are quick to anger and ready to fight at the slightest provocation. But don't forget the principle: these Gauls have a secret weapon, their famous magic potion that fills them with assurance and ambition…

The General Exposition: wines from all over Burgundy are presented here.

The Great Dates of the Auction

In the mid-19th century, the first editions of the wine auction of the Hospices de Beaune took place in the magnificent courtyard of the Hôtel-Dieu. Later, it would be held in a room inside the building: the King's Chamber. Then for a while it would be in the very winery where the products were made. Since 1959, the covered marketplace has housed the event. It has therefore left the historic building, even if it hasn't gone very far. It is just on the other side of the cobblestone street! As for the date of the event, it was definitively chosen in 1925: the third Sunday of November. The wine auction would thus follow the flurry of activity around Dijon's gastronomic fair, letting visitors to the region kill two birds with one stone, so to speak. Its increasing fame would not protect it from dark times: in 1910, 1956, and 1968 the harvests were so poor that the auction wasn't even held. In 1916 and from 1939-1942, war prevented it from taking place.

The Negociant:
An Important Role in Burgundy

Not very well known, and sometimes not very well liked, negociants nevertheless fill a prominent role in Burgundy. They are responsible for commercializing almost 60% of the region's wines. These impact of these local institutions reaches across 150 countries. Their historical contribution to the international renown of the region was vital. The negociants can be thought of as successors to the Cistercian abbeys that promoted Burgundy's wines outside the region during the Middle Ages. It is undoubtedly this prestige that inspired popes and cardinals in 14th century Avignon gladly to fill their cellars with the wines of Beaune. The negociants are also heirs to the Valois dynasty of dukes of Burgundy, who built a stellar reputation for their region's wines throughout Europe by supplying them to various royal courts at the dawn of the Renaissance.

The first negociants appeared in the mid-18th century. Their creation was often tied to the textile trade; merchants would pass through Beaune on their way to Flanders, where the cloths were produced. Some of them decided to settle in or near Beaune and ended up specializing in wine. In the following century, the booming negociant business in Burgundy became standard: the region has 200 negociants that were established in the late 19th century. These outfits benefited from a number of factors: the wine trade was boosted by the free-trade policy of Napoleon III. Railroads were also being developed at this time; the proliferation of routes led to an appreciable drop in the cost of transport and allowed for quick access to new markets. The negociants exclusively controlled the commercialization of Burgundian wine, which was also the case for a large part of the 20th century.

One thing is sure: the oldest bottles of Burgundy still around today are sleeping in the cellars of Beaune's negociants. The vignerons only handled commercialization of their wines quite late in the game. This is because the development of estate bottling is quite recent; it only became common in the 1970s.

As transportation gradually progressed and the reputation of Burgundy's wines spread, the negociants began to open new markets. The notable conquests of the post-war era were the American market (second only to England in value) and Japan (which completes the podium). Today, the negociant business is prospecting numerous markets where people are just beginning to consume wine: Russia, China, Brazil, Scandinvia, South Korea, etc.

Negociant Eleveur and Negociant... Vigneron!

To reduce Burgundy's negociant activity to its purely commercial role and its exploration of new markets would be erroneous. These firms are also deeply involved in production (vinification and vineyard management). From a winemaking standpoint, the heart of the negociant business is elevage, a prerogative that they hold very dear. In Burgundy, negociants buy wines in barrel and provide the ideal conditions and the necessary care for them to blossom. Finally, they determine the best time for bottling. All these steps require experience and savoir faire.

Most of today's 130 negociants also own vineyards. The total surface area owned by negociants comes to more than 2,000 hectares; they work almost 40% of the grand crus of the Côte de Nuits and the Côte de Beaune. Some of the biggest estates in the region are controlled by negociants and undeniably enjoy a reflection of their prestige. Louis Jadot (150 hectares), Bouchard Père et Fils (130 ha), Faiveley (120 ha), Joseph Drouhin (105 ha), Louis Latour (50 ha), etc.

Many negociants also buy grapes and must (unfermented grape juice) from vignerons and make the wine themselves, a formula that developed relatively recently. By overseeing the entire vinification, a firm can thus print its own style on the wine starting earlier in the process.

In other words, the division between negociants and vignerons is not so clear in Burgundy. All the more so since many reputed vignerons also purchase from their colleagues to meet demands...

The General Exposition of the Great Wines of Burgundy

A taster's paradise: more than 3,000 wines presented and 10,000 bottles for sale during the weekend of the auction. This sizable show, which is open to the public, is designed to present the new vintage to negociants and foreign buyers, but it is also an opportunity for a large audience to discover the appellations of Burgundy: Chablis, Côte de Beaune, Côte de Nuits, Côte Châlonnaise, Mâconnais, but also Beaujolais crus. About twenty circular stands allow visitors easily to locate the various wine-producing areas of Burgundy. At the door each guest receives a catalog listing all the estates present. This is the only moment of the year when all of the region's appellations are brought together, the only occasion to explore the famous diversity of Burgundy's terroirs.

The Cellar of the Year 2000

CEO of Patriarche (Beaune) and an emblematic figure of the auction, André Boisseaux was also a true visionary. Almost 40 years ahead, he predicted the "2000 effect"! In June 1963, he had more than 2,000 bottles of the best appellations in Burgundy (Chambertin, Clos de Vougeot, etc.) put away in a cellar. He gave instructions not to open it until the arrival of the new millennium, as a gift from the men of the 20th century to those of the 21st. The last turn of the key was executed by the famous Canon Kir, deputy-mayor of Dijon. There were three keys: one at Patriarche, a second at the town hall, and the third entrusted to the Hospices de Beaune. Its unveiling on the weekend of the auction in 2000 was quite the event. All the more because the tastings that followed made good on all their promises. The excellent 1959 vintage, from some of the best terroirs of Burgundy, had evolved remarkably. André Boisseaux was no longer of this world, but he continued to dazzle with his ability to make a splash.

Presidents of the Wine Auction of the Hospices de Beaune from 1950 to 2008

1950 M. de Salis, Swiss Ambassador to France.
1951 David K. Bruce, United States Ambassador to France.
1952 Sir Oliver Harvey, English Ambassador to France.
1953 William Tyler representing C. Douglas Dillon, United States Ambassador to France (ill on the day of the auction).
1954 Prince Bernhardt of the Netherlands.
1955 Sir Gladwyn Jebb, English Ambassador to France.
1956 *No auction held.*
1957 M. Gras, doyen vigneron of the Hospices (86 years old), replacing Paul-Henri Spaak, Secretary General of NATO (ill the day of the auction).
1958 Pierre Micheli, Swiss Ambassador to France.
1959 Doctor Eugène Aujaleu, French Director General of Public Health.
1960 Baron Jaspar, Belgian Ambassador to France.
1961 Sir Pierson Dixon, British Ambassador to France.
1962 Charles E. Bohlen, United States Ambassador to France.
1963 Baron Bentinck Van Shoonheten, Dutch Ambassador to France.
1964 Archduke Otto von Habsburg.
1965 Sir Patrick Reilly, British Ambassador to France.
1966 William Tyler, United States Ambassador to The Hague.
1967 Pierre-Jean Moatti, Prefect of Burgundy.
1968 *No auction held.*
1969 Pierre Dupont, Swiss Ambassador to France.
1970 Giovanni-Franco Pompéi, Italian Ambassador to the Vatican.
1971 Princess Margrethe of Denmark (now queen of Denmark).
1972 Richard Hatfielf, Prime Minister of New Brunswick (Canada).
1973 Prince Edward, Duke of Kent (Great Britain).
1974 Alain Decaux (historian).
1975 Duke Carl of Württemberg and his wife, Princess Diane of Orleans.
1976 Count de Kerchove de Denterghem, Belgian Ambassador to France.
1977 Prince Bertil of Sweden and his companion Lilian.
1978 Lino Ventura (actor).
1979 Prince Paul-Alfons of Metternich-Winneburg.
1980 Katsuichi Ikawa, Japanese Ambassador to France.
1981 Peter Ustinov (actor, director, writer).
1982 Baron Paternotte de la Vaillée, Belgian Ambassador to France.
1983 Marie-José Nat, Jean-Claude Brialy, Victor Lanoux (actors).
1984 Mstislav Rostropovitch (cellist).
1985 Professeur Roger Guillemin (Nobel prize winner in medicine, 1977).
1986 Princess Marie Astrid of Luxembourg and her husband Carl Christian of Austria.
1987 Professor Luc Montagnier (co-discoverer of the AIDS virus and Nobel prize winner in medicine, 2008)
1988 Princess Alix de Foresta.
1989 Carole Bouquet (actress).

1990 Dominique Lapierre (writer).
1991 Florence Arthaud (navigator).
1992 Barbara Hendricks (singer).
1993 Lambert Wilson (actor).
1994 Admiral Leighton Smith (Commander in Chief of the United States Naval Forces) and Michèle Alliot-Marie (French Minister of Youth Affairs and Sports).
1995 Catherine Deneuve (actress).
1996 Claudie André-Deshayes (astronaut).
1997 Thierry Lhermitte (actor).
1998 Sandrine Kiberlain and Anouk Aimée (actresses).
1999 Kristin Scott Thomas (actress).
2000 Inès Sastre (model and actress) and Charles Berling (actor).
2001 Amira Casar (actress) and Julien Clerc (singer)
2002 Chiara Mastroianni and Elsa Zylberstein (actresses).
2003 Marlène Jobert and Jean Réno (actors).
2004 Charlotte Rampling (actress), Jonathan Nossiter (filmmaker)
2005 Catherine Jacob (actress), Sonia Rykiel (fashion designer).
2006 Fanny Ardant, Jocelyn Quivrin, and Alice Taglioni (actors).
2007 Richard Berry (actor), Maréva Georges, Linda Hardy, and Sonia Rolland (Miss France winners).
2008 Jean-Pierre Marielle and Michel Blanc (actors).

Sonia Rolland (Miss France 2000) was president of the auction in 2007.

Beaune Aspect de la
cour l' Hotel Dieu pendant la vente des

S VINS
NE
DE SALINS
NE CONTROLÉE
PAR
ARCHE
ET FILS
13% VOL.
TS A BEAUNE (COTE-D'OR)
Hospices d
19
POMM
Appellation Po
Cuvée Cy
le troisième
de Novembre,
célèbre vente aux
à la chandelle des
Vins du Domaine
Hospices, constitué tout
long des siècles grâce à
généreuses donations.
grands vins en tonneaux
pris en charge par les
qui ont la délicate
de les élever et de les
mettre en bouteilles.
13,5% vol.
MIS
ANTONIN RODET, NÉGOCIANT-ÉLEVEUR A MER

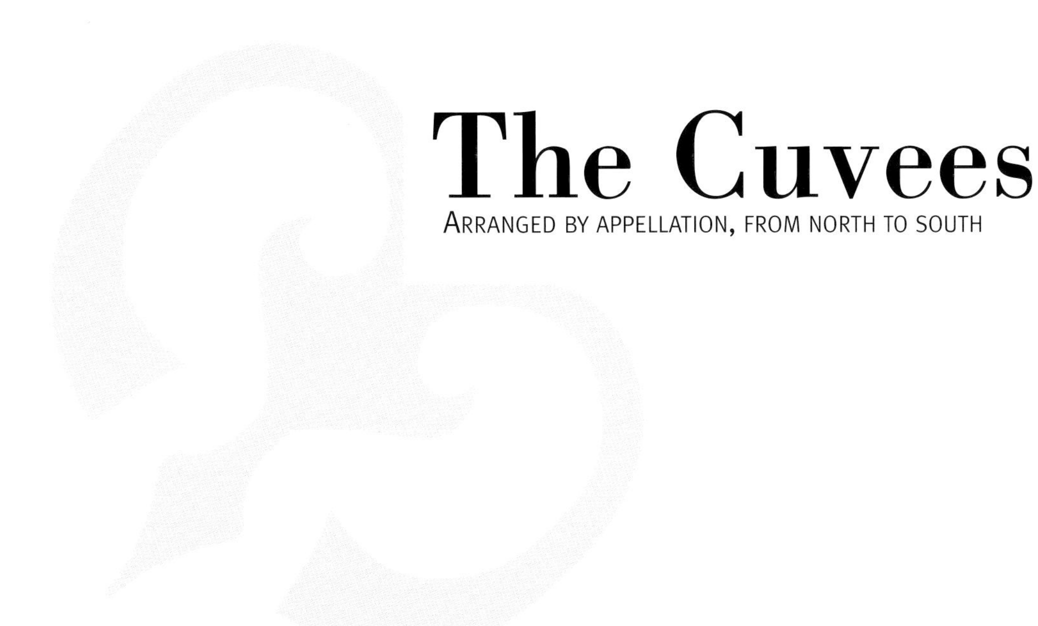

The Cuvees

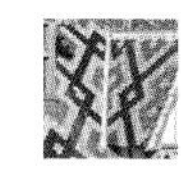

ARRANGED BY APPELLATION, FROM NORTH TO SOUTH

Double previous page:
The first editions of the auction were held in the courtyard of the Hôtel-Dieu.

Left page:
Various vintages of Hospices wines. Starting in 1969, labelling was standardized regardless of the buyer. Labels are provided by the Hospices.

THE REDS

Mazis-Chambertin grand cru cuvée Madeleine Collignon

Composition: Mazis
Vineyard Area: 1.74 hectare

■ *History*

This vineyard was entrusted to the Hospices de Beaune in 1976 by a certain Jean Collignon, who wished the cuvee produced from them to carry his mother's name. Madeleine Collignon was the descendant of an old negociant family from Gevrey-Chambertin that also owned vineyards.

■ *Terroir*

Mazis-Chambertin is the closest grand cru to the village of Gevrey-Chambertin. This *terroir* is under the refreshing influence of the Lavaut combe (a deep, narrow valley). Grapes ripen rather slowly and the harvest is late here. The soil is made up of magnificent limestone lava with veins of quartz, in theory a poor soil (certain analyses have shown the opposite) that drains well. Situated on the middle slopes, the vineyard is exposed east-southeast. In short, all the elements necessary for a great wine are in place. The Mazis-Chambertin is rich, elegant, unusually complex, and at once powerful and "fresh."

© Pitiot-Servant - Coll. Pierre Poupon

© Pitiot-Servant - Coll. Pierre Poupon

Clos de la Roche grand cru cuvée Cyrot-Chaudron

Composition: Les Froichots
Vineyard Area: 0.22 hectare

■ *History*

In 1979, Raymond and Suzanne Cyrot-Chaudron left vineyards (also see the Beaune cuvee of the same name) as well as a significant sum of money to the Hospices de Beaune. With these funds and those from the Kritter family, a parcel of this grand cru was acquired in 1991.

■ *Terroir*

The Clos de la Roche is one of the four grand cru 'clos' (walled vineyards) in the commune of Morey-Saint-Denis (between Gevrey-Chambertin and Chambolle-Musigny). The vineyards belonging to the Hospices are in the upper slopes of the appellation. These parcels give wines with great elegance and minerality, while the lower slopes, with deeper soil, give wines with more wild, animal aromas. The vineyards of the Hospices are planted on rather thick, clayey soils that give full-bodied wines.

Clos de la Roche grand cru cuvée Georges Kritter

Composition: Les Froichots
Vineyard Area: 0.22 hectare

© Pitiot-Servant - Coll. Pierre Poupon

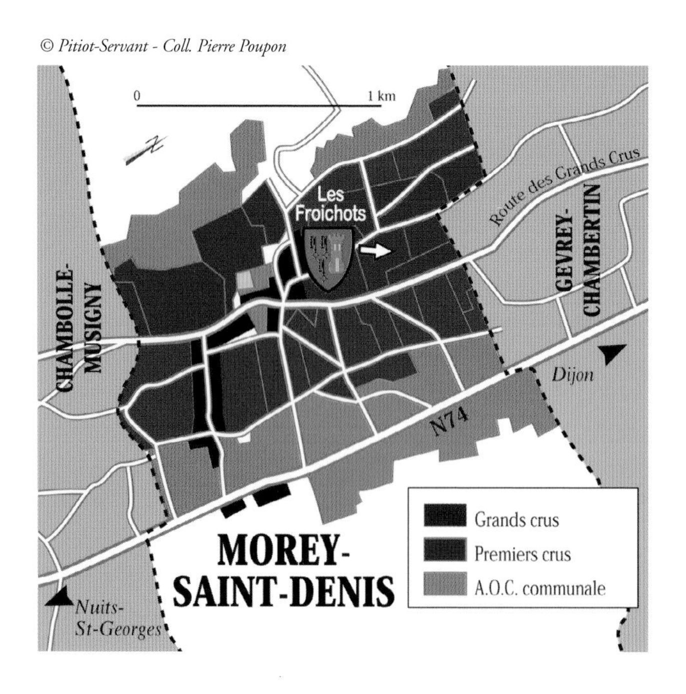

■ *History*

The creation of this cuvee in 1991 was intimately linked to the last one (Clos de la Roche "Cyrot-Chaudron"). The combined legacies of these two families would allow the purchase of this prestigious vineyard. It is more precisely the widow of Georges Kritter who made the donation a reality. Georges Kritter was the cousin and collaborator of André Boisseaux, an important figure in the Beaune negociant business after the Second World War. At the head of the winery Patriarche Père et Fils, Boisseaux was one of the main buyers at the auction throughout his career.

■ *Terroir*

This parcel is contiguous to the Cyrot-Chaudron vineyards and shares exactly the same characteristics. The grapes are even vinified in the same vat. As a result, only the *elevage* carried out by the negociants after the purchase of the cuvee produces the differences between the flavor profiles of the two wines.

Corton grand cru cuvée Docteur Peste

Composition: Les Chaumes et la Voierosses, Les Bressandes, Les Grèves, Les Fiètres
Vineyard Area: 2.60 hectares

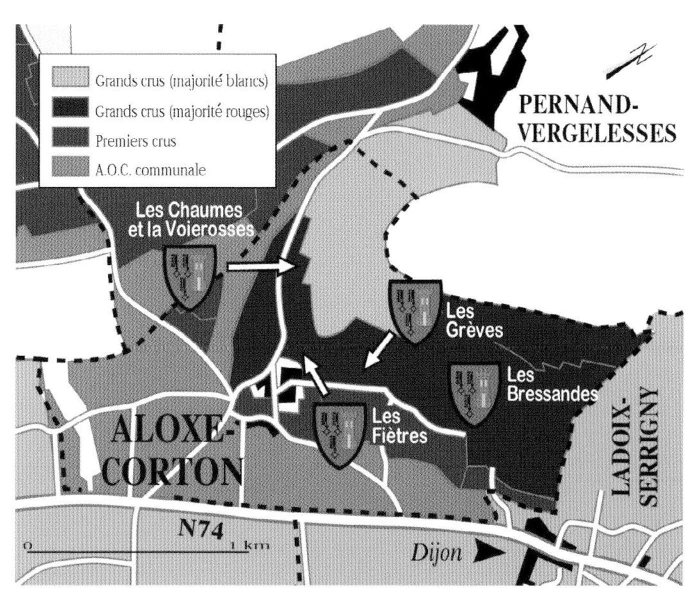

© Pitiot-Servant - Coll. Pierre Poupon

■ *History*

The records do not reveal whether the patients of Jean-Louis Peste were frightened when they saw that they would be treated by a man by the name of Doctor "Plague"! It is nevertheless certain that this doctor, born in Savigny, performed his job at the Hospices quite capably in the mid-19th century. He was even the mayor of Beaune. His daughter made a significant donation to the estate in 1924. The name of this cuvee assures him a place in history.

■ *Terroirs*

"*Terroirs*" has to be plural in this case because the grand cru vineyards in Corton make up a vast property. There are four grand crus in this cuvee, all near the village of Aloxe-Corton. They create a good summary of what this sector can give. Les Chaumes et la Voierosses, with its full southern exposure, contributes the main part of this cuvee. The other important vineyard in this wine is Les Bressandes, which is also on the middle of the slopes but has full eastern exposure. The blend is rather delicate and elegant.

Corton grand cru cuvée Charlotte Dumay

Composition: Les Renardes, Les Bressandes
Vineyard Area: 2.66 hectares

■ *History*

In 1534 Charlotte Dumay made a considerable donation of vineyards for the "purification and salvation of her soul." At least, this is what is mentioned in a document, written on parchment in gothic lettering, composed in the presence of the director of the Hôtel-Dieu. The benefactress was the childless wife of the keeper of the king's mint in Dijon, who was charged with the casting and circulation of coins.

© Pitiot-Servant - Coll. Pierre Poupon

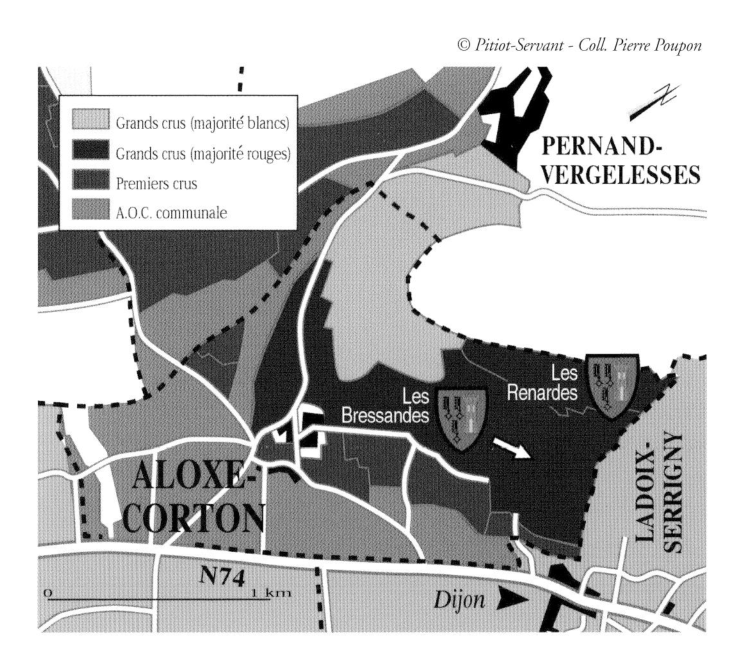

■ *Terroirs*

Here, we are in the heart of the Corton appellation. The parcels in the middle slopes (Les Bressandes) and the upper slopes (Les Renardes) enjoy the same full eastern exposure. Vines thrive on soils of varying depths around the hillside. The Corton proposed by the Hospices nevertheless shows more finesse than structure.

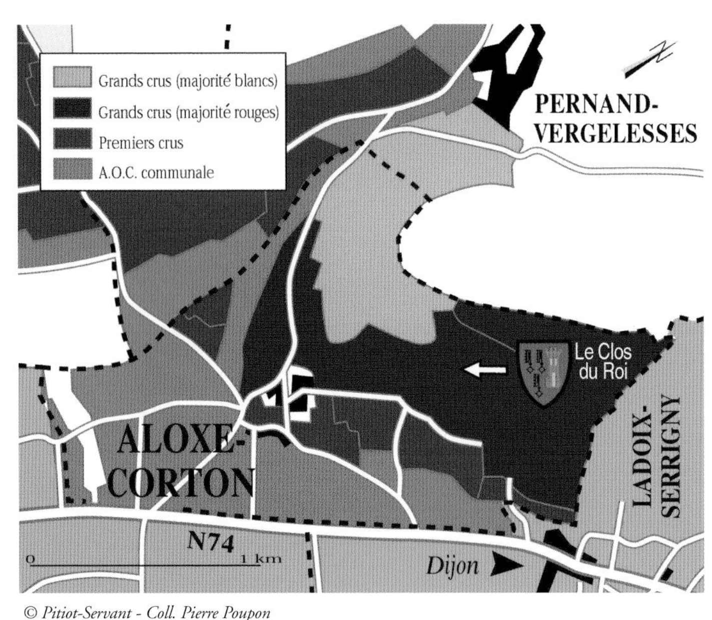

© Pitiot-Servant - Coll. Pierre Poupon

Corton Clos du Roi grand cru cuvée Baronne du Baÿ

Composition: Clos du Roi
Vineyard Area: 0.84 hectare

History

This name first appeared in the catalog of the Hospices de Beaune in 2007 even though the estate has owned the vineyards since 1924. This is because the fruit from this parcel was previously blended into the Corton cuvee "Docteur Peste." When the Hospices decided to vinify this parcel separately, the institution named the cuvee after the daughter of Doctor Peste, who had made the donation in her father's memory.

Terroir

On the upper slopes of Corton, with eastern exposure, the Clos du Roi vineyard gives some of the most archetypal Cortons. These structured, full-bodied wines require long aging to reveal their full complexity. This parcel is planted with very high-quality vines that give remarkably well-composed grapes.

© Pitiot-Servant - Coll. Pierre Poupon

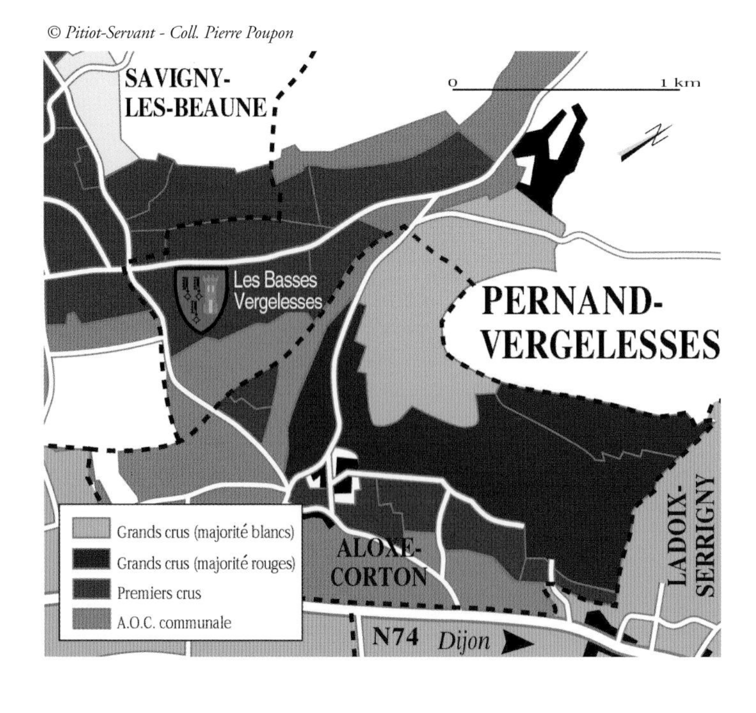

Pernand-Vergelesses cuvée Rameau-Lamarosse

Composition: Les Basses-Vergelesses
Vineyard Area: 0.70 hectare

History

The name of the Lamarosse family is closely tied to the vineyards of Beaune. There are mentions as early as 1626 of a barrel-maker of this name from Beaune. In the 19th century, his descendants exported the wines of Burgundy to several continents. In 1940, the last representative of the family left these vineyards and the family house to the Hospices de Beaune.

Terroir

Like many other communes in the region, Pernand carries the name of one of its most renowned vineyards: Les Vergelesses. Catching the very first rays of the morning sun and enjoying a rich, thickly clayey soil, this sector gives the best reds of the commune. This cuvee is rather austere and strict. It requires time in the cellar.

Savigny-lès-Beaune premier cru cuvée Arthur Girard

Composition: Les Peuillets
Vineyard Area: 1 hectare

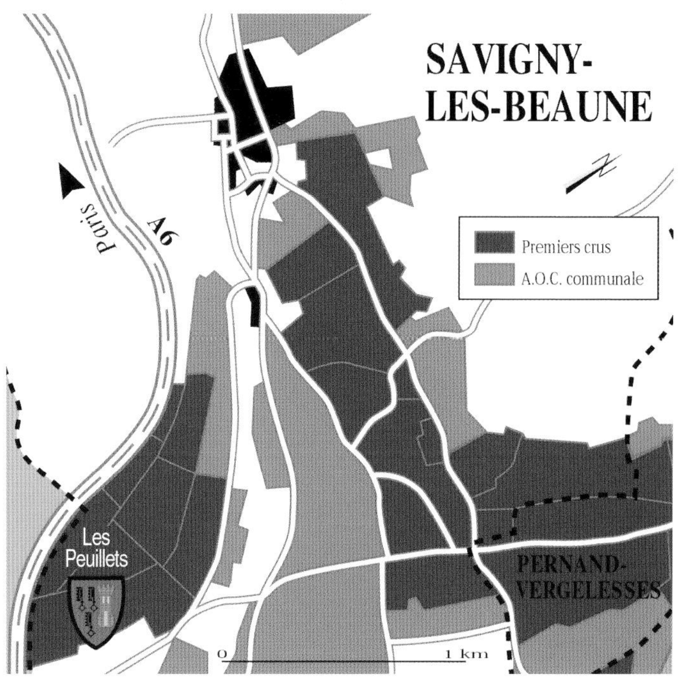

History

In 1936 a certain Arthur Girard left part of his property to the Hospices de Beaune, including a wide range of vineyards in Savigny-lès-Beaune (a commune adjacent to Beaune) in both village and premier cru appellations.

Terroirs

Of the many vineyards donated by Arthur Girard, only the Premier cru Les Peuillets contributes to this cuvee, which recently became a mono-*terroir* wine (in 2006). These vineyards are in the southern part of the appellation, in a continuation of the vineyards of Beaune. It is an early-ripening sector with thick clay soils that give the most robust wines of Savigny.

Savigny-lès-Beaune premier cru cuvée Forneret

Composition: Les Vergelesses, Les Gravains
Vineyard Area: 1 hectare

History

What an astonishing man Xavier Forneret was: romantic poet, violinist, writer, a master of black humor and eccentricity…. This native of Beaune had his hour of glory (André Breton admired him) but his work would not be known to posterity. He wrote: "The heart must give of itself, just as life must give itself up." This is precisely what his mother, Eléonore, did when she left her vineyards to the Hospices in 1842.

Terroirs

Unlike the cuvee "Arthur Girard," which is marked by its *terroir* in the southern part of the appellation, this cuvee is sourced from two parcels in northern Savigny. Situated on the upper slopes and enjoying good sun exposure, these vineyards generally give supple wines. This *terroir* has the distinction of a soil that is sandy and therefore drains well.

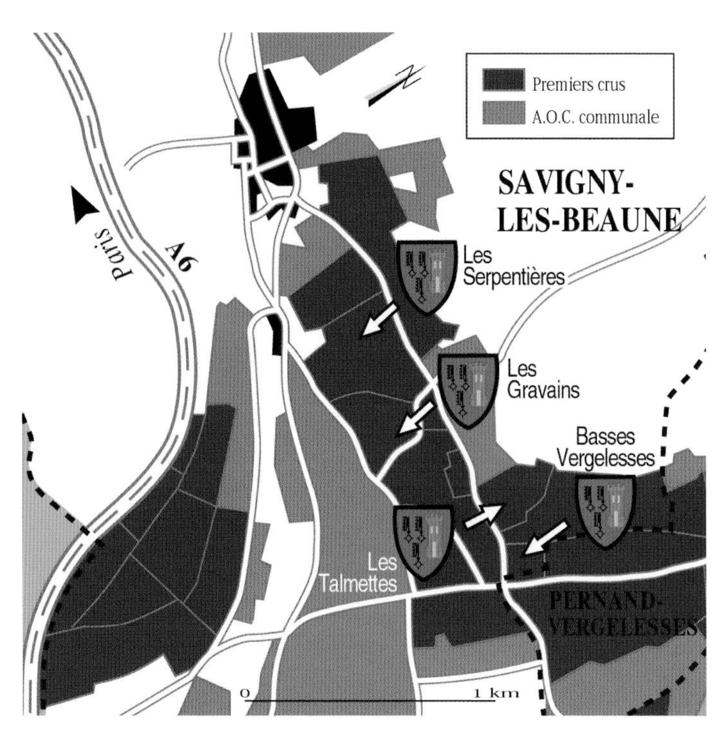

© Pitiot-Servant - Coll. Pierre Poupon

Savigny-lès-Beaune premier cru cuvée Fouquerand

Composition: Les Serpentières, Les Talmettes, Basses-Vergelesses, Les Gravains
Vineyard Area: 1.07 hectare

■ *History*

Coming from donations received in 1832 and 1844, this cuvee is among the estate's oldest. We owe its existence to Denis-Antoine Fouquerand and his wife. Several premier cru parcels in the commune of Savigny have thus expanded the Hospices' holdings.

■ *Terroirs*

Another premier cru Savigny, another character. This time the vineyards providing the better part of the cuvee are on the south-facing slope. The lighter, rockier soils here give wines of finesse. The very quintessence of what this appellation can give.

Beaune premier cru cuvée Guigone de Salins

Composition: Les Bressandes (1.20 hectare), Les Seurey, Champs Pimont
Vineyard Area: 2.64 hectares

© Pitiot-Servant - Coll. Pierre Poupon

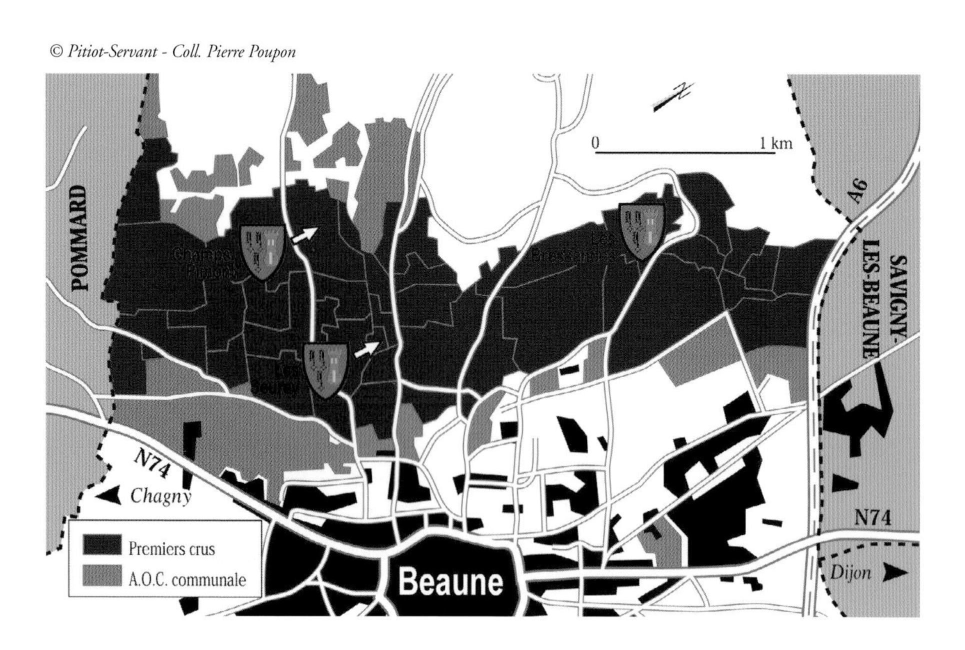

■ *History*

The Hospices naturally began to build its vineyard holdings in the heart of the vineyards of Beaune. This cuvee carries the name of the co-founder of the Hôtel-Dieu. Descended of the nobility of the Franche-Comté, Guigone de Salins took over the direction of the institution upon the death of her husband, Nicolas Rolin, and settled in Beaune in 1461. She would devote herself to the sick and live in the Hôtel-Dieu until her death at 82 years of age.

■ *Terroirs*

This cuvee is from three different parcels, but Les Bressandes dominates the blend. This vineyard is right in the middle of the hillside, on a light soil that drains well. The slope here is quite steep! The resulting wine has great finesse.

Beaune premier cru cuvée Nicolas Rolin

Composition: Les Cent Vignes, En Genêt, Les Bressandes, Les Grèves, Les Teurons
Vineyard Area: 2.65 hectares

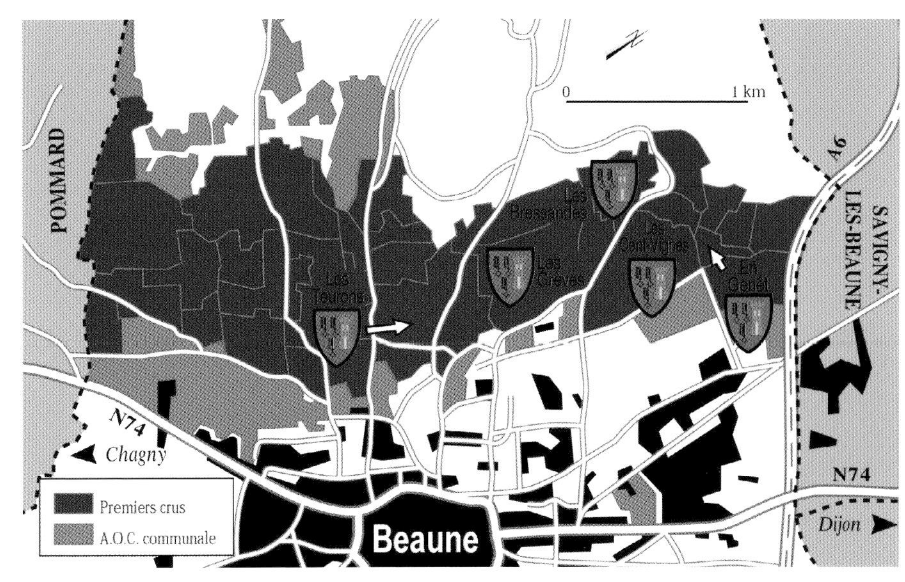

© Pitiot-Servant - Coll. Pierre Poupon

■ *History*

Les Cent Vignes is first mentioned in the institution's archives in 1497. It is therefore in the historic heart of the estate of the Hospices. This premier cru Beaune carries the name of the co-founder of the Hospices de Beaune, who was also chancellor to the duke of Burgundy. The cuvee was expanded thanks to a donation received in 1963. The widow of Maurice Pallegoix, an eminent local man, was the donor.

■ *Terroirs*

If the cuvee "Guigone de Salins" generally gives a feminine wine, the cuvee carrying her husband's name is more… masculine. It is marked by a tight, firm tannic structure. The wine of the chancellor to the duke of Burgundy is sourced, once again, from several different *terroirs*. A parcel in the Cents-Vignes vineyard, at the foot of the slopes of Beaune and on rather deep soil, makes up half of the cuvee.

Beaune premier cru cuvée Dames Hospitalières

Composition: Les Bressandes, La Mignotte, Les Teurons
Vineyard Area: 2.75 hectares

■ *History*

Those who are partial to this cuvee had better not arrive at the auction late as the event traditionally opens with the "Dames Hospitalières." The name of this wine, which means "Women of the Hospital," is a tribute to the nuns who cared for the sick right from the establishment of the Hôtel-Dieu. They arrived in 1452 from Valenciennes in northern France.

■ *Terroirs*

Here again we find the vineyard of Les Bressandes (see the cuvee "Guigone de Salins"). The cuvee is mainly associated with another *terroir* of Beaune, however: La Mignotte, which assures that the wine will be well structured.

© Pitiot-Servant - Coll. Pierre Poupon
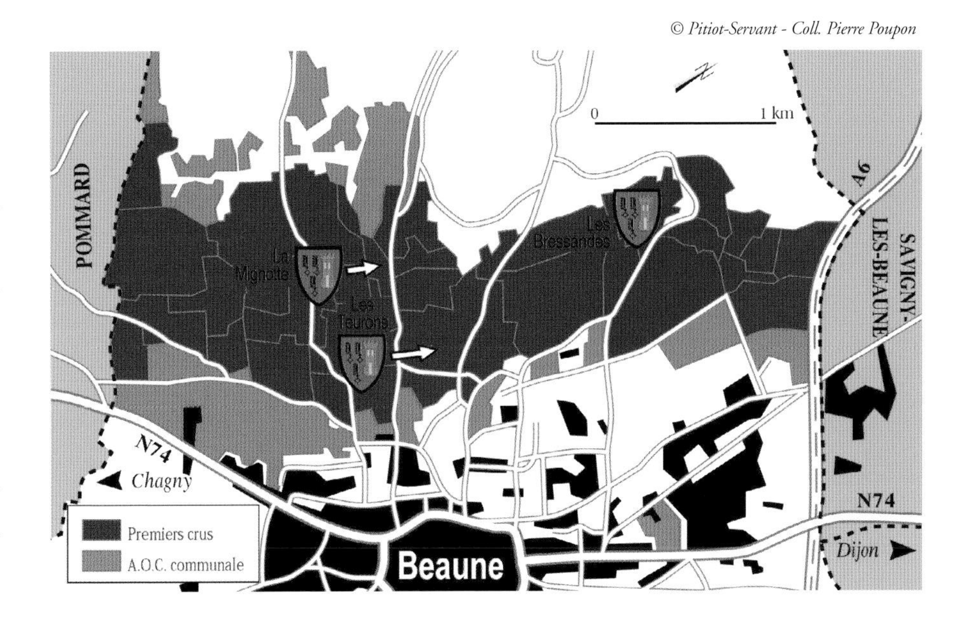

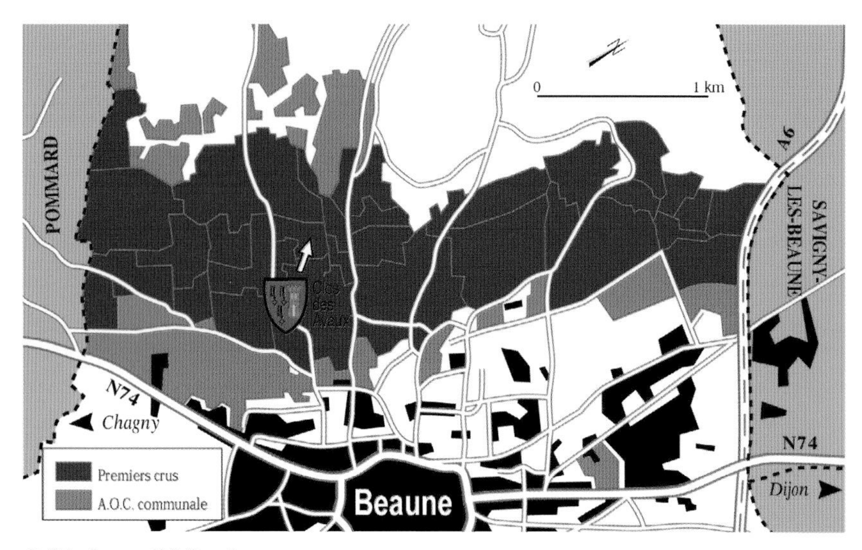

© Pitiot-Servant - Coll. Pierre Poupon

Beaune premier cru Clos des Avaux

Composition: Clos des Avaux
Vineyard Area: 1.87 hectare

■ *History*

This vineyard had a surprising destiny given that it was previously owned by another local institution: the Hospice de la Charité (founded in 1645). After the French Revolution the two Hospices merged (also see the cuvee "Rousseau-Deslandes"). This is the only cuvee that does not carry the name of a donor or a historical reference related to the Hospices de Beaune.

■ *Terroir*

The name "Avaux" is a distortion of the name of the Vaux (or Val) vineyard. As the name indicates ("val" meaning valley), the parcel is placed at the mouth of a combe in the southern part of the vineyards of Beaune. From a plot that drains well but is not very steep, the wines made from the (old) vines are full-bodied without being rustic. Part of the vineyard was replanted recently. This cuvee therefore comes mainly from young vines.

Beaune premier cru cuvée Maurice Drouhin

Composition: Les Avaux, Les Grèves, Champs Pimont, Les Boucherottes.
Vineyard Area: 2.69 hectares

■ *History*

In the first half of the 20th century, Maurice Drouhin was at the head of one of Beaune's most famous negociants: Joseph Drouhin. He was also vice-president of the administrative council of the Hospices de Beaune starting in 1941. Wanted by the occupying forces for his role in the Resistance during the Second World War, he fled to the Hôtel-Dieu, where the nuns hid him for six months. To express his thanks, he donated vineyards to the institution in 1947.

© Pitiot-Servant - Coll. Pierre Poupon

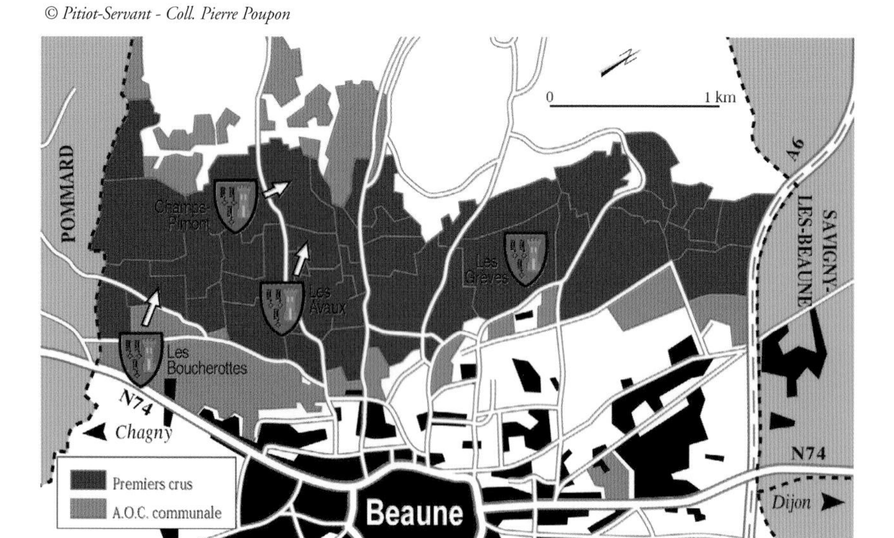

■ *Terroirs*

Like many of the Beaune cuvees, this wine is a blend from various *terroirs*. Between the vineyards on the lower slopes – Les Avaux (which dominates the cuvee) – and those perched on the steep Champ-Pimonts, this cuvee gives an overview of the character of the central part of the Beaune appellation. The soils here are generally rich and rather heavy, producing powerful wines that are austere in their youth. This Beaune approaches the character generally expected of a Pommard. Spicy aromas and herbaceous notes can often be detected in this wine.

Beaune premier cru cuvée Hugues et Louis Bétault

Composition: Les Grèves, Clos des Mouches, Les Aigrots, La Mignotte
Vineyard Area: 1.88 hectare

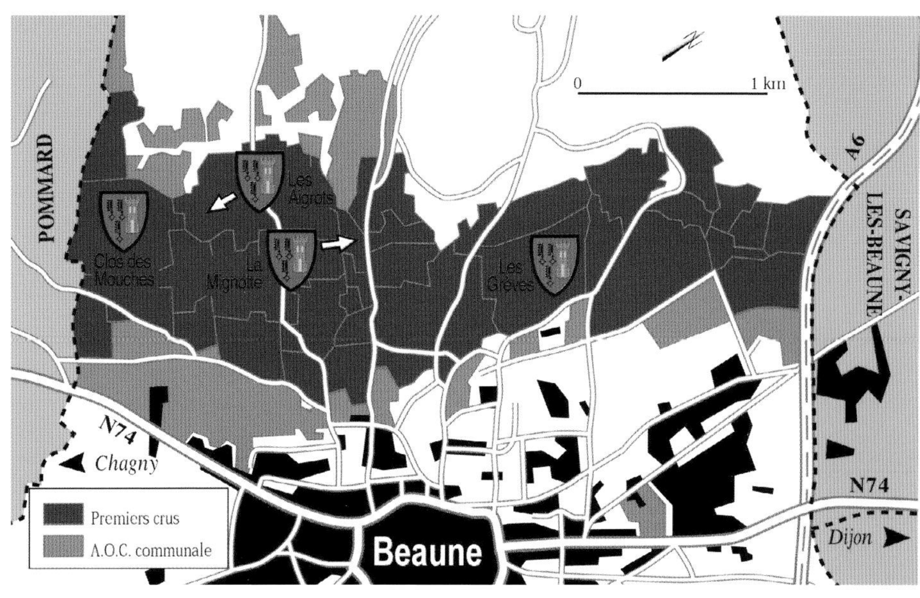

■ *History*

Hugues Bétault was one of the most important benefactors of the Hôtel-Dieu de Beaune when it experienced a difficult period in the 17th century. He was an officer and secretary to the king of France. His brother, Louis, would take over his duties upon his death in 1652 and would also make several donations. Their memory is also kept alive by a plaque with their family's coat of arms in the Saint Louis room in the Hôtel-Dieu.

■ *Terroirs*

Two of the best premier cru *terroirs* of Beaune are united in this cuvee. To the north, the vines in Les Grèves are about fifty years old; to the south, the Clos des Mouches boasts one of the best-established *terroirs* of the appellation. These two sectors generally give structured, powerful wines.

Beaune premier cru cuvée Cyrot-Chaudron

Composition: Les Montrevenots
Vineyard Area: 1.40 hectare

■ *History*

This name can also be found on one of the cuvees of Clos de la Roche. Unlike this other wine (which comes from a purchased vineyard), the Beaune Premier cru "Cyrot-Chaudron" comes directly from a donation from the Cyrot-Chaudrons, a husband and wife, in 1979.

■ *Terroir*

This is one of the rare mono-*terroir* Beaune cuvees of the Hospices. The parcel borders the Pommard appellation, perched high above the Clos des Mouches. The vineyard is partly comprised of very old vines (planted in 1929).

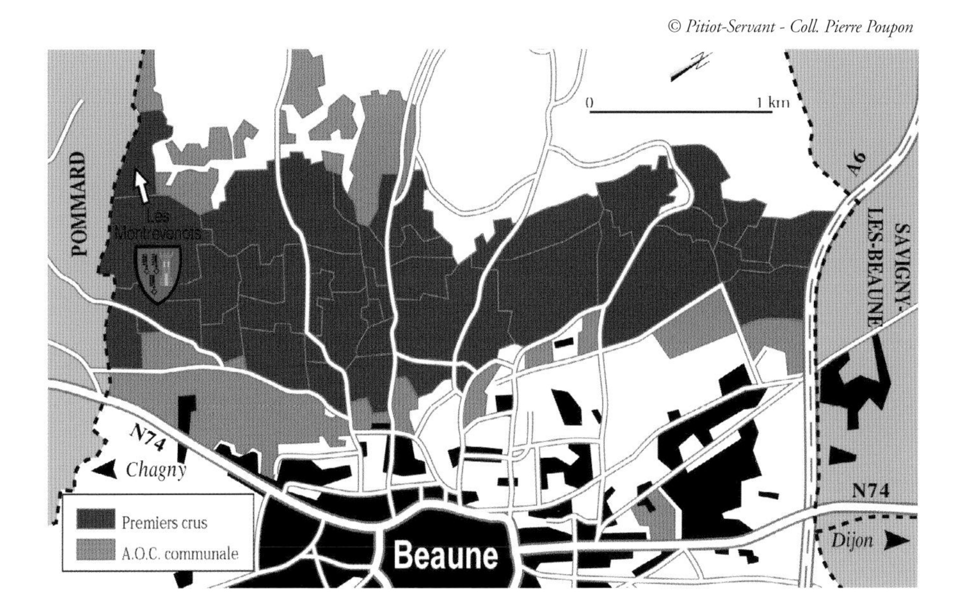

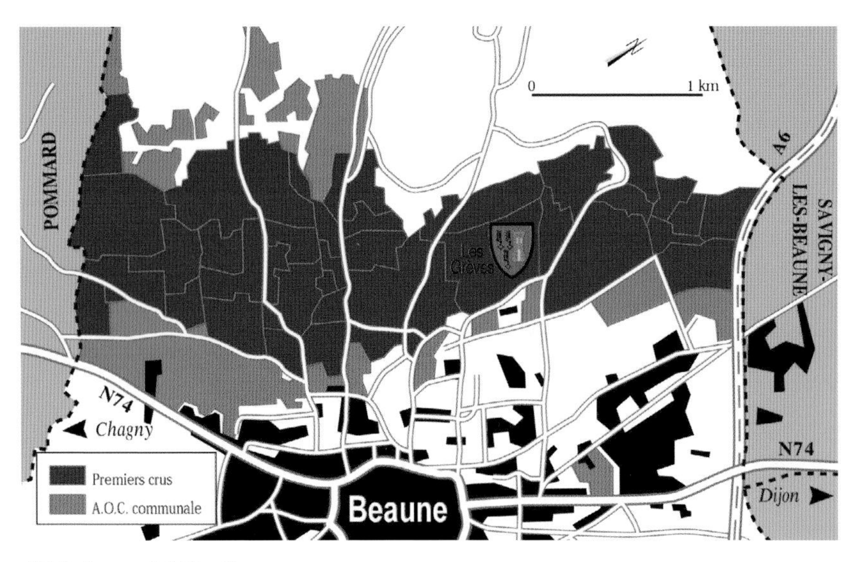

© Pitiot-Servant - Coll. Pierre Poupon

Beaune Grèves premier cru cuvée Pierre Floquet

Composition: Les Grèves
Vineyard Area: 0.77 hectare

■ *History*

This is the newest member of the large family of Beaune cuvees of the estate of the Hospices, acquired at the same time as a donation from Pierre Floquet, in 1997. This cuvee was first put up for auction in 2004.

■ *Terroir*

With no less than 31 hectares from the top to the bottom of the slope, the premier cru Les Grèves is quite large. It is also one of the most famous vineyards of Beaune. The vineyards of the Hospices constitute two parcels right in the heart of this sector. This *terroir* gives wines of great elegance and finesse. Patience is often called for since this cuvee tends to be rather closed when young.

Beaune premier cru cuvée Brunet

Composition: Les Bressandes, Les Cent Vignes, Le Bas des Teurons
Vineyard Area: 1.47 hectare

© Pitiot-Servant - Coll. Pierre Poupon

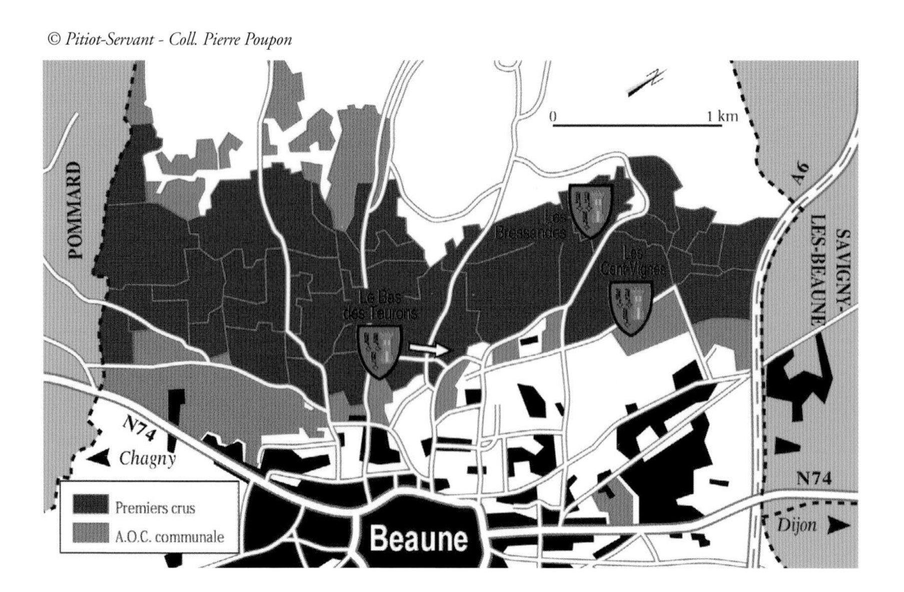

■ *History*

This cuvee carries the name of an important family in the history of Beaune. Many of its members have made donations to the local institution. The most extraordinary destiny in this family was that of Suzanne Brunet, a nun at the Hôtel-Dieu during the French Revolution. Condemned to the guillotine for anti-revolutionary activity, she escaped her sentence thanks to the death of Robespierre.

■ *Terroir*

Three *terroirs* are almost equally represented in this cuvee. With Les Bressandes and Les Cents Vignes, the northern part of the appellation is dominant. Finesse and fullness are the principal characteristics of this blend. The wine tends more toward elegance than concentration.

Beaune cuvée Rousseau-Deslandes

Composition: Les Cent Vignes, Les Montrevenots, La Mignotte
Vineyard Area: 2.09 hectares

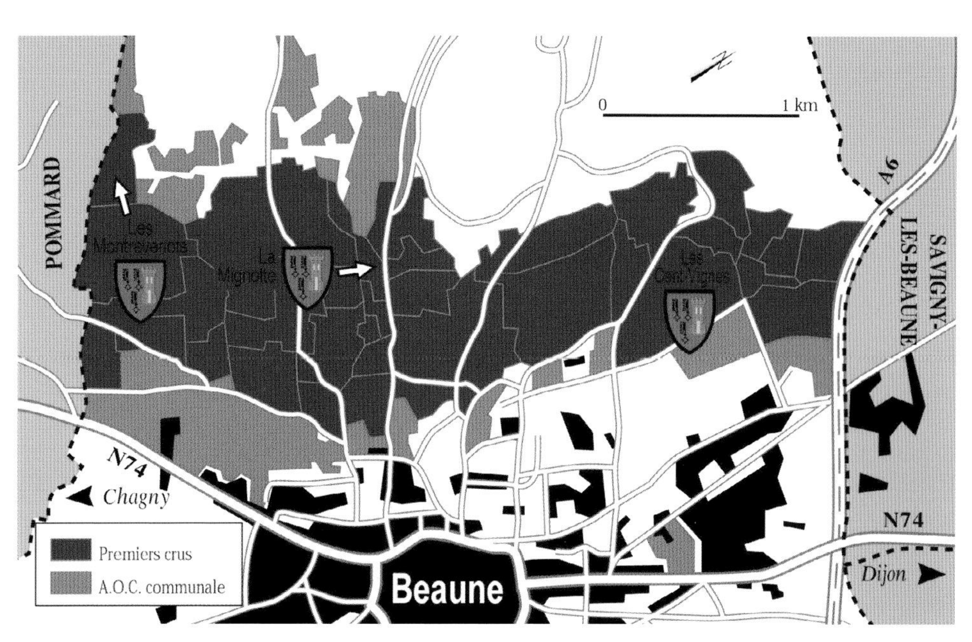

© Pitiot-Servant - Coll. Pierre Poupon

■ *History*

In 1645, against a backdrop of war and plague, the Hospice de la Trinité was born in Beaune (it would later become the Hospice de la Charité). The foundation was initiated by Antoine Rousseau and Barbe Deslandes. The institution would be placed under the control of the Hôtel-Dieu after the French Revolution (1805), as would its vineyards.

■ *Terroir*

Once again it is a trio of *terroirs* that makes up this cuvee. Les Cents Vignes dominates with just less than half of the cuvee, but the wine remains a balanced image of this vineyard, which gives full-bodied wines, and les Montrevenots. The latter is on white soil on the upper slopes, where ripening is more difficult. La Mignotte adds a plump, fleshy quality to the blend.

Pommard premier cru cuvée Dames de la Charité

Composition: Les Petits Épenots, Les Combes Dessus, La Refène, Les Rugiens Bas, Les Rugiens Hauts
Vineyard Area: 1.54 hectare

© Pitiot-Servant - Coll. Pierre Poupon

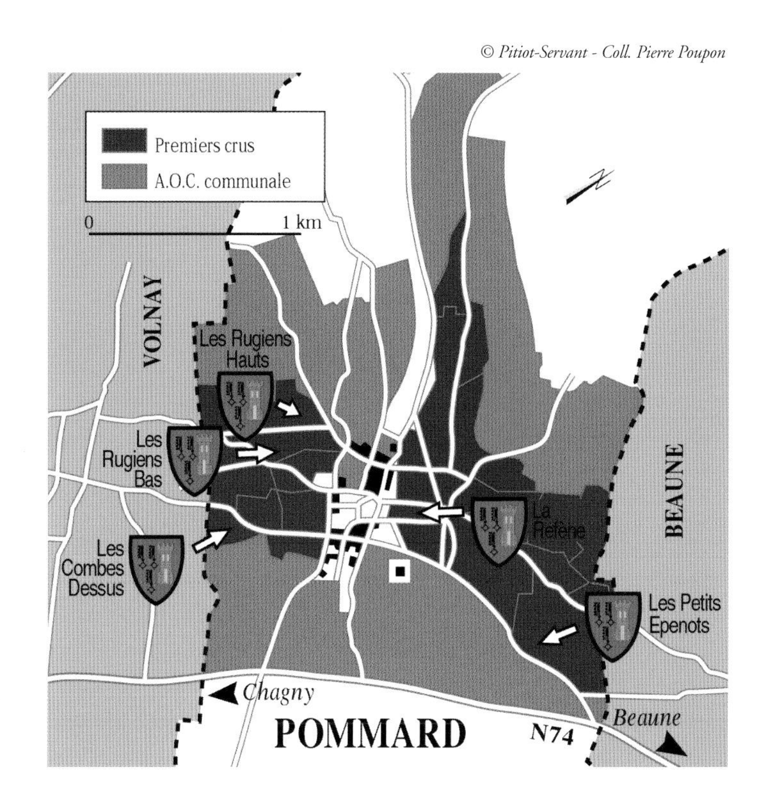

■ *History*

The "Dames de la Charité" or Women of Charity in question are, of course, the nuns who ran the society of the same name in Beaune, caring for the sick. This institution would merge with the Hôtel-Dieu in 1805. Not only were the sisters indispensable for their dedication to their work, but some of them also left vineyards and other belongings to the Hospices.

■ *Terroir*

This cuvee was revamped in 2005 and is now made up exclusively of premier cru vineyards, including two of the most respected *terroirs* of the appellation: Les Rugiens and Les Petits Epenots. The latter (0.42 hectares out of a total of 1.46 hectares) brings finesse. This cuvee is nevertheless one of the most robust wines of the Hospices de Beaune. Rather typical of Pommard, it is deeply colored and concentrated, with "rustic" tannins.

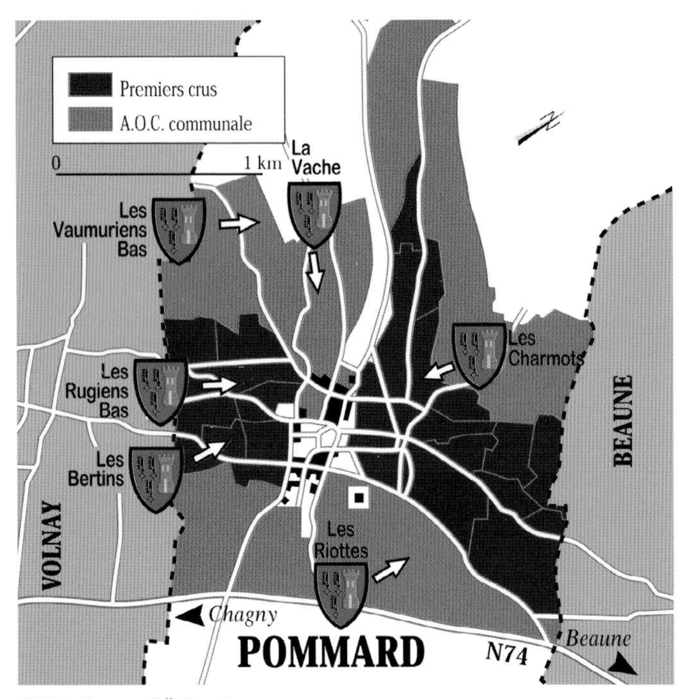

© Pitiot-Servant - Coll. Pierre Poupon

Pommard cuvée Raymond Cyrot

Composition: Les Charmots, Les Riottes, Les Rugiens bas, Les Bertins, La Vache, Les Vaumuriens Bas
Vineyard Area: 1.83 hectare

■ *History*

This is one of the cuvees resulting from the donation of the Cyrot-Chaudrons in 1979 (see the Beaune Premier cru Clos de la Roche and the Pommard "Suzanne Chaudron").

■ *Terroirs*

This cuvee is like a jigsaw puzzle, or even confetti. Six *terroirs*, three of which are premier crus, contribute to its production. Les Riottes has the potential to make up the largest part of the cuvee, but a significant part of the vineyard was torn up and replanted. As a result, none of the parcels has provided more than half a hectare in recent vintages. Only the premier cru Les Charmots comes near. The blend is dominated by a relatively young vineyard that gives a delicate Pommard, unlike the norm for the appellation.

© Pitiot-Servant - Coll. Pierre Poupon

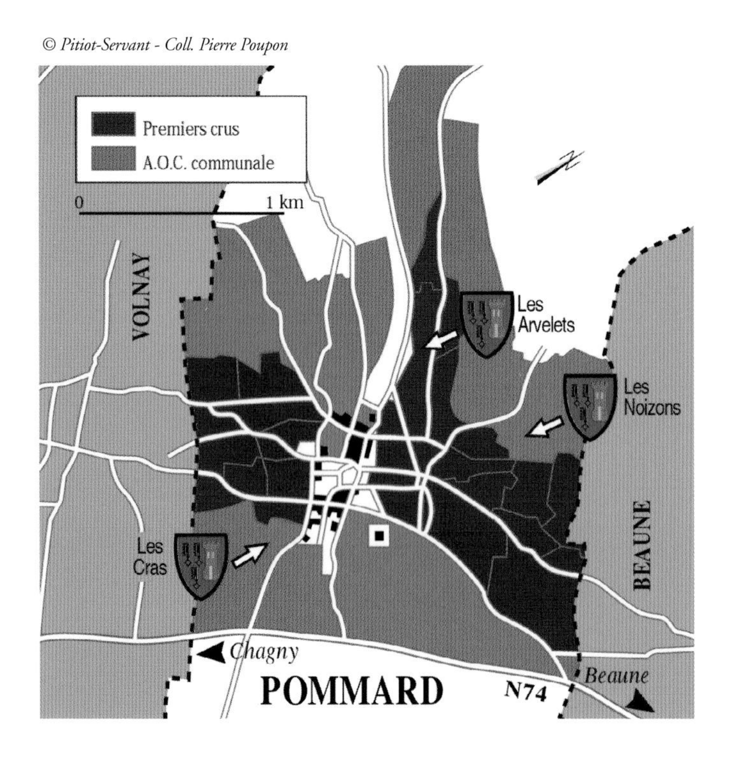

Pommard cuvée Billardet

Composition: Les Arvelets, Les Noizons, Les Cras
Vineyard Area: 1.34 hectare

■ *History*

Two celebrated doctors of the Hospices de Beaune are honored here. Antoine Billardet practiced at the Hôtel-Dieu during the French Revolution. His son Charles, a surgeon, would dedicate himself to the same institution for fifty years. Their daughters and granddaughters would make significant donations to the hospital.

■ *Terroirs*

Three *terroirs* are blended here, but the parcel in Les Cras contains just a few vines. Les Noizons, a site on the mid-slopes, and Les Arvelets therefore play the lead roles. Les Arvelets is a premier cru situated high up on the south-exposed face of a steep combe. A *vigneron* must wait patiently to see his grapes ripen here. The result is a delicate Pommard.

Pommard cuvée Suzanne Chaudron

Composition: Les Petits Noizons, La Chanière, Les Noizons, Les Petits Épenots, La Croix Planet, En Poisot, Rue au Port
Vineyard Area: 1,88 hectare

■ *History*
This cuvee joined the estate of the Hospices de Beaune with the famous legacy of Raymond Cyrot and Suzanne Chaudron (1979), a copious donation that generated four cuvees in all.

■ *Terroirs*
Three *terroirs* make up the bulk of this cuvee, with the majority of the vines coming more specifically from the sector of Les Noizons, a high-lying vineyard on white soil. The southeastern exposure here is ideal for vines.

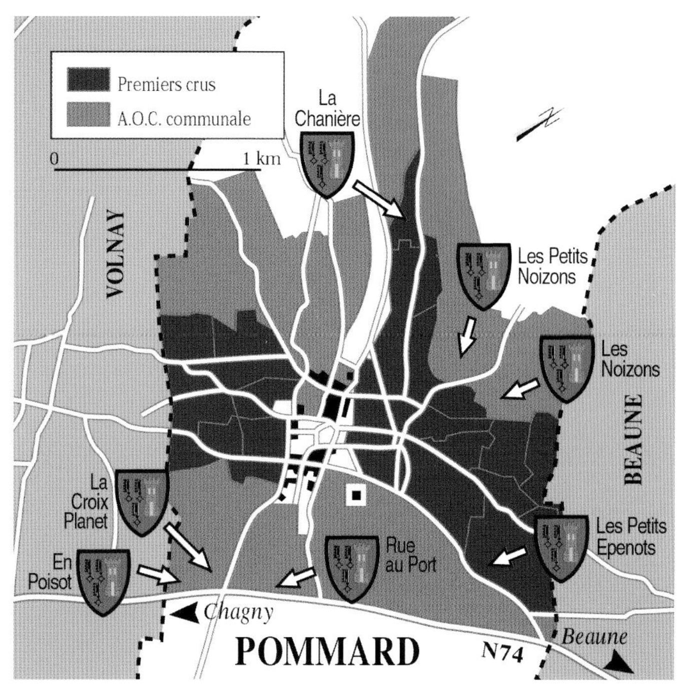

Pommard premier cru Épenots cuvée Dom Goblet

Composition: Les Petits Épenots
Vineyard Area: 0.70 hectare

■ *History*
This is one of the most recent additions to the estate's lineup of wines. This cuvee was created in 2008 after the vineyard Les Petits Epenots, one of the best plots in Pommard, was separated out. It had previously been blended into the cuvee "Billardet." Dom Goblet was the last monk responsible for the finances of the Clos de Vougeot.

■ *Terroir*
The finesse of the wines from the *terroir* Les Epenots conflicts with the image of Pommard. No angular tannins or robust character here; on the contrary, the tannins are incredibly delicate. This *terroir* in the northern part of the appellation is on a narrow ledge on the mid-slopes.

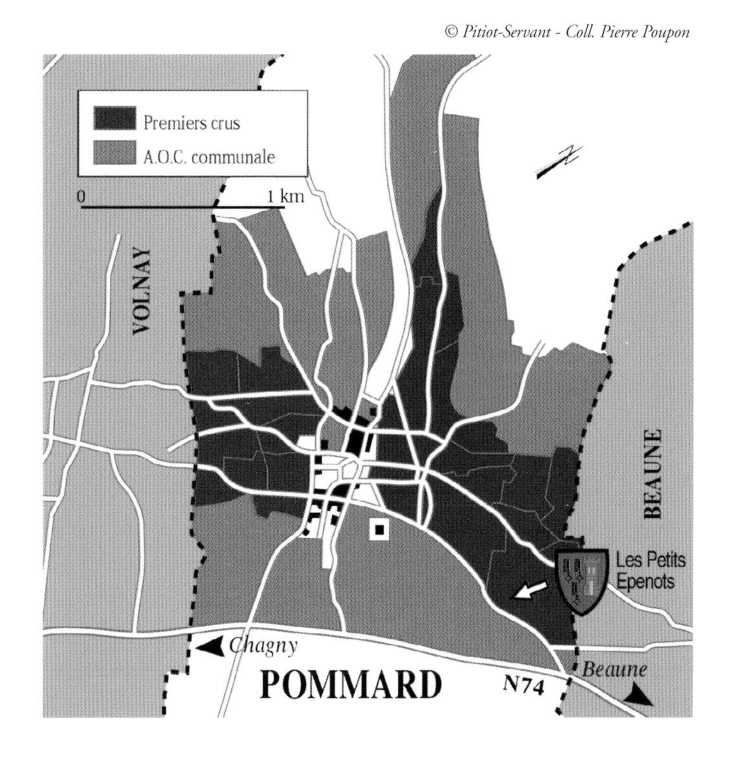

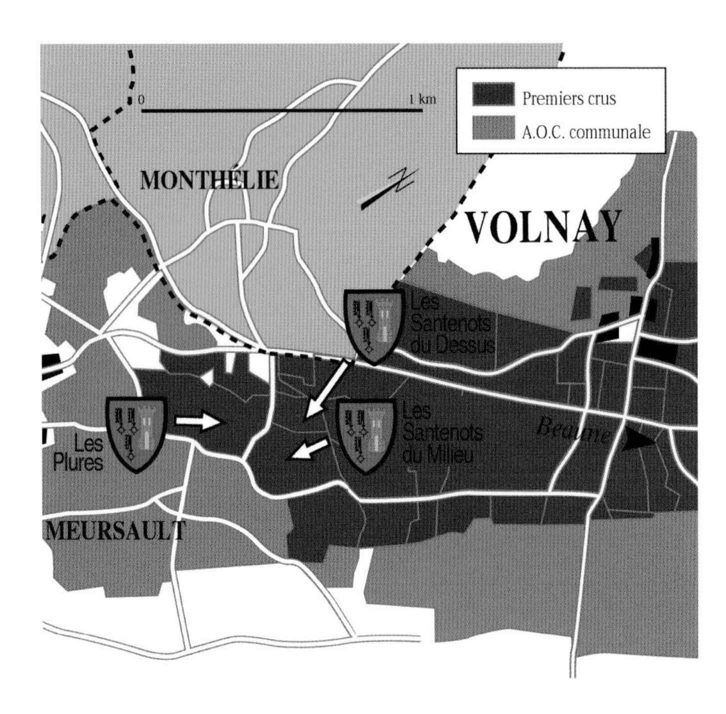

Volnay-Santenots premier cru cuvée Jehan de Massol

Composition: Les Santenots du Dessus (93 ares), Les Santenots du Milieu, Les Plures
Vineyard Area: 1.54 hectare

■ *History*
"Massol" comes from the Italian Mazzoli, the name of a doctor who came from beyond the Alps in the 15th century. The legend tells that he fell in love with Beaune during a journey and decided to settle here. One of the descendants of Augustino Mazzoli, the magistrate Jehan de Massol, would leave his property to the Hospices.

■ *Terroirs*
This is quite simply one of the best "red" *terroirs* of the Côte de Beaune, a parcel where grapes take time to ripen. The reward: an uncommon complexity and purity. The wines grown here also have a suave, pleasing side thanks to the mouthfeel of velvety tannins. This vineyard has the potential of a grand cru.

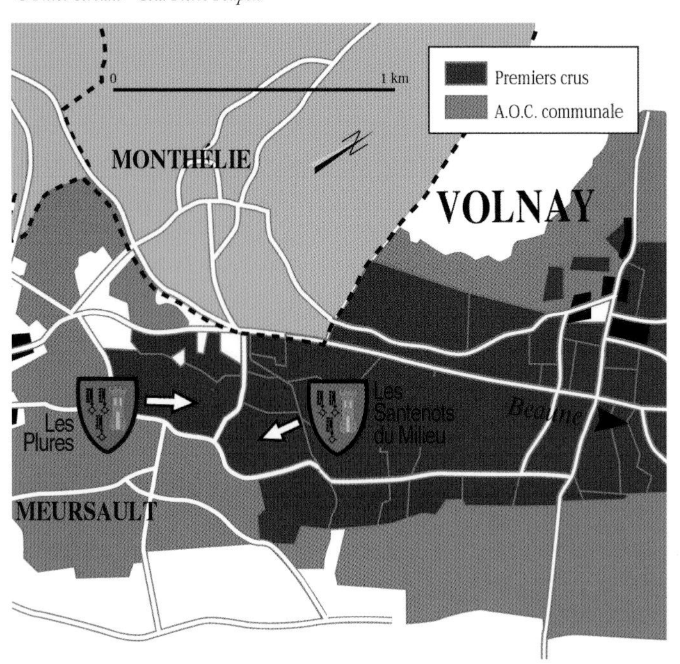

Volnay-Santenots premier cru cuvée Gauvain

Composition: Les Plures, Les Santenots du Milieu
Vineyard Area: 1.4 hectares

■ *History*
The Gauvain family was one of the most generous benefactors of the Hospices de Beaune. In 1804, Bernard Gauvain left all of his belongings to the institution. His widow would later donate one of the grandest residences of Beaune (Place Carnot), which now houses the Federation of Negociants of Burgundy.

■ *Terroirs*
The same prestigious origins as the cuvee "Jehan de Massol" (Les Santenots) and the same level of quality. Here we are in the heart of one of the most auspicious sectors of the entire Côte de Beaune for producing great red wines. The parcel is on the mid-slopes, with a deep soil that is remarkably balanced between limestone and clay. The stones present in the soil ensure its aeration.

Volnay premier cru cuvée Blondeau

Composition: Les Champans, Taille Pieds, En L'Ormeau, En Roncerets
Vineyard Area: 1.81 hectare

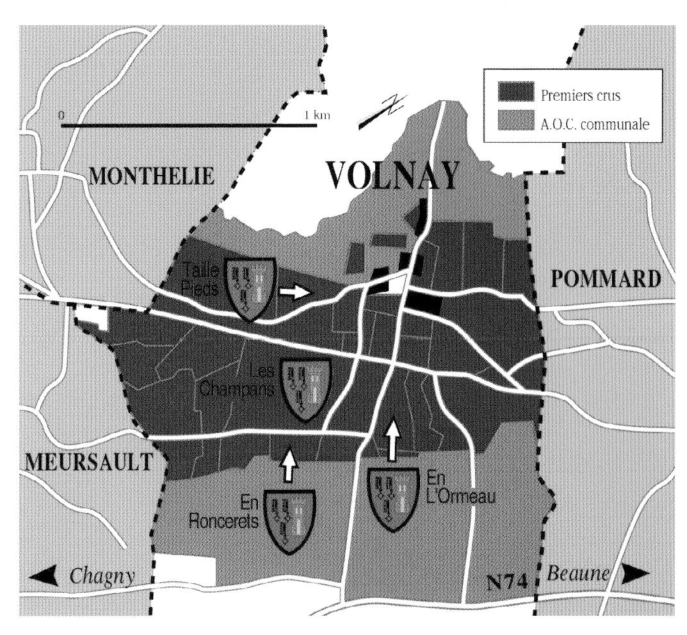

© Pitiot-Servant - Coll. Pierre Poupon

■ *History*

The generosity of François Blondeau is unquestionable: he was nicknamed "the saint of Volnay." He had a school built, the church of Volnay restored, etc. In 1809 he named the Hospices de la Charité as inheritor of his vineyards, hoping thus to ensure the care of five elderly people in perpetuity.

■ *Terroirs*

Two of the best *terroirs* of Volnay are united here (Les Champans and Taille Pieds). Together they represent two thirds of the cuvee. The finesse and generosity of the wines of Volnay are brilliantly displayed here, but without lacking structure.

Volnay premier cru cuvée Général Muteau

Composition: Le Village, Carelles sous Chapelle, Les Fremiets, Taille Pieds, Les Caillerets Dessus
Vineyard Area: 1.69 hectare

© Pitiot-Servant - Coll. Pierre Poupon

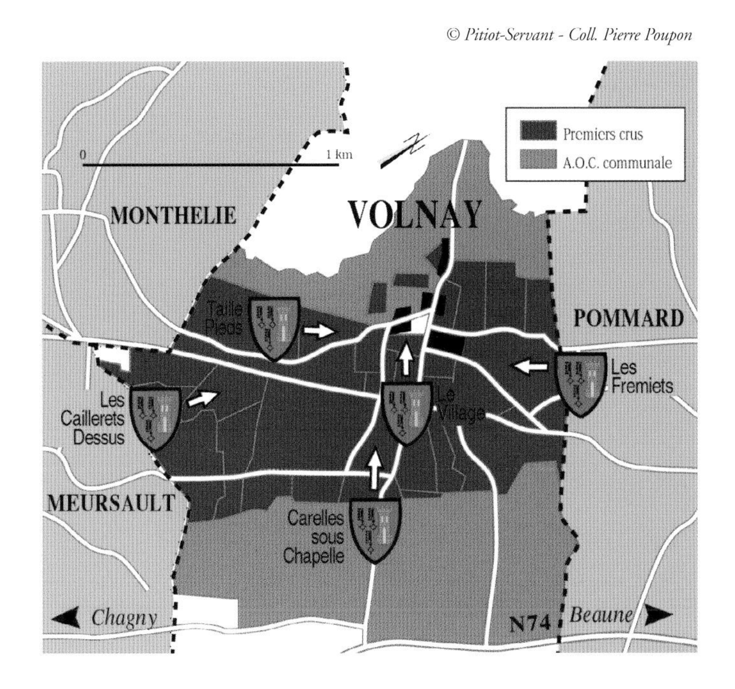

■ *History*

This martial name evokes tragic times in the history of France: the First World War. General Muteau, a native of Chalon-sur-Saône, was an officer under Marshal Foch. Having no children, he left numerous donations to the Hôtel-Dieu on his death.

■ *Terroirs*

This wine is a blend of five premier crus. Despite the scattered nature of the parcels that go into this cuvee, it has the particularity of coming from sites within a relatively small area. Many of them are around the village of Volnay – the name of the dominant parcel (0.77 hectares), Le Village, bears witness. The result is a nicely structured Volnay, sometimes even austere in its youth.

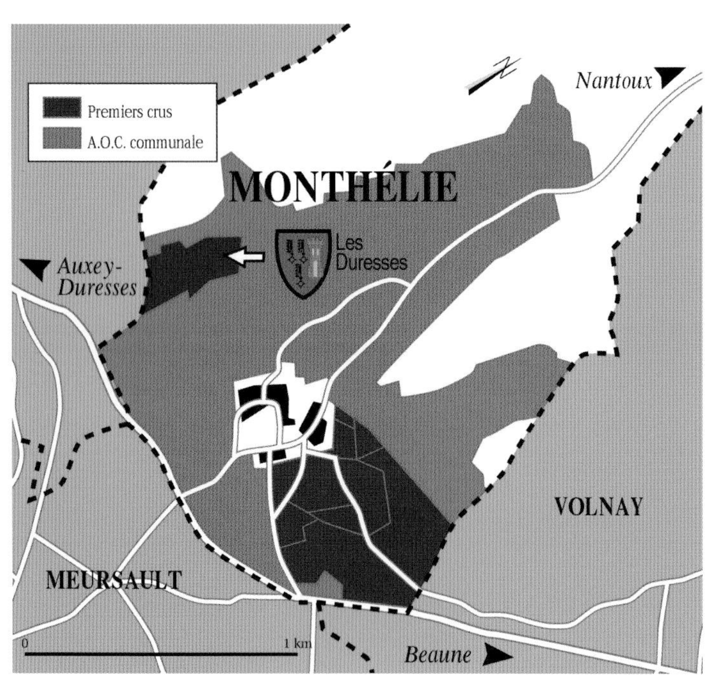

Monthélie premier cru cuvée Lebelin

Composition: Les Duresses
Vineyard Area: 0.89 hectare

■ *History*

Lebelin is one of the names that has marked the history of Beaune. In the 16th century, no less than seven mayors of the town were from this family. A certain Etienne Lebelin, a priest, was the first to preside over the chapel of the Hospices de la Charité in the 17th century. Jean-Jacques and Marguerite Lebelin would donate a large sum in 1704.

■ *Terroir*

Towering over the vineyards of Meursault, Monthélie is one of the picturesque villages that lend such charm to the Côte de Beaune. The vineyards retreat in a combe. There, near the commune of Auxey and enjoying a nearly full southern exposition, is the vineyard of Les Duresses. Despite this favorable exposure, the *terroir* remains cold since it is under the influence of the combe. This vineyard gives delicate wines for medium aging.

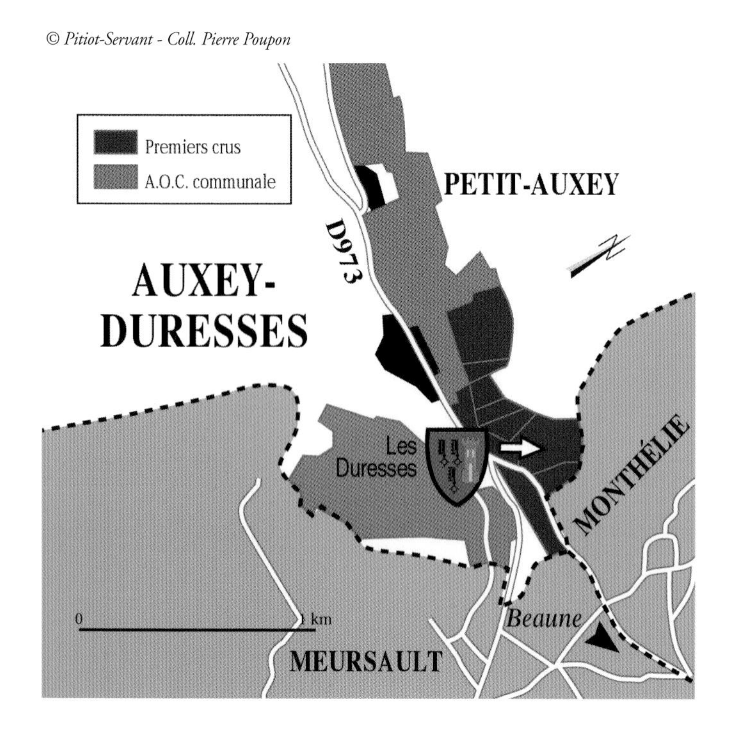

Auxey-Duresses premier cru cuvée Boillot

Composition: Les Duresses
Vineyard Area: 0.66 hectares

■ *History*

In 1898 Antoinette Boillot, having no children, left her family estate to the Hospices de Beaune. It included vineyards in Auxey-Duresses, Meursault, and Volnay, that her husband had worked until his death a few years before. Today it is not uncommon to see the name Boillot among the producers of the Côte de Beaune.

■ *Terroir*

Here again we find the *terroir* Les Duresses, which also gives a cuvee of Monthélie. Continuing deeper into the combe, the vineyard crosses the border of Auxey. In the late 19th century the villagers of Auxey chose this vineyard to add to the name of their commune, a testament to how highly they prized this *terroir*. This wine is generally quite structured, with firm tannins.

THE WHITES

Corton-Vergennes grand cru cuvée Paul Chanson

Composition: Les Vergennes
Vineyard Area: 0.28 hectare

■ *History*

A bon vivant and an indefatigable ambassador of the wines of Burgundy, Paul Chanson was president of the eponymous negociant, which is a historic name in Beaune. He also made a donation, in 1974, of one of his best vineyard plots.

■ *Terroir*

Les Vergennes is its own *terroir*. Planted on the famous hill of Corton, in the heart of a vineyard predominantly planted for red wine production, it gives a very distinct wine. Where Corton-Charlemagne is chiseled and frank, Corton-Vergennes seduces with its opulence and richness. Notes of exotic fruit bring a lively character to the wine.

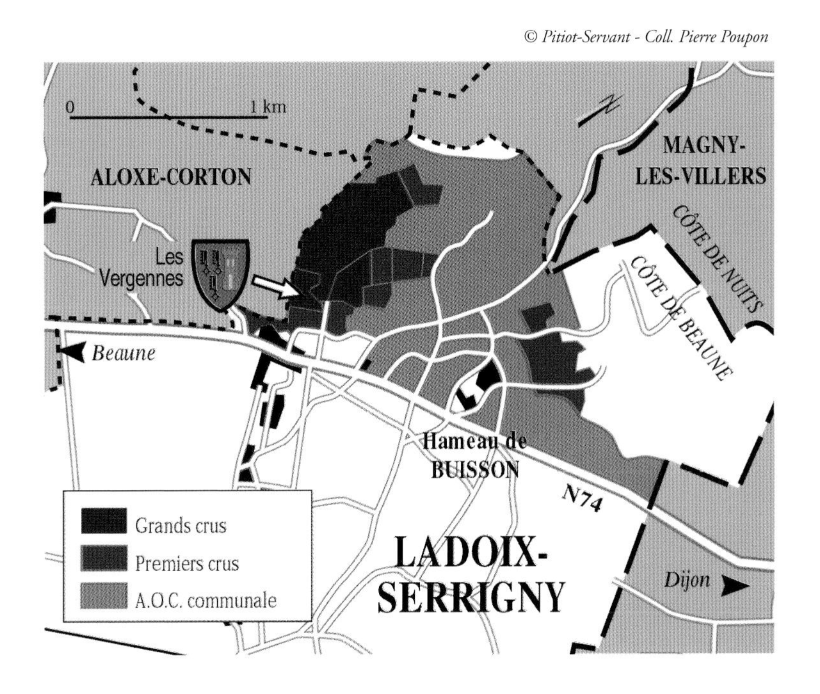

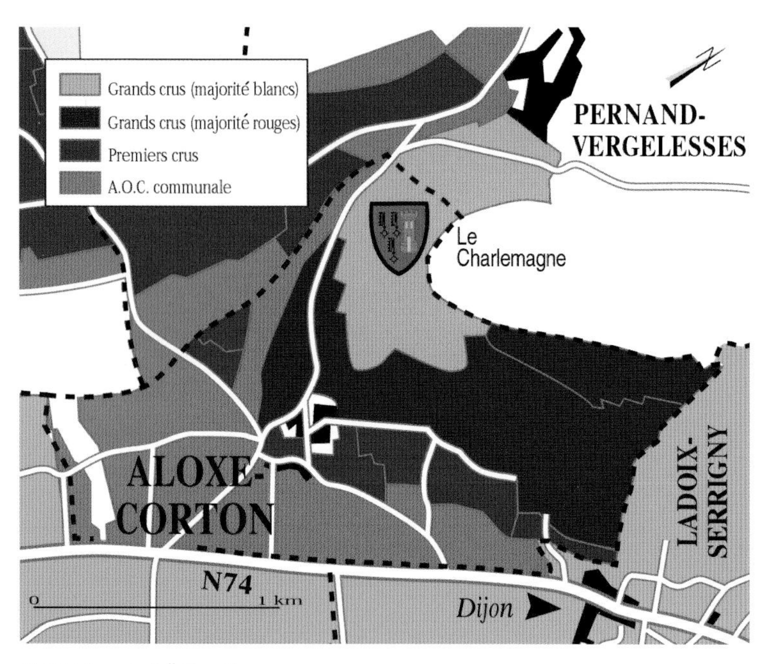

Corton-Charlemagne grand cru cuvée François de Salins

Composition: Le Charlemagne
Vineyard Area: 0.48 hectare

■ *History*

The name of de Salins inevitably evokes the co-founder of the Hospices, Guigone de Salins. Her family would remain a prominent local fixture for centuries to come. For example, a certain Doctor Jean-Baptiste de Salins would manage the Hôtel-Dieu in 1695. François de Salins, a priest and canon at Notre-Dame de Beaune, comes from the same family. In 1745 he made a donation of vineyards in Savigny-lès-Beaune and Aloxe-Corton.

■ *Terroir*

It is the vineyard Le Charlemagne, in the very heart of Corton-Charlemagne, that gives this cuvee. This hillside puffs out its chest to face south. The soil is poor, with a great deal of limestone that gives the wine a wonderful minerality.

Corton-Charlemagne grand cru cuvée Charlotte Dumay

Composition: Les Renardes
Vineyard Area: 0.34 hectares

■ *History*

A parchment dated 1534 in gothic lettering attests to this gift. A certain Charlotte Dumay donated these vineyards in 1584. The cuvee, however, is a recent creation (it first appeared at the auction in 2004). Given its considerable holdings in this vineyard (more than 2 hectares), the Hospices decided to replant one parcel to Chardonnay in 2001.

■ *Terroir*

At the northern end of the Aloxe-Corton appellation, Les Renardes is on the upper slopes of the hill of Corton. The soil is rather lean on this steep slope that sees the first morning rays of sun. All of these characteristics contribute to the outstanding potential of this grand cru. It generally gives a more opulent wine than the cuvee "François de Salins," another Corton-Charlemagne produced by the Hospices.

Saint-Romain cuvée Joseph Menault

Composition: Sous la Velle et Au village
Vineyard Area: 0.75 hectare

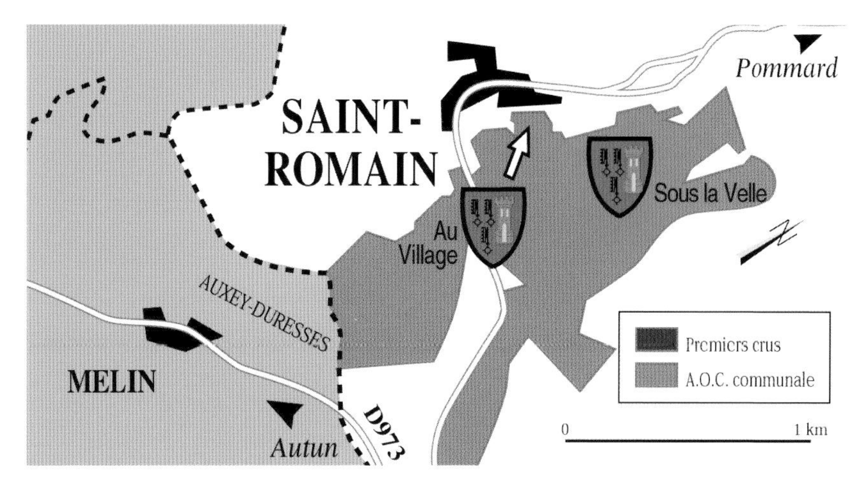

© Pitiot-Servant - Coll. Pierre Poupon

■ *History*
Sold at the auction for the first time in 2009, this cuvee is the newest addition to the lineup of wines produced at the Hospices de Beaune. It carries the name of the man who donated the vineyards: Joseph Menault, a *vigneron* and bachelor from the village of Saint-Romain. The donation was made in 1992, but at that time the vineyards were rented out. The Hospices finally began working them in 2006. The 2006 and 2007 vintages were produced by the Hospices but were not included in the famous auction.

■ *Terroirs*
The spectacular vineyards of Saint-Romain have the particularity of being on the upper slopes of the Côte de Beaune. Their highest point is at about 400 meters in altitude, on a limestone cliff. The result: grapes ripen slowly here, so these vineyards are among the last to be harvested. The wines therefore display freshness and finesse. Planted near the village of Saint-Romain, the two parcels that make up this cuvee have full eastern exposure and enjoy the first rays of the morning sun.

Meursault-Charmes premier cru cuvée Albert Grivault

Composition: Les Charmes Dessus
Vineyard Area: 0.55 hectare

© Pitiot-Servant - Coll. Pierre Poupon

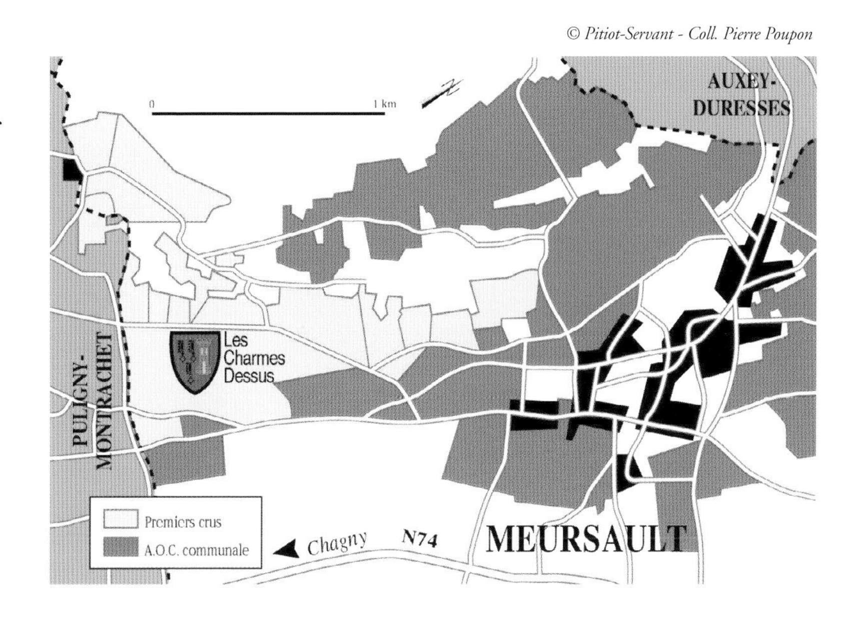

■ *History*
Albert Grivault is a well-known name among enthusiasts of Meursault. The estate of the same name works the Clos des Perrières vineyard, one of the most famous *terroirs* of the appellation. The Hospices has this family to thank for the plot in Les Charmes that has belonged to the estate since 1904.

■ *Terroir*
A gentle slant on the south-facing slopes of Meursault. This is the heart of white wine country. Les Charmes Dessus offers ideal exposition and a rather lean, stony soil. Everything is in place to give an unusually harmonious white wine with great length.

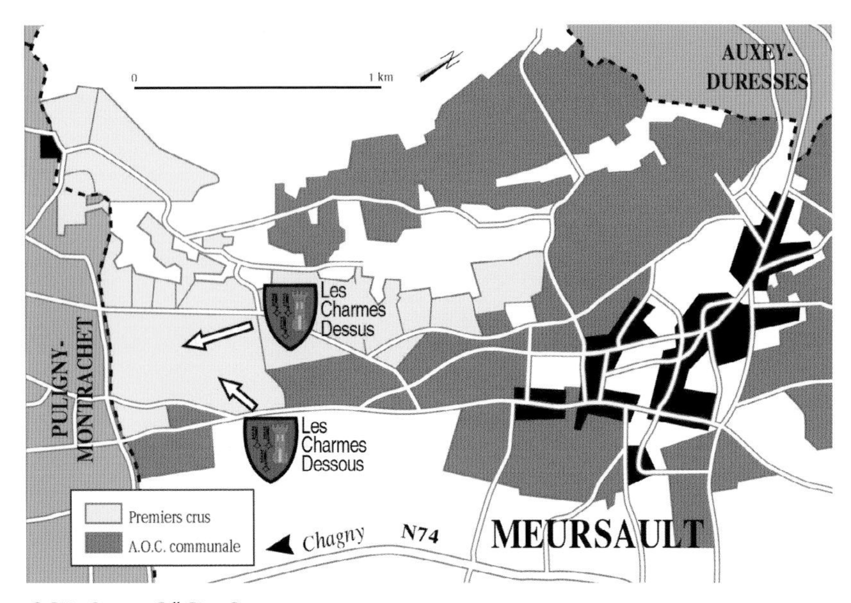

Meursault-Charmes premier cru cuvée de Bahèzre de Lanlay

Composition: Les Charmes Dessus, Les Charmes Dessous
Vineyard Area: 0.88 hectare

■ *History*

His name may not be easy to pronounce, but Louis Bahèzre de Lanlay is remembered by the Hospices as one of its principal benefactors. An inspector of telegraph lines, he was the descendant of a family from Finistère in Brittany. He left his fortune to the Hospices de Beaune in 1884. His brother Emile, also born in Beaune, is another benefactor of the Hospices. Their father had created a respected wine estate with vast vineyard holdings.

■ *Terroirs*

Many of the subtleties of the Burgundian *terroirs* emerge in this cuvee. The upper and lower parts of the premier cru Les Charmes contribute almost equal parts. Les Charmes Dessous (meaning "below") brings a round, rich character to the wine. Les Charmes Dessus (meaning "above"), just a few dozen yards up the hillside, gives finesse and minerality. The cuvee offers a synthesis of these qualities.

Meursault-Genevrières premier cru cuvée Philippe le Bon

Composition: Les Genevrières dessous
Vineyard Area: 0.44 hectare

■ *History*

Philanthropist, friend of the arts, and gastronome, Philip the Good was the duke of Burgundy who made possible the foundation of the Hospices de Beaune in 1443. He and his chancellor, Nicolas Rolin, governed Burgundy for a long and prosperous period.

■ *Terroir*

Once again, we are in the presence of one of the best premier crus of Meursault, known for its delicate wines. The cuvee of the Hospices comes from the dessous or lower part of the vineyard, where the soil is rather thick. The wines are characterized by an uncommon density and length, without ever being heavy. Note that this cuvee will potentially include a parcel of Les Genevrières Dessus, which was torn up in 2006 and therefore will not be in production for a few more years.

Meursault-Genevrières premier cru cuvée Baudot

Composition: Genevrières Dessus, Genevrières Dessous
Vineyard Area: 1,48 hectare

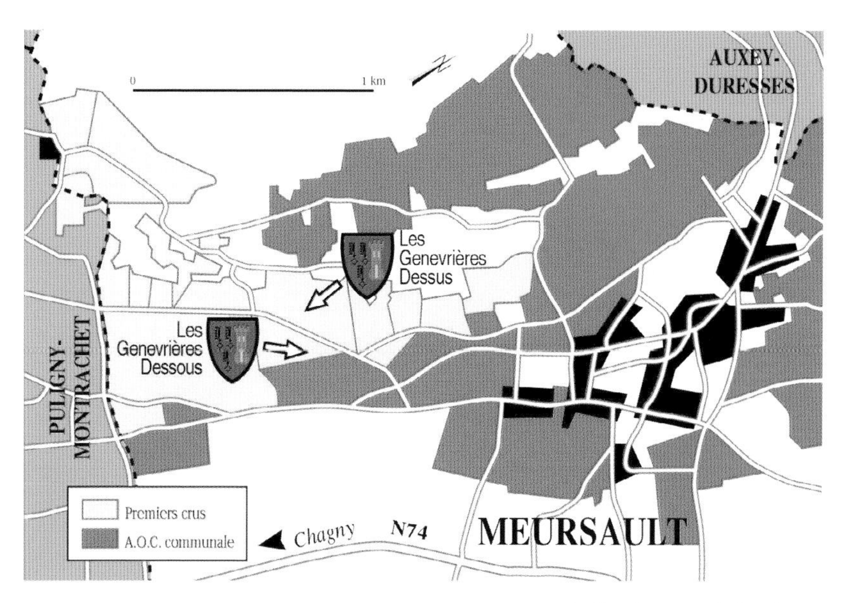

© Pitiot-Servant - Coll. Pierre Poupon

■ *History*

Felix Baudot was an art connoisseur, an atavism since the Baudots, an old parliamentary family of Burgundy, were known for their taste in art and literature. His collection of stained glass, Antique pillars, and other archeological pieces was auctioned off in 1882. According to his wishes, the revenue from the sale went to the Hospices de Beaune.

■ *Terroirs*

The cuvee "Baudot" is to Les Genevrières what the cuvee "Bahèzre de Lanlay" is to Les Charmes: a union of the characteristics found in the upper and lower parts of the vineyard. This parcel is one of the most renowned of Meursault. The two areas give almost equal parts of the cuvee. There is one noteworthy difference from Les Charmes: Les Genevrières is higher on the slopes, giving the wines an outstanding delicacy and elegance.

Meursault-Porusots premier cru cuvée Jehan Humblot

Composition: Les Porusots
Vineyard Area: 0.56 hectare

© Pitiot-Servant - Coll. Pierre Poupon

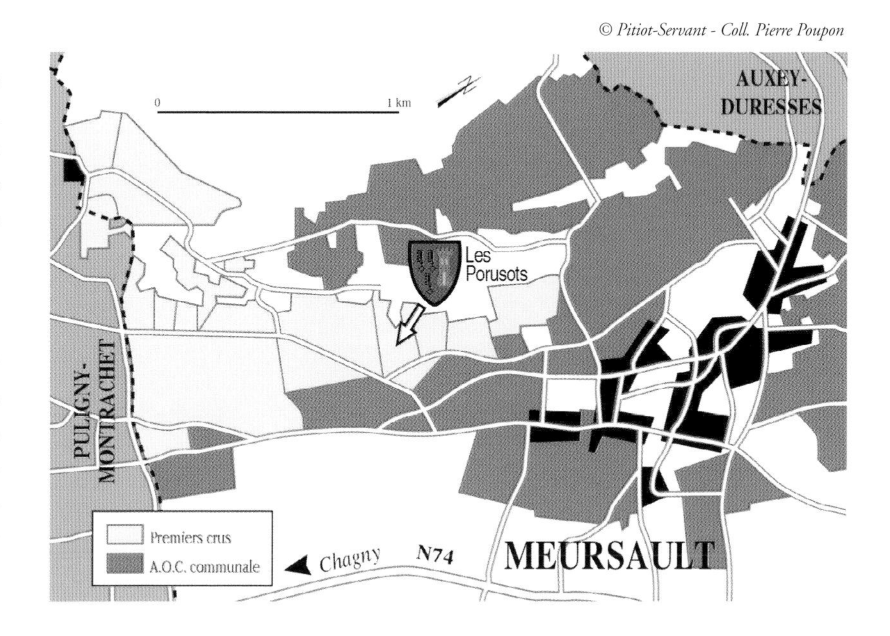

■ *History*

This is one of the oldest white wines of the Hospices de Beaune. It carries the name of a royal attorney and notary who owned a seigneury near Beaune. Having no children, he donated it to the Hospices in 1600. Since 2005, this has been a mono-*terroir* cuvee: only the premier cru Les Porusots is now used in its production.

■ *Terroir*

Just south of the town of Meursault, on a rather steep slope, is the premier cru Les Porusots. The soil here is rather deep and rocky. All of the vines are over 40 years old, and some are even over 70 years. The wine is chiseled, direct, even strict in its youth, characteristics that make it look like a cousin of the Corton-Charlemagne cuvee "François de Salins."

Meursault cuvée Goureau

Composition: Les Porusots, Les Peutes Vignes, Les Grands Charrons
Vineyard Area: 0.56 hectare

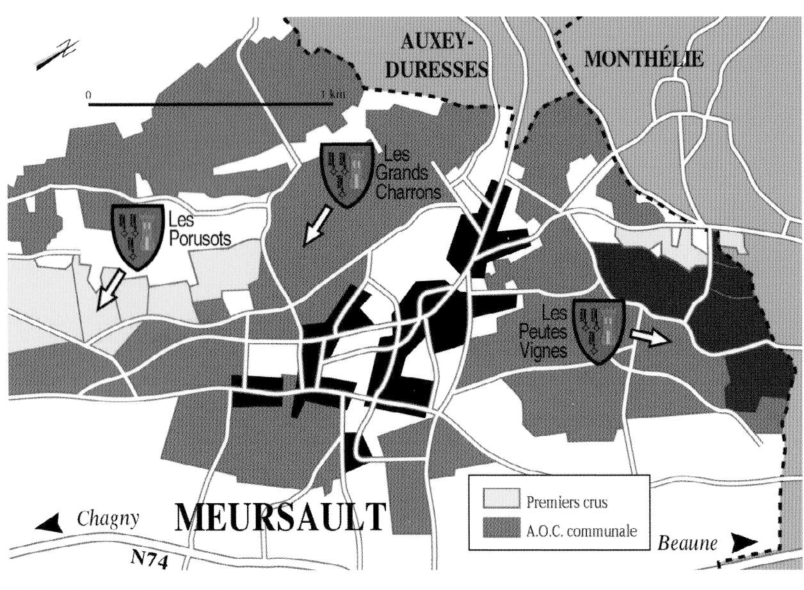

© Pitiot-Servant - Coll. Pierre Poupon

■ *History*

This cuvee carries the name of a benefactor of the Hospice de la Charité (an institution merged with the Hôtel-Dieu after the French Revolution). Mademoiselle Goureau made a gift of several estates located on the plain of Beaune.

■ *Terroirs*

Here again we encounter the premier cru Les Porusots, which is responsible for half of this cuvee. In fact, this plot is immediately adjacent to the one that gives the cuvee "Humblot." These two cuvees therefore share a common characteristic: a certain austerity. Nevertheless, the vineyard Les Peutes Vignes, in the northern part of the appellation on a generous soil, brings great opulence to this cuvee.

Meursault cuvée Loppin

Composition: Les Criots, Les Cras.
Vineyard Area: 0.4 hectare

© Pitiot-Servant - Coll. Pierre Poupon

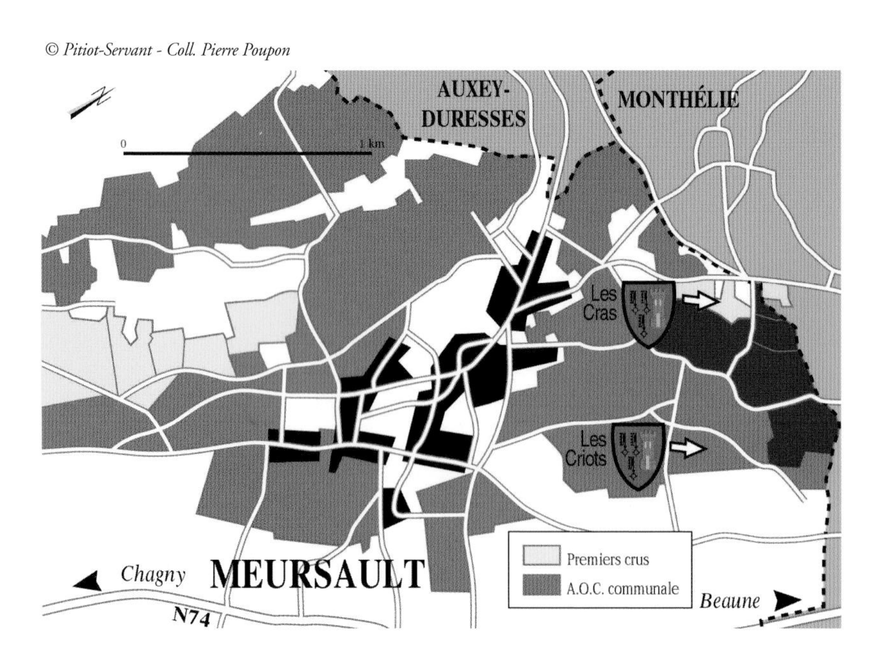

■ *History*

The name of Loppin can be found several times in the index of donors to the Hospices de Beaune. They were an important local family. A certain Jéhan Loppin was archdeacon of the collegiate church of Beaune in 1656. He welcomed a young king to Beaune, the 20-year-old Louis XIV who was on his way to Lyons. During his stay the king visited the Hôtel-Dieu, which is why the "King's Chamber" there is so named.

■ *Terroirs*

Officially this cuvee is in a village appellation, but about half of the contributing vineyards are classified premier crus (Les Cras). This proportion was achieved recently when some vines in the other vineyard, Les Criots, were torn up. These vines were replanted in 2009. Regardless of their classification, these two *terroirs* gives excellent Meursaults that are more delicate than opulent.

Bâtard-Montrachet grand cru cuvée Dames de Flandres

Vineyard Area: 0.29 hectare

© Pitiot-Servant - Coll. Pierre Poupon

History

With this cuvee, the Hospices de Beaune has a foothold in the "Who's Who" of Burgundy's best dry white wines. This is one of the vineyards purchased by the institution (in 1989). Its name, meaning "Women of Flanders," is a tribute to the first nuns who cared for the sick at the Hôtel-Dieu. This cuvee has drawn record bids at the auction, going for about 5,000€ per barrel on average, or 165€ per bottle (not including taxes or the cost of bottling).

Terroir

Situated just below his big brother Le Montrachet, Le Bâtard-Montrachet lies midway up the hillside on a gentle slope. The vineyards of the Hospices are in the upper part of the appellation, where the earth is thick and the light slope allows for good drainage. The very old vines here produce small grapes, and yields are very low. All of these elements explain why tasting this cuvee is always an event.

Pouilly-Fuissé cuvée Françoise Poisard

Composition: Les Plessys, Les Robées, Les Chevrières
Vineyard Area: 1.41 hectare

History

This recent donation (1994) allowed the Hospices de Beaune to gain a foothold in the Mâconnais, the southern zone of Burgundy. They started at the top: these vineyards are in Pouilly-Fuissé, the most prestigious sector of the appellation. Françoise Poisard's donation also included fields and two houses.

Terroir

These are the southernmost vineyards of the estate of the Hospices de Beaune, more than 55 miles from the winery. This meridional position explains why they are the first to be harvested. This cuvee consists of three parcels in the commune of Chaintré, where the soils and exposures are varied. This Pouilly-Fuissé is often rather opulent (more than average for the appellation) yet with a certain mineral severity when young. This wine ages beautifully.

© Pitiot-Servant - Coll. Pierre Poupon

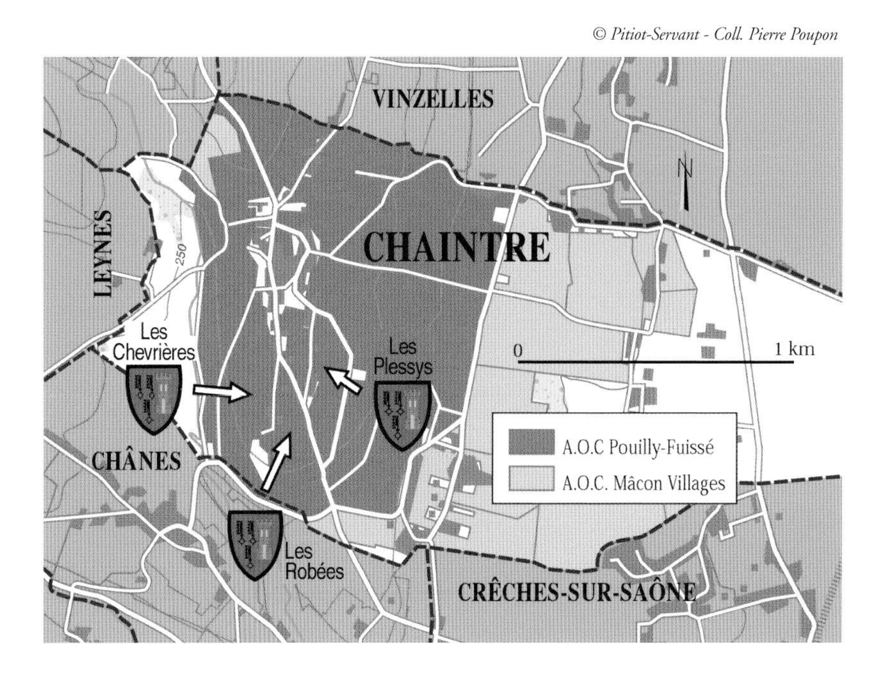

Tasting Notes

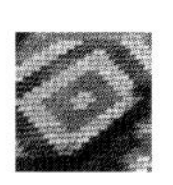

Chapter 6

Double previous page:
A walled vineyard in the southern part of the Beaune appellation.

Left page:
Winter light on the vineyard trellising.

THE REDS

Mazis-Chambertin grand cru cuvée Madeleine Collignon

Mazis hauts

Vintage tasted 2004

A fresh fruit profile featuring redcurrant aromas rises out of the glass. A vegetal note typical of the vintage is present without dominating. Distinguished, structured tannins on the palate. This Mazis-Chambertin is direct, with a good backbone. Quite a success for this difficult vintage.

Maison Michel Picard
Château de Chassagne
21190 Chassagne-Montrachet
Phone: (+33) (0)3 80 21 98 57
www.michelpicard.com

Clos de la Roche grand cru cuvée Cyrot-Chaudron

Les Froichots

Vintage tasted 2002

A deep, brilliant ruby color. The complex nose of blackberry and cherry is pure and intense. A svelte, fresh, fruity wine that gradually unfurls on the palate. The tight tannins on the finish invite a few more years of cellaring.

Vintage tasted 2004

Notes of blackberry jelly are followed by a floral touch on the complex nose. The mouthfeel is silky, with more finesse than power. All in all, a well-made grand cru despite the difficult vintage.

"Réserve Particulière" of the Hospices de Beaune

Clos de la Roche grand cru cuvée Georges Kritter

Les Froichots

Vintage tasted 2001

Nice aromatic complexity: fresh fruit notes are supported by a delicate oakiness. The concentration is worthy of a great vintage, but the tannins are delicate. A streak of acidity brings vigor and length. An elegant wine that is developing serenely. Drink in 4-5 years.

Maison Patriarche
5 - 7, rue du Collège
21200 Beaune
Phone: (+33) (0)3 80 24 53 01
www.patriarche.com

Corton grand cru cuvée Docteur Peste
Les Chaumes et la Voierosses, Les Bressandes, Les Grèves, Les Fiètres

Vintage tasted 2005
A complex, intense perfume of black fruit. The nose becomes more pure and expansive with aeration, indicating that this wine deserves to be aged. On the palate, the mellow yet concentrated tannins are braced by a nice vivacity. A dense, solid wine that needs another ten years.

Pierre André
Château de Corton André
21420 Aloxe-Corton
Phone: (+33) (0)3 80 25 00 00
www.pierre-andre.com

Corton grand cru cuvée Charlotte Dumay
Les Renardes, Les Bressandes

Vintage tasted 2005
A gourmand wine from start to finish. The superb nose features violet aromas and both fresh and overripe fruit. The palate is nice and full but shows more length than density.

"Réserve Particulière" of the Hospices de Beaune

Pernand-Vergelesses cuvée Rameau-Lamarosse
Les Basses-Vergelesses

Vintage tasted 1994
Brick red. Persistent oak and a slightly gamey note confirm that this wine is quite evolved (the vintage was difficult). The palate is nicely concentrated, with firm tannins. The wine seems already to have given its best.

"Réserve Particulière" of the Hospices de Beaune

Savigny-lès-Beaune premier cru cuvée Arthur Girard
Les Peuillets

Vintage tasted 2007
The intense fruit character on the nose suggests that these grapes were quite ripe. The tender palate is girded by crisp, delicate tannins. The wine exudes elegance and distinction. While it is showing well now, it will continue to develop for another 3-4 years.

"Réserve Particulière" of the Hospices de Beaune

Savigny-lès-Beaune premier cru cuvée Forneret
Les Vergelesses, Les Gravains

Vintage tasted 2001
The color shows a hint of evolution but is still a relatively bright ruby red. Candied red berries are accompanied by a hint of underbrush on the nose. The palate is round and soft. A nice wine to drink today and through the early 2010s.

Champy
5, rue du Grenier à sel
21200 Beaune
Phone: (+33) (0)3 80 25 09 99
www.champy.com

Beaune premier cru cuvée Guigone de Salins
Les Bressandes, Les Seurey, Champs Pimont

Vintage tasted 2003
Ripe cherry aromas greet the nose. With aeration a floral note emerges (peony, rose). Extremely suave tannins are softened by the natural sweetness of the vintage. Yet the wine is not heavy. A great pleasure to drink, it is drinking well today but has all the elements necessary to age gracefully.

Michel Picard
Château de Chassagne
21190 Chassagne-Montrachet
Phone: (+33) (0)3 80 21 98 57
www.michelpicard.com

Beaune premier cru cuvée Nicolas Rolin
Les Cents Vignes, En Genêt, Les Bressandes, Les Grèves, Les Teurons

Vintage tasted 2006
A complex nose evokes red berry coulis. A hint of oaky vanilla and some wild notes come out with aeration. The tannins are rather firm, but it is the wine's full, fresh character that carries it.

Albert Bichot
6, boulevard Jacques Copeau
21200 Beaune
Phone: (+33) (0)3 80 24 37 37
www.bichot.com

Joseph Drouhin
7 rue d'Enfer
21200 Beaune
Tel. 03 80 24 68 88
www.drouhin.com

Beaune premier cru cuvée Dames Hospitalières

Les Bressandes, La Mignotte, Les Teurons

Vintage tasted 1999

A surprisingly youthful color – still a brilliant ruby after ten years. Ripe cherry aromas mingle with underbrush on the nose. The palate is expressive and dense. A pronounced oaky note makes the finish a bit tight.

Louis Latour
18, rue des Tonneliers
21204 Beaune
Phone: (+33) (0)3 80 24 81 10
www.louislatour.com

Beaune premier cru cuvée Clos des Avaux

Clos des Avaux

Vintage tasted 2002

An intense, expressive nose. With aeration it yields aromas of cherry pits, underbrush, and spices. Silky tannins. A concentrated wine that nevertheless shows finesse and harmony.

Champy
5, rue du Grenier à sel
21200 Beaune
Phone: (+33) (0)3 80 25 09 99
www.champy.com

Beaune premier cru cuvée Maurice Drouhin

Les Avaux, Les Grèves, Champs Pimonts, Les Boucherottes.

Vintage tasted 2005

This wine's illustrious origins are obvious from the first whiff. The nose features deep, alluring notes of black fruit, all with the nice ripeness typical of this vintage. The tannins are tight and dense without being aggressive. A suave finish with a note of licorice. A clean, deep, and unusually concentrated wine.

Beaune premier cru cuvée Hugues et Louis Bétault

Les Grèves, Clos des Mouches, Les Aigrots, La Mignotte

Vintage tasted 2006

This wine is a true delicacy and might be considered one of the great achievements of the vintage. A deep, intense nose with notes of fresh blackberry. Suave tannins. The long finish shows notes of licorice.

Dufouleur Frères
Au Château, 1 rue de Dijon
BP5 - 21700 Nuits-Saint-Georges
Phone: (+33) (0)3 80 61 00 26
www.dufouleur-freres.com

Beaune premier cru cuvée Cyrot-Chaudron

Les Montrevenots

Vintage tasted 2001

A beautiful, deep color with glints approaching an evolved brick red. The nose has a roasted quality but the aromas are quite present. Good structure and firm tannins on the palate.

Albert Bichot
6, boulevard Jacques Copeau
21200 Beaune
Phone: (+33) (0)3 80 24 37 37
www.bichot.com

Beaune premier cru cuvée Brunet

Les Bressandes, Les Cents Vignes, Le Bas des Teurons

Vintage tasted 2003

The generosity of this vintage is evident. Aromas of overripe fruits suggest prunes and even figs. Harmonious and well balanced even though the wine does not fully show the typicity of Burgundy. Suave and gourmand.

Bouchard Père et fils
Rue du Château
21200 Beaune
Phone: (+33) (0)3 80 24 80 24
www.bouchard-pereetfils.com

Beaune cuvée Rousseau-Deslandes

Les Cent Vignes, Les Montrevenots, La Mignotte

Vintage tasted 2005

A wine of great elegance and finesse. The nose shows floral notes (peony) along with a hint of vanilla. The tight tannins are a bit firm on the finish. A harmonious, generously aromatic wine. Still young, it should age for at least another 5 years.

Louis Latour
18, rue des Tonneliers
21204 Beaune
Phone: (+33) (0)3 80 24 81 10
www.louislatour.com

Pommard premier cru cuvée Dames de la Charité

Les Petits Épenots, Les Combes Dessus, La Refène, Les Rugiens Bas, Les Rugiens Hauts

Vintage tasted 2002

This classy, voluptuous wine seduces from start to finish. Aromas of candied cherries with a hint of vanilla delight the nose. The dense, slightly firm palate is complemented by fleshy tannins.

"Réserve Particulière" of the Hospices de Beaune

Pommard cuvée Raymond Cyrot

Les Charmots, Les Riottes, Les Rugiens Bas, Les Bertins, La Vache, Les Vaumuriens Bas

Vintage tasted 2005

A robust wine with tight tannins, just as you generally expect from a Pommard. Dense and solid, but still quite harmonious. Smoky aromas on the nose. Needs at least 5 more years aging.

Pommard cuvée Billardet

Les Arvelets, Les Noizons, Les Cras

Vintage tasted 2003

The intensity and heat of the vintage have been tamed in this wine. The nose is expressive and ripe but retains a certain aromatic freshness. On the palate the tannins are fine and velvety. Long and suave. A success.

Bouchard Ainé et fils
4, boulevard Maréchal Foch
21200 Beaune
Phone: (+33) (0)3 80 24 24 00
www.bouchard-aine.fr

Pommard cuvée Suzanne Chaudron

Les Petits Noizons, La Chanière, Les Noizons, Les Petits Épenots, La Croix Planet, En Poisot, Rue au Port

Vintage tasted 2006

An intense nose of blackberry jelly, with floral notes adding to the complexity of this first impression. A strong tannic backbone and great concentration on the palate. The finish is tight and firm.

Dufouleur Frères
Au Château - 1 rue de Dijon
BP5 - 21700 Nuits-Saint-Georges
Phone: (+33) (0)3 80 61 00 26
www.dufouleur-freres.com

Pommard premier cru Épenots cuvée Dom Goblet

Les Petis Épenots

Vintage tasted 2007

An old expression claims that the wines of Burgundy unfurl on the palate like a peacock's tail. That comparison works perfectly for this Pommard, which fills the mouth with a caressing touch and beautifully pure aromas. This cuvee is one of the great triumphs of the vintage.

"Réserve Particulière" of the Hospices de Beaune

Volnay premier cru Santenots cuvée Jehan de Massol

Santenots du Dessus, Santenots du Milieu, Les Plures

Vintage tasted 2006

Wild black fruit and a hint of chocolate on the nose. A dense mat of mellow tannins coats the mouth. A nice stroke of acidity and a very long finish. Dense and vigorous.

Bouchard Père et Fils
Rue du Château
21200 Beaune
Phone: (+33) (0)3 80 24 80 24
www.bouchard-pereetfils.com

Volnay premier cru Santenots cuvée Gauvain

Les Plures, Santenots du Milieu

Vintage tasted 2005

Complexity and intensity from start to finish. Pleasant notes of rose and peony on the nose. On the palate supple tannins repose against a tense, vigorous foundation. A cellaring wine to be opened through 2015.

Champy
5, rue du Grenier à sel
21200 Beaune
Phone: (+33) (0)3 80 25 09 99
www.champy.com

Volnay premier cru cuvée Blondeau

Les Champans, En Taille Pieds, En L'Ormeau, En Roncerets

Vintage tasted 2003

The nose seduces with notes of black fruit coulis (blackcurrant) and a nice intensity. The palate is a bit more serious, with dense, firm tannins. A good cellaring wine to drink around 2012.

Bouchard Ainé et fils
4, boulevard Maréchal Foch
21200 Beaune
Phone: (+33) (0)3 80 24 24 00
www.bouchard-aine.fr

Volnay premier cru cuvée Général Muteau

Le Village, Carelle sous Chapelle, Les Fremiets, Taille Pieds, Les Caillerets Dessus

Vintage tasted 2002

There is no heavy artillery in this wine; it shows harmony and elegance from start to finish. Notes of very ripe cherries bloom on the nose. The full-bodied palate is blanketed in round tannins. Drinking well now.

Louis Jadot
Rue Eugène Spuller
21200 Beaune
Phone: (+33) (0)3 80 22 10 57
www.louisjadot.com

Monthélie premier cru cuvée Lebelin

Les Duresses

Vintage tasted 1999

A deep color. Notes of fresh leather rise to the nose. Fine tannins and a concentrated mouthfeel. A touch of chocolate on the finish brings the wine a certain bearing. Drink now.

"Réserve Particulière" of the Hospices de Beaune

Auxey-Duresses premier cru cuvée Boillot

Les Duresses

Vintage tasted 2006

The superb nose is immediately seductive with its unrestrained expression of red berries. Full, robust tannins. A generous wine with plenty of character. Drink through 2015.

Pierre André
Château de Corton André
21420 Aloxe-Corton
Phone: (+33) (0)3 80 25 00 00
www.pierre-andre.com

THE WHITES

Corton-Vergennes grand cru cuvée Paul Chanson

Les Vergennes

Vintage tasted 1999

Notes of ripe, almost exotic fruit on the nose attest to the vigor of this wine despite its age. Remarkably full-bodied. A mineral finish with a flinty tone concludes the tasting. A powerful, gourmand wine.

Chanson Père et Fils
10, rue Paul Chanson
21200 Beaune
Phone: (+33) (0)3 80 25 97 97
www.vins-chanson.com

Corton-Charlemagne grand cru cuvée François de Salins

Le Charlemagne

Vintage tasted 2004

This wine's greatness is clear right from the first whiff. Very pure citrus notes (mainly lemon), and the palate follows in the same delicate, crystalline spirit. The finish is exceptionally long. The expression of the *terroir* is unmistakable. A very great white Burgundy.

Bouchard Père et Fils
Rue du Château
21200 Beaune
Phone: (+33) (0)3 80 24 80 24
www.bouchard-pereetfils.com

Saint-Romain cuvée Joseph Menault

Sous la Velle et Au cillage

Vintage tasted 2006

This vintage gave many powerful, expressive whites. This is the case for this cuvee that evokes overripe white fruit (peach) on the nose. The palate is supple and opulent. This Saint-Romain is "muscular," or at least more structured than is generally the case in this appellation.

Vintage tasted 2007

Superb notes of honeysuckle greet the nose. A vanilla touch imparted by the *elevage* in barrel assures great complexity. Brilliance, purity, and freshness join forces on the palate. To find a Saint-Romain of this caliber is an excellent surprise, especially from such a complicated vintage.

"Réserve Particulière" of the Hospices de Beaune

Meursault-Charmes premier cru cuvée Albert Grivault

Les Charmes Dessus

Vintage tasted 2002

An evolved nose with cinnamon and roasted apples. The palate is well balanced, with a fine and delicate mouthfeel.

Louis Jadot
Rue Eugène Spuller
21200 Beaune
Phone: (+33) (0)3 80 22 10 57
www.louisjadot.com

Meursault-Charmes premier cru cuvée Bahèzre de Lanlay

Les Charmes Dessus, Les Charmes Dessous

Vintage tasted 2005

As is typical of the highly concentrated reds produced in 2005, this wine needs time to become more refined and to unleash its ripe fruit notes. The palate shows a nice balance between substance and freshness. A long finish.

Pierre André
Château de Corton André
21420 Aloxe-Corton
Phone: (+33) (0)3 80 25 00 00
www.pierre -andre.com

Meursault-Genevrières premier cru cuvée Philippe le Bon

Les Genevrières Dessous

Vintage tasted 2004

A precise, vigorous wine from start to finish. The nose, which is a bit restrained at the moment, features notes of citrus zest. The

palate shows more finesse than body but leaves a pleasant sensation of energy. To be cellared until at least 2012.

Bouchard Père et Fils
Rue du Château
21200 Beaune
Phone: (+33) (0)3 80 24 80 24
www.bouchard-pereetfils.com

Meursault-Genevrières premier cru cuvée Baudot

Genevrières Dessus, Genevrières Dessous

Vintage tasted 2006
A very classy bouquet. Delicate notes of white flowers mingle with well-integrated oak and vanilla. Harmonious on the palate. A delicate, satiny mouthfeel supported by a nice minerality. A distinguished wine.

Domaines et Saveurs Collection
(*elevage* by Méo-Camuzet Frère et Sœurs)
165, route de Dijon
21200 Beaune
Phone: (+33) (0)3 80 22 58 16
www.ds-collection.com

Meursault cuvée Goureau

Les Porusots, Les Peutes Vignes, Les Grands Charrons

Vintage tasted 2006
Very pure notes of citrus rind on the nose. The palate, unctuous and mineral at the same time, slowly reveals its power. Promising on the whole, but it needs time to mellow out and become more spontaneously charming. A cellaring wine.

Albert Bichot
6, boulevard Jacques Copeau
21200 Beaune
Phone: (+33) (0)3 80 24 37 37
www.bichot.com

Meursault cuvée Loppin

Les Criots, Les Cras

Vintage tasted 2004
Roasted notes of coffee and toast mark the nose. The palate is full and gourmand. An unctuous, opulent wine to enjoy now.

Michel Picard
Château de Chassagne
21190 Chassagne-Montrachet
Phone: (+33) (0)3 80 21 98 57
www.michelpicard.com

Bâtard-Montrachet grand cru cuvée Dames de Flandres

Vintage tasted 2005
White wines can occasionally have an almost tannic finish, which is the case in this Bâtard-Montrachet. Deep notes of candied grapes dominate the nose. A bit austere on the whole, but with an exceptional density. This perfect archetype of the appellation needs another ten years of aging.

Michel Picard
Château de Chassagne
21190 Chassagne-Montrachet
Phone: (+33) (0)3 80 21 98 57
www.michelpicard.com

Pouilly-Fuissé cuvée Françoise Poisard

Les Plessys, Les Robées, Le Chevrières

Vintage tasted 2006
This wine perfectly expresses the qualities of its vintage and appellation: the mouthfeel is creamy and unctuous. The nose presents aromas of yellow fruit, acacia flower, and the peach notes that are typical to the whites of the Mâconnais. Full-bodied. A true delicacy.

Albert Bichot
6, boulevard Jacques Copeau
21200 Beaune
Phone: (+33) (0)3 80 24 37 37
www.bichot.com

PRACTICAL INFORMATION

WHERE TO BUY THE WINES OF THE HOSPICES DE BEAUNE

At the Auction

There are two ways to acquire wines of the Hospices de Beaune during the annual auction (the third Sunday of November). Firstly, by going through a negociant that regularly bids (see "Tastings" for contact information); the company will take a purchase order specifying the cuvee desired and the maximum to bid. Secondly, by contacting the auction house directly (Christie's since 2005).

In both cases a lot is comprised of a minimum of one *pièce* or barrel, or a little more than 300 bottles. Certain negociants offer to group potential buyers together for the same cuvee, allowing their clients to buy just half of a *pièce*. Christie's advises individuals who wish to purchase smaller volumes of wine to register jointly with friends or family members. Bids may be placed by telephone or online, on the condition that the bidder has registered ahead of time.

The auction lasts throughout the afternoon (starting at 2:30pm) and into the early evening. The wines are sold in series (several barrels of a single cuvee). The winning bidder decides the number of barrels he wishes to purchase, anywhere from a single one to the entire series (sometimes as much as ten barrels). Any remaining barrels are immediately put up for auction until the entire series has been sold.

Regardless of how the wine is purchased, it must complete its *élevage* in barrel for another 12-20 months. If a cuvee is purchased through a negociant, that winery will naturally be responsible for the aging (beginning no later than the January 15th following the auction) and bottling. If the buyer contacted the auction house directly, Christie's will direct him or her to one of the negociants (preferably a winery that purchased other barrels of the same cuvee). It is advisable to find out about the costs of *élevage* and bottling from several companies beforehand, as each one has its own policy in this matter.

Retail

The negociants that regularly buy wines at the auction of the Hospices generally propose a small selection of bottled Hospices wines (see “Tasting”).

The wines of the Hospices are regularly presented at wine fairs for high-volume distribution. Major French supermarket chains such as Leclerc, Intermarché, Système U, and Cora are usually among these buyers.

Several retail shops in Beaune also permit individuals to leave with a “souvenir” to taste, such as:
- the gift shop at the Hôtel-Dieu;
- L’Athenaeum;
- Le Marché aux Vins;
- the display cellars of la Reine Pédauque;
- Jean-Luc et Paul Aergerter.

Online, two sites propose wines of the Hospices de Beaune throughout the year:

- Hospices de Bourgogne: www.hospicesdebourgogne.com
- L’Athenaeum: www.athenaeumfr.com

The Prices

Prestige and charity generally dictate that the wines of the Hospices de Beaune be sold at higher prices than equivalent appellations from most other local estates and negociants. It is possible, however, to get quite a good price at the auction. For example, in 2005 – an excellent vintage – the Beaune cuvee “Nicolas Rolin” sold for an average of 2,600 euros per barrel or only 9 euros a bottle. Moreover, the estate proposes a wide range of wines, including some appellations that are relatively unknown to the general public and therefore proportionately less expensive than certain famous names. A bottle of wine from the Hospices de Beaune can just as easily cost under 30 euros retail (Monthelie, Saint-Romain, etc.) as over 300 euros (Bâtard-Montrachet, Mazis-Chambertin), depending on the vintage.

THE FESTIVITIES

Tastings

In addition to the street fair that takes place, numerous tastings and wine tourism activities are held in Beaune on the weekend of the auction of the Hospices.

Hospices de Beaune
The public tasting of the Hospices wines takes place in the old cellar (behind the Hôtel-Dieu). It is open Saturday from 8:30-9:30am and from 2-3:00pm, and Sunday from 8:30-9:30am. Paid entry.
www.hospicesdebeaune.com

General Exposition of Wines
The Viticultural Committee of the Côte d’Or brings together winemakers from throughout Burgundy for a tasting of the current year’s wines as well as a few wines already in bottle. Saturday and Sunday mornings at the Palais de Congrès in Beaune. Paid Entry.

Patriarche Père et Fils
This estate proposes a tasting of about a dozen wines, including older vintages. On the menu: cuvees of the Hospices de Beaune and house wines. Saturday and Sunday. Paid entry.
www.patriarche.com

Caves des Cordeliers
Just a few feet from the Hôtel-Dieu, this cellar built into an 18th-century convent proposes a tasting of prestigious appellations, including wines of the Hospices. Paid entry.

Bouchard Ainé et Fils
This estate proposes a “Tour of the Five Senses,” which presents a playful introduction to the secrets of wine tasting, including a chance to practice on a dozen wines, including older vintages. Paid entry.
www.bouchard-aine.fr

The Display Cellar of La Reine Pédauque
This estate was a pioneer in receiving the public in Beaune. All weekend, it proposes a tasting of a dozen wines, including cuvees from the Hospices de Beaune and old – or even very old – vintages from the house cellars. Paid entry.
www.reine-pedauque.com

Maison Champy Père et Fils
This estate presents a tasting of the wines of the Hospices de Beaune as well as a few samples of its own production. Saturday all day and Sunday morning. Paid entry.
www.champy.com

Marché aux Vins
This cellar, established more than thirty years ago just a few steps away from the Hôtel-Dieu, proposes tastings rich in older vintages. Saturday and Sunday. Paid entry.

Practical Information

Where to Stay and Eat:
The weekend of the wine auction is the event of the year in Beaune. Many locals like to have house guests at this time of year. The auction also draws many visitors (even if access to the auction hall is reserved for buyers). The town is relatively small (23,000 residents) compared to its fame, and its capacity to accommodate visitors is limited. It is advisable to book hotels (especially) and restaurants well in advance.

Getting Around
The center of town is closed to traffic on Sunday. Parking is available along the circular boulevard surrounding the old city and in parking lots just outside of the center of town.

Tourist Information
The Tourist Information Center of Beaune
www.beaune-tourisme.fr

Visiting the Estate of the Hospices the Rest of the Year
Throughout the year the Hospices proposes group visits of the old winery. An expert explains the origins of the estate, how it functions, the auction, the cuvees, etc., then shows you through the cellars of the Hôtel-Dieu. A tasting of five "Réserve Particulière" wines is led by estate personnel. Reservation required.
Email: hospices.beaune@wanadoo.fr

RESULTS OF THE AUCTION OF THE HOSPICES DE BEAUNE FROM 1950 TO 2008

Year	Total Revenue of the Auction (in euros)	Number of Barrels Sold	Average Price per Barrel (in euros)	Change in Average Price per Barrel	Average Price per Barrel in Hours of Work Paid at That Year's French Minimum Wage (in euros)
1950	49 310	494	99,82	/	839,4
1951	39 804	353	112,76	12,97 %	738,6
1952	58 278	332	175,54	55,68 %	1 151,40
1953	79 458	467	170,15	-3,07 %	1 114,90
1954	56 501	535	105,61	-37,93 %	575
1955	67 169	354	189,74	79,67 %	986,4
1956	No auction held due to poor vintage				
1957	90 750	246	368,90	94,42 %	1 873,20
1958	47 234	311	151,88	-58,83 %	663,2
1959	264 126	738	357,89	135,64 %	1 465,90
1960	131 277	484	271,23	-24,22 %	1 084,70
1961	226 206	372	608,08	124,23 %	2 461,20
1962	229 855	442	520,03	-14,49 %	1 886,50
1963	239 954	670	358,14	-31,13 %	1 248,10
1964	325 867	782	416,71	16,35 %	1 416
1965	67 024	294	227,97	-45,30 %	745,2
1966	350 099	752	465,56	104,28 %	1 453,30
1967	214 450	574	373,61	-19,74 %	1 140
1968	No auction held due to poor vintage				
1969	260 017	305	852,51	128,15 %	1 707,30
1970	394 187	679	580,54	-31,90 %	1 112,60
1971	446 385	341	1 309,05	125,47 %	2 327,90
1972	1 147 133	755	1 519,38	16,07 %	2 555,40
1973	1 216 116	871	1 396,23	-8,10 %	2 154,80
1974	513 997	490	1 048,97	-24,88 %	1 405,70
1975	293 189	267	1 098,09	4,69 %	1 356,50
1976	839 392	560	1 498,91	36,50 %	1 658
1977	990 461	586	1 690,21	12,76 %	1 705,70
1978	926 432	361	2 566,29	51,83 %	2 364,30
1979	1 507 873	712	2 117,80	-17,47 %	1 753,90
1980	1 129 647	643	1 756,84	-17,05%	779,2
1981	1 013 664	429	2 362,85	34,49 %	872,7
1982	1 863 613	712	2 617,43	10,77 %	845,9
1983	2 102 576	688	3 056,07	16,76 %	897,8

Double previous page:
The roofs and the basilica of Beaune, as seen from the Hôtel-Dieu.

Year	Total Revenue of the Auction (in euros)	Number of Barrels Sold	Average Price per Barrel (in euros)	Change in Average Price per Barrel	Average Price per Barrel in Hours of Work Paid at That Year's French Minimum Wage (in euros)
1984	2 421 805	636	3 807,87	24,59 %	1 024,50
1985	3 795 294	555	6 838,37	79,59 %	1 722,60
1986	2 860 248	714	4 005,95	-41,42 %	976,1
1987	2 192 674	506	4 333,35	8,17 %	1 021
1988	3 799 182	701	5 419,66	25,07 %	1 188,60
1989	4 434 894	659	6 729,73	24,17 %	1 382,10
1990	3 335 279	663	5 030,59	-25,25 %	1 010,35
1991	1 959 274	553	3 542,99	-29,57 %	711,6
1992	1 765 816	663	2 663,37	-23,07 %	524,9
1993	1 628 308	759	2 145,33	-21,29 %	404
1994	1 836 553	558	3 291,31	53,43 %	607,1
1995	2 004 704	565	3 548,15	7,80 %	629,4
1996	2 853 083	719	3 968,13	11,84 %	686,6
1997	3 585 524	617	5 811,22	46,45 %	966,7
1998	3 765 338	577	6 525,72	12,30 %	1 064,30
1999	4 732 600	729	6 491,91	-0,52 %	1 045,80
2000	5 272 997	727	7 253,09	11,73 %	1 132,20
2001	3 846 000	696	5 525,86	-23,81 %	829,1
2002	3 480 000	691	5 036,18	-8,87 %	737,3
2003	3 423 600	560	6 113,57	21,39 %	850,2
2004	3 026 000	699	4 329,04	-29,18 %	568,8
2005	3 789 800	789	4 803,30	10,95 %	568,8
2006	3 780 800	680	5 560,00	15,76 %	672,3
2007	4 286 550	607	7 061,86	27,01 %	836,7
2008	2 826 800	544	5 196,32	-26,42 %	551,8

The Records
- Highest total auction revenue: 5 272 997€(year: 2000)
- Average sale price per barrel: 7 253€ (year: 2000)
- Highest sale price for the "Charity Barrel": 200 000€ (Beaune Premier Cru "Dames Hospitalières," sold to the Belvedere company and to actor Jean Reno) profits went to the Princess Margarita of Romania Foundation and the Children's Health Federation.
- Biggest increase of average sale price per barrel: + 135,64% (year: 1959)
- Biggest drop of average sale price per barrel: - 58,83% (year: 1958)

GLOSSARY

Left page:
The town hall of Meursault.

Appellation: All of the vineyards of the Hospices de Beaune fall within "controlled origin" appellations (*appellations d'origine contrôlée* or AOCs). AOC wines are subject to laws intended to guarantee their provenance from a strictly delimited production area. Production methods are also regulated to ensure that the character of the wines is the result of natural and human factors inherent to their place of origin.

Variety: The type of vine. The variety has a strong influence on the characteristics of the grapes and therefore of the wine. It is also responsive to its environment (climate and *terroir*). This is especially the case for the Burgundian varieties: Pinot Noir (for the red wines) and Chardonnay (for the white wines).

Cru (Premier Cru or Grand Cru): The word cru is French for "growth" and is used to refer to individual vineyards. A *premier cru* therefore literally means "first growth" and a *grand cru*, "great growth."
The hierarchy of wine appellations in Burgundy forms a pyramid with four levels. At the base are the regional appellations (e.g., Burgundy - Côte Chalonnaise); then come the village appellations (e.g., Pommard). On the second-highest level are the premier crus (e.g., Pommard Premier Cru Epenots). The peak of the pyramid holds the grand crus (e.g., Clos de la Roche). The vast majority of the vineyards owned by the Hospices are classified premier cru or grand cru.

Vatting: This is the period when grapes destined for red wine production are in vats. Vatting generally lasts anywhere from fifteen days to three weeks. Alcoholic fermentation (the transformation of the sugars in the grape into alcohol) takes place during this period. When vatting is completed the wine is placed in oak barrels.

Cuvee: In the strict sense of the word, a cuvee is all of the wine from the same cuve or vat. In practice, it depends on the volume and the number of parcels produced by each individual Burgundian winery. At the Hospices de Beaune, the composition of the cuvees is defined above all by donations, which are the result of the segmentation of the vineyards of Burgundy. A cuvee can thus be a combination of several *terroirs* within the same appellation. Wines from different appellations are never mixed at the Hospices, which strictly adheres to the AOC framework. The Hospices de Beaune also vinifies "mono-*terroir*" cuvees. The cuvees are generally named after donors and benefactors.

Vinification: The process that turns the must (grape juice) into wine. For red wines, the grapes are pressed and put in vats with the grape solids for the maceration, during which valuable elements of the solids are leached into the juice. The must is kept in vats for the alcoholic fermentation. For white wines the grapes are pressed and the juice is immediately separated from the solids. The juice is then transferred to barrels (only 12-48 hours after the grapes arrive at the winery) for alcoholic fermentation.

Elevage: The period following alcoholic fermentation when a wine ages and matures, usually in barrel. During this stage there are various changes to its chemical composition that soften it and make it more appealing. This phase of 10-20 months requires the permanent care and attention of the winemaker to ensure that the process goes smoothly.

Bottling: The wine is ready for its final container: a bottle. There are two possible cases in Burgundy: either the cuvee is bottled by the producer who vinified it or it has already been bought in bulk by a "negociant-eleveur" that handles the packaging and then the commercialization.

Negociant: Burgundy's negociants are generally large wineries that purchase grapes or newly vinified wine that they then complete with vinification (in the first case), *elevage*, bottling, and commercialization. Today most negociants also own vineyards that contribute a part of their production. (For a more detailed explanation, see the section 4 inset entitled "Negociant *Eleveur* and Negociant... *Vigneron*!")

Pièce: The Burgundian term for a barrel containing 228 liters, or about 300 bottles, of wine. This unit is used in commercial transactions (prices are established per *pièce*). In speaking of the container, most professionals use the word *fût* or barrel.

Charity Barrel, aka President's Barrel: At each auction, one barrel of the harvest of the Hospices de Beaune is put up for sale for the profit of one or several charitable organizations. A representative of each organization is present at the event. The Charity Barrel comes from one of the most prestigious cuvees produced by the Hospices, but the cuvee selected varies from one year to the next.

Supervisor: The supervisor is the head of the winery. He may have many skills, as he is responsible for the technical and sometimes also the commercial workings of the winery. The supervisor of the estate of the Hospices de Beaune leads its team of *vignerons* and oversees vinification. The quality of the cuvees depends largely on his work. His commercial role is also significant since it is up to him to present the wines of the year to buyers and to the press.

Terroir: This word is used frequently in Burgundy! A *terroir* is a vineyard area recognized for its capacity to give a wine a specific flavor profile that is consistent from one year to the next. The notion of *terroir* encompasses geology, soil type, and climate but also includes human expertise.

Vigneron: Unlike the English word "winemaker," the French title of *vigneron* focuses more on the work in the vineyard than the work in the cellar and could be loosely translated as "winegrower."

ACKNOWLEDGEMENTS

I would like to thank:

- Roland Masse, for his warm welcome under all circumstances;
- Antoine Jacquet for his enthusiasm in perpetuating the original missions of the Hospices de Beaune;
- Denis Duveau for his informed view of the stakes of the auction and for organizing the tasting;
- Anne Caillaud and Laurent Waldspurger for their advice and professionalism;
- Laure Gasparotto, witness to the first steps of this project, for his dynamic encouragement;
- Valérie and Sylvain Pitiot for sharing their memories of their "Hospices years" and for the precious cards (thank you also to graphic artist Luc Groffier);
- Pierre Poupon for having motivated me to take on a published project;
- Odile Hadey for her editorial advice;
- Lionel Georgeot for his availability and generosity…;

… and the whole team of ÉcriVin for their valuable and regular expressions of support.

Thank you also to everyone who so kindly offered their testimony and their help:
Albéric Bichot, Monique Boisseaux, Yann Colette, Valérie Dolat and the Municipal Archives of Beaune, Laurent Dechaume, Frédéric Drouhin, Robert Drouhin and his assistant Pascale Doussot, Daniel Gossot, Benoit Goujon, Louis-Fabrice Latour and his assistant Marie-José Baudouin, André Masson, Stéphane Murat, André Porcheret.

This work was also composed with the hospital personnel in mind. May national solidarity, even more than charity, give them the means to complete their missions with humanity.

INTERSTATE
25

CONTENTS

Left page:
Harvesting in the Meursault premier cru Les Genevrières.

Photographs:

- p. 2, 4, 6, 8, 10, 11, 12, 16, 17, 20 (bottom) , 26, 27, 30 (bottom), 31, 32, 33, 36, 37, 40, 42, 44, 45, 46, 47, 48, 49, 50, 51, 52, 53, 55, 57, 58, 59, 60, 61, 62, 63, 64, 65, 66, 67 (bottom), 68, 71, 72, 73 (top), 74, 75, 76, 78, 83, 84, 85, 86, 87, 88, 89, 90, 91, 92, 93, 94, 95, 96, 97, 98, 99, 100 (top), 102, 103 (top),104, 106, 107, 108, 110, 111, 112, 113, 114, 115, 116, 118, 119, 120, 124, 125, 127, 129, 130, 131, 132, 133, 134, 135, 136, 139, 142, 159, 166, 168, 176, 180, 184, 188, 190: © Thierry Gaudillère/ ecrivin.fr
- p. 7, 70, 73 (bottom), 79, 80, 81, 82, 103 (bottom), 104: © Lionel Georgeot/ ecrivin.fr
- p. 104 (bottom), 109, 121, 123: © David Clémencet/ ecrivin.fr
- p. 100 (bottom), 101 (bottom): © DR
- p. 13, 14, 19, 24, 29, 30, 35: © RMN / Gérard Blot
- p. 15: © RMN / Franck Raux
- p. 20, 23, 34: © RMN / Agence Bulloz
- p. 21: ©) RMN / Hervé Lewandowski
- p. 22: ©) RMN / All rights reserved
- p. 25: © The National Gallery, London, Dist. RMN / National Gallery Photographic Department
- p. 28, 38: © RMN / Christian Jean

Maps:

All vineyard maps are taken from *Les Vins de Bourgogne* and *The Wines of Burgundy* by Sylvain Pitiot & Jean-Charles Servant (Pierre Poupon Collection - Hameau de Chevignerot - 21200 Beaune Vignobles - www.collection-pierrepoupon.fr) with the kind permission of the authors.

ISBN : 978-2-35156-049-5

Book Design: Walid Salem, Perfecto
Monitoring: Perfecto, Bordeaux, France

Printed in Italy, October 28, 2009
Legal Deposit in November 2009